MEDIA & OPEN SOCIETIES

MEDIA & OPEN SOCIETIES

Cultural, Economic and Policy Foundations for Media Openness and Diversity in East and West

Jan van Cuilenburg & Richard van der Wurff
(eds.)

Het Spinhuis
2000

Publication of this book is financially supported by the Netherlands Press Institute.

The Expert Meeting on Media and Open Societies was financially supported by The Amsterdam School of Communications Research *ASCoR*, The Netherlands Organisation for Scientific Research NWO, the Faculty of Social and Behavioural Sciences of the University of Amsterdam, and the University of Amsterdam.

ISBN 90-5589-179-7

Cover design: Jos Hendrix
Lay-out: Hanneke Kossen / René de Ree

Het Spinhuis Publishers, Oudezijds Achterburgwal 185, 1012 DK Amsterdam, The Netherlands

Table of Contents

Part II

SOCIAL RESPONSIBILITIES OF MEDIA IN A CHANGING SOCIETY

Media and Open Societies

An Introduction

JAN VAN CUILENBURG AND RICHARD VAN DER WURFF
The Amsterdam School of Communications Research *ASCoR*,
University of Amsterdam, The Netherlands

Introduction

> The concept of the Open Society is facing new challenges, mostly in connection with new communication and information technologies which one the one hand provides more options for individual uses and access to information and on the other hand creates new obstacles which cannot be resolved individually [...]. On the threshold of the Third Millennium the emerging Knowledge Society provides huge amounts of information and ways of access. It is a historic challenge to open it to all nations, all regions, all social, ethnic, and gender groups and individuals. It is a historic challenge, and it can be faced and resolved only through developing Global Open Society, Global Glasnost. (Zassoursky and Vartanova, 1999: 261-262).

Thus summarise Yassen Zassoursky and Elena Vartanova the conclusions of the first Expert Meeting on Media, Communications and the Open Society. This meeting was organised in Moscow in November 1998 by the Faculty of Journalism of Moscow State University and The Amsterdam School of Communications Research *ASCoR* of the University of Amsterdam. The present volume presents the proceedings of the follow-up Expert Meeting that was organised by both parties in Amsterdam in October 1999. The central theme of this Second Expert Meeting on Media and Open Societies was the role of *communications policies* in supporting the development of open societies, of global *glasnost.*

Communications Policies, Media and Open Societies

Communications policies are changing in East and West. Though the historic contexts in these areas are very different, the dynamics in media and communications policies are becoming more similar. Internationalisation, digitisation and convergence have changed the media sector around the globe. Individualisation, the emergence of an Information Society and the 'end' of the era of ideologies, change policy making in Russia as well as in the Netherlands. Traditional, national and medium-specific regulatory models in communications policy have become outdated. They are being replaced by new, medium-neutral and internationally oriented regulatory models. This necessitates a rethinking of policy objectives and choice of instruments. The main question of our meeting, and of this book, is how new regulatory models can contribute to the emergence of an open society – that is, a society in which all have access to society's information and communication resources in a non-discriminatory and affordable way.

The revision of communications policy objectives that is taking place today centres around the notion of the individual, independent, mature and responsible citizen. It gives rise to a new regulatory model that shows affinity with the traditional print or press model (Pool, 1983; Latzer, 1998; KPMG, 1996). Limitations of governments and policy making are well recognised, and competition and self-regulation are viewed upon favourably. Quality of media tend to be assessed less in terms of abstract (and sometimes paternalist) notions of 'culture' and 'participation', and more in terms of individual opportunities and needs satisfaction. Access to and choice from a diverse palette of information and communication options are becoming more important media performance criteria than quality of information and communication in normative terms. This shift in thinking on policy objectives of course has its repercussions for the choice of policy instruments. Economic mechanisms are increasingly relied upon, because these mechanisms are considered to be best suited to the combined tasks of creating equal opportunities for actors and allocating scarce (information and communication) resources in a neutral, transparent and non-paternalist manner.

Communications Policies in East and West

Transparent and objective as we want or argue communications policies to be, discussions on communications policy never do take place in a simple objective and transparent way. Too many and too important values and interests are at stake, that complicate and invigorate discussions. Differences between East and West still play a major role here. Though the dynamics of media and communications policy are becoming more similar, they are still looked at from different perspectives.

The discussions at our Expert Meeting and the papers presented in this volume are no exception to this. Several authors discuss for example the role of states in communications policy, or the role of advertising in media financing. In both East and West, states are retreating, and advertising is becoming a growing source of income for media. In the Netherlands, we view these changes with nostalgic ambivalence, because we tend to consider the state (or better, the government) as a benevolent force that upholds quality of media. In Russia, these changes are viewed with impatient anticipation. There the state is viewed with suspicion, and advertising is much more favourably looked upon as an independent source of income that could relieve media from the dominance of political factions.

These and other issues related to communications policies, media and open societies are critically examined in this volume by experts from the Faculty of Journalism of Moscow State University, The Amsterdam School of Communications Research *ASCoR* of the University of Amsterdam, and other experts from Finland, the United Kingdom and Belgium. Reflecting convergence in communications policies dynamics, we all focus on the same issues that we believe are key to the development of communications policies for open societies in East and West. These are:

1 the social responsibilities of media in a changing society;
2 the role of competition in stimulating media innovation and diversity; and
3 the potential of new media in strengthening user's autonomy and empowerment.

Expressing our different historical contexts, we do however approach these issues from different perspectives. Hopefully the mix will help in elaborating communications policy that really can contribute to the development of global openness.

Outline of the Book

The papers in this volume are organised in five sections. Section One contains two key note speeches that were delivered by Jan van Cuilenburg from *ASCoR* and Yassen Zassoursky of the Faculty of Journalism of Moscow State University. Both key notes raise the issue of how socially responsible media in a competitive environment can contribute to 'openness'.

JAN VAN CUILENBURG starts by arguing that in an 'open society' media should contribute to *open-mindedness* and *receptiveness* of their audiences. Heterodox people and minorities should not only be permitted and tolerated in society; they should be appreciated and invited to participate in social and political dialogue and to take joint responsibility for society. He then distinguishes two routes for research on how communications policy can contribute to realising this difficult aim. One approach focuses on media market forces that may contribute to diversity. The other approach focuses on social responsibilities of media and journalists. Van Cuilenburg argues that journalists and media have a role to play in enhancing audiences' capabilities to adapt receptively to ever increasing pluralism in society.

YASSEN ZASSOURSKY also addresses the issues of social responsibility and competition, but from a very different historical perspective. His argument starts with the initial 'golden age' of the free press in which media contributed to the opening up of Russian society. He then discusses how in more recent years the contribution of 'free' media towards openness and democracy in Russia is threatened both by government officials and media owners. Government officials mistakenly equate 'social responsibility of the media' with accountability to the state; owners and advertisers substitute 'freedom of the press' by permissiveness and a lack of concern for the just requirements of morality. Zassoursky concludes that mechanisms need to be found to maintain and develop freedom of information as a basic human right in modern democratic society, against etatism and permissiveness.

Social Responsibilities of Media in a Changing Society

Section Two contains five papers that focus more in particular on the issue of social responsibilities of media in a changing society. One major conclusion that emerges from these papers is that in defining social responsibilities of media in an open society we should find a balance; a balance between (individual and societal) needs on the one hand, and expected or required (individual and societal) contributions and commitments (or norms), on the other hand.

KAARLE NORDENSTRENG, from Tampere University in Finland, reminds us that democracy is the ultimate goal to which media (policy) should contribute. He reviews contemporary theories of democracy, investigates the role that these theories attribute to the media, and distils a number of requirements that are placed on media by the principles of democracy. Discussing these requirements, Nordenstreng points out the dilemmas involved in finding an appropriate balance between individual and societal needs and commitments: not all citizens always want to be informed about all ideas. On the contrary, although from a democratic point of view we may want media to reflect all possible ideas in society, from an individual point of view we tend to disregard diverging opinions. This dilemma is touched upon several times in this book.

YASSEN ZASSOURSKY, from Moscow State University, elaborates the dilemmas involved in finding an appropriate balance between individual and societal needs while defining the social responsibilities of media in a different way. He argues that the concept of the 'social responsibility' of the press is a vague and ambiguous concept that can be interpreted in different ways and used for various purposes. He points to Fascist, Soviet and US interpretations of the social responsibility theory to substantiate his case. In order to make 'social responsibility' a useful concept, one has to define to whom in particular (e.g. the state, elites, the individual, the group) and according to what criteria media need to be responsible. Zassoursky concludes by arguing that journalists, editors and owners should be responsible to individuals, to the citizens.

Thirdly, IRINA NETCHAEVA, from Moscow State University, discusses how journalists in South Africa reinterpret their social responsibilities in the post-*Apartheid* period. She describes the unequal development of ICT and the social-economic polarisation in this country, and argues that the general assumptions that underlie the 'open society' concept do not easily apply to this situation. Journalists in South Africa have to play different roles than is common in Western countries. They need first of all to be mediators, between the information rich and poor in South Africa, and between Sub-Sahara Africa and the industrialised world. Reflecting these needs, Netchaeva advocates a community-centred definition of the social responsibility of media.

The issue of individual contributions and norms is also taken up by ANDREI RASKIN, again from Moscow State University. Raskin discusses the role of new media and journalists in armed conflicts. New information and communication technologies increase opportunities to improve global media coverage of conflicts, and increasing media coverage in principle may act as an impediment to human rights violations. Yet the way ICTs are currently deployed by media organisations actually reduces openness in conflict situations and increases the grip of parties to the conflict on reporting. Journalists should aim to prevent this and maintain open, unbiased media coverage.

Finally, JO BARDOEL, KEES BRANTS and RENÉ PLUG, all three from *ASCoR*, complement the preceding papers by presenting empirical evidence on how social responsibilities of media are actually defined and redefined in governmental documents in the Netherlands. Their paper suggests how the redefinition of social responsibilities follows more general normative changes in Dutch society. These include a shift from political to cultural aims, from collectivist to individualist aims, from a national to a multicultural perspective, and from an ambiguous to a positive assessment of economic forces.

Competition, Media Innovation and Diversity

The role of economic forces in shaping media systems that cater in a balanced way for both individual and societal needs and that strengthen both individual and societal commitments is discussed in Section Three. Here the authors focus on three specific and partially contradictory objectives of media (policy): quality, open diversity and reflective diversity; and on media competition as primary economic force that is at play in the media sector. The question that these authors raise is whether media competition stimulates media companies to innovate products and processes and to offer an optimal mix of high quality and diverse information and entertainment to audiences. The main conclusion that emerges from these papers is that media competition indeed will trigger media innovation and diversity, but that a too competitive environment on the contrary reduces quality and stimulates content replication rather than diversity.

Supporting this overall conclusion, ELENA VARTANOVA, from Moscow State University, argues that in Russia commercialisation and politi-cisation threaten media diversity. Growing competition in the media sector in post-Soviet Russia is accompanied by an increasing number of media companies and available media products. During the first stages of liberalisation, the growing number of media outlets improved diversity. More recently, competition tends to result in tabloidisation. In addition, the lack of (diverse) sources of income, and especially income from advertising, makes media organisations extremely dependent on political capital. Both developments, tabloidisation and politicisation, reduce access of Russians to diverse media content.

RICHARD VAN DER WURFF, JAN VAN CUILENBURG and GENEVION KEUNE, from *ASCoR*, argue that a distinction should be made between moderate and ruinous competition. When media companies can and do adopt different strategies, competition is moderate and media output is diverse. Yet when companies adopt similar strategies, competition becomes ruinous and programming becomes more similar. The number of firms and the extent of new entry are among the factors that determine which strategies are adopted. Results of a case study on competition and programming in the Netherlands are presented to substantiate the argument. This case study shows, surprisingly similar to developments in Russia if we take the very different contexts in both countries into account, that increasing commercialisation first increased and later reduced diversity in the Netherlands, too.

In a similar vein, ELS DE BENS from Ghent University analyses media competition in Flanders. She argues, too, that whereas moderate competition stimulates innovation and diversity, in a highly competitive media market media organisations tend to offer similar content to the same audiences on the basis of similar marketing studies. Hence strong competition leads to replication and tabloidisation. Empirical evidence from Flemish television and newspaper markets supports this argument.

ROBERT PICARD, from the Turku School of Economics and Business Administration, Finland, offers in his paper an explanation for why strong competition has a negative effect on media content quality. Strong competition implies a large and growing number of media outlets. This reduces subsequently average audience size, average revenues per media outlet and average capacity to invest in content. A lowering of content finally will reduce audience size even more, hence initiating a negative cycle of declining audiences, investments and quality of content. According to Picard, governments need to provide specific financial incentives to bring this negative cycle to a hold; a conclusion that is supported by the results of the Flemish and Dutch case studies. However, the Russian case study clearly reminds us of the dangers involved in too much governmental involvement, too. Hence in each case a balance between moderate competition and moderate governmental involvement needs to be found.

The papers included in this section all show, in one way or the other, that a further clarification of operational definitions of competition and diversity is required to improve our analysis of the relationships between competition and diversity. This issue is taken up in the paper by IORDAN IOSSIFOV from *ASCoR*, who presents a research outline for a study into competition, innovation and diversity in newspaper markets.

New Media and Empowerment

Sections Two and Three focus on the supply side of media systems. They focus on the responsibilities of media organisations and on their economic interactions as determinants of how media meet social and individual needs. Complementing these perspectives, the papers in Section Four analyse the demand side. They address the issue of users' access to and use of new media. The conclusions that emerge from these papers are somewhat ambiguous in terms of access and usage patterns.

Yet they reinforce the conclusions of the previous sections that quality and diversity are not any more the sole responsibility of media organisations and/or governments, but the outcome of (partly commercial) interactions between users and suppliers of media content and infrastructure.

First, PIET BAKKER from *ASCoR*, shows how national communities that do not have their own nation states, use the Internet to reinforce community ties and strengthen communication between members that are spread around the globe. All the websites studied show similar elements that together constitute a virtual nation: maps, symbols, historical accounts and news. New media here offer communities means to organise themselves that did not exist before.

MARIA LOUKINA from Moscow State University also presents a relatively optimistic view of how the Internet offers improved means of communication to non-elites in Russian society. She shows how the Internet in Russia is growing, how it expands the reach of newspapers, radio and television, and how Internet usage changes information provision. Combined, these developments bring more openness and diversity in Russia's media system.

IVAN ZASSOURSKY, from Moscow State University, in turn, shows how the concept of an 'open society' is introduced at the level of Russian politics as well. The 'open society' has become part of the *leitmotiv* of the liberal 'new city generation'. Media and the Internet, more than traditional political parties, play an important role in spreading these ideas. Unfortunately, media and the Internet also spread less liberal, more totalitarian ideas.

COLIN SPARKS, from Westminster University in London, shows a gloomier picture than especially Bakker and Loukina in his analysis of Internet access. He shows how patterns of access to the Internet in its current state very closely map on existing distributions of wealth and power. A reinvention of the Internet as entertainment medium on a WebTV basis might change this access pattern but would also destroy the democratic potential of the current Internet technology, he argues.

These papers thus sketch an ambiguous picture of how new media empower marginalised social groups in society. On the one hand, Bakker and Loukina argue how Internet technology increase communication opportunities for these marginal groups. On the other hand, Sparks clearly shows that the same marginal groups lack access to the Internet. These seemingly paradoxical results raise the question of whether access to the Internet is restricted to, and potentially a source of power for, emerging elites within traditionally marginalised social groups. Further research into these issues and in particular into group-specific usage patterns of Internet applications (www, email, newsgroups) is highly needed.

Communications Policies for the Future

Both our Expert Meeting and this volume end with a concluding key note of DENIS MCQUAIL, emeritus professor of Communication at the University of Amsterdam. McQuail points out that the contribution of media to openness, equality, and political and human rights (i.e. democracy) depends upon other political actors and factors. This sets limits to what media can bring about; a logical yet frequently neglected conclusion. Second, he enumerates a number of conditions that are necessary or conducive for media to contribute to democracy, as well as a number of positive and negative forces that can create or break up these conditions. Positive forces include economic and moral support for media from audiences, a secure income from advertising, transparency, technological innovation and increasing professionalism. Negative forces include concentration, ruinous competition, politicisation, and either a lack or over-abundance of advertising. Public policy can reinforce positive forces and reduce negative forces in various ways, thereby strengthening the role of media in stimulating openness, equality and, political and human rights. He gives a number of suggestions of what policies could focus upon and concludes:

> The means for achieving some of these goals in practice are more limited than they used to be, for a number of reasons. Nevertheless, the dependence of democracy on adequate mass media is too important for public policy to be allowed to wither away. (McQuail, 2000: 262).

We hope that the ideas presented in this book will contribute to developing such communications policies.

References

KPMG

1996 *Public Issues Arising from Telecommunications and Audiovisual Convergence. Summary report.* <http://www.ispo.cec.be/infosoc/promo/pubs/exesum.html>.

Latzer, M.
1998 European mediamatics policies. *Telecommunications Policy* 22 (6): 457-466.
McQuail, D.
2000 Concluding notes. Media policy for the Open Society. In J. van Cuilenburg and R. van der Wurff (eds.), *Media and Open Societies*, pp. 257-262. Amsterdam: Het Spinhuis.
Pool, I. de Sola
1983 *Technologies of Freedom.* Cambridge, Mass.: Harvard University Press.
Zassoursky, Y.N. and Vartanova, E. (eds.)
1999 *Media, Communications and the Open Society.* Moscow: Faculty of Journalism/Publishing IKAR.

Part I

MEDIA FOR OPEN SOCIETIES:

RESPONSIBILITY AND RECEPTIVENESS

Media for an Open and Receptive Society

On the Economic and Cultural Foundations of Open and Receptive Media Diversity

JAN VAN CUILENBURG
The Amsterdam School of Communications Research *ASCoR*,
University of Amsterdam, The Netherlands

Introduction

21-23 October 1999 The Amsterdam School of Communications Research *ASCoR* and the Faculty of Journalism of Moscow State University organised the Second Expert Meeting on *Media and Open Societies.* The first expert meeting on this theme was held in Moscow, 12-14 November 1998. The central question of the second expert meeting was, how communication policies can contribute to the creation and maintenance of openness in communication systems East and West.

In this keynote article, I want to address the theme of the expert meeting starting from *ASCoR*'s mission statement. *ASCoR*'s mission statement directs *ASCoR*'s research toward the theme of *Communication Toward Open Societies.* Research in *ASCoR* focuses on the social, political and economic context, functions and meaning of the production, distribution and reception of symbolic messages in society. *ASCoR*'s mission statement stresses both the empirical and the normative character of communication science teaching and research. The ultimate objective of communication research within the *ASCoR* framework is to build a body of knowledge on the role of social communications and information provision for enhancing openness in society. Against this background, the social communications system is studied from the perspective of social, cultural and political diversity and tolerance between divergent social groups, categories and minorities in a plural society.

The theme of this second expert meeting on *Media and Open Societies* was the need for a reorientation in communications and media policies. This theme emerged from the discussions during the first *Media and Open Societies* meeting in Moscow last year. Technological, economic and social developments within and outside the media sector urge for a revision of communications policy and regulatory models. Traditional, national and medium-specific policy and regulatory models need to, and indeed are already being replaced by new, medium-neutral and more internationally oriented models. A very important question is, whether these new models do indeed contribute to the emergence and strengthening of open societies. In different sessions we will as scientists explore this socially and politically very important question.

Communication Toward Open Societies

Studying *Communication Toward Open Societies* can be done in very divergent ways and into very distinct directions. Without excluding other possible lines of research, in this keynote I want to make a plea for a research agenda that might be labelled as *media for an open and receptive society*. Obviously, such a theme has a strong relationship with the late Karl Popper's work on *The Open Society and its Enemies* (1945). When Popper's famous book was published, World War II had just ended and fascism had just been wiped out by the Allies from the East and the West, by the Soviet Union and by Western democracies under the leadership of the United States and the United Kingdom. At that time, the communist Soviet Union and its leader, Joseph Stalin, by many people in the Western world were looked upon as liberators and good friends. But, as we all know, this warm relation did not last for a long time: the 1948 Berlin crisis made enemies out of friends, the Iron Curtain was spun, and the Cold War began.

Popper

The euphoria in Europe just after the World War for many people pushed aside a clear view of the inherent totalitarian character of communism. Nazism just being defeated with blood, sweat and tears, apparently made people blind to new political dangers. With the exception of individuals like Karl Popper. To Popper there was a strong similarity between fascism and communism: their closed ideology and their epistemological position on truth and knowledge, on the historical necessity and predictability of the future, made both fascism and communism to enemies of open and democratic societies. The post-war history of communism world-wide has often tragically underlined the adequacy of Popper's analysis at that time.

Virtually all Popper's post-war work has been a fight against closed thinking, in science, in politics, and in the media. Against the 'closed society' Popper ardently pleaded for an 'open society' in which personal responsibility and piecemeal social engineering are shaping a solid foundation for society. An open society according to Popper is characterised by an intellectual and political climate that favours creative, dynamic, inventive thinking and trial-and-error based searching for solutions to social problems, solutions that are never considered as final, but as just for the time being, in the understanding that every solution already from the very beginning inherently contains problems once again. Unorthodox, creative, open social thought and political thinking constitute the decisive difference to a closed and dogmatic society.

Open societies demand from their citizens that they take responsibility in full freedom, that they accept and cope with the inevitability of acting under conditions of uncertainty, that they make social and political choices and accept the consequences therefrom. No small claim. History shows that this demand for large numbers of people often is too heavy a burden. Lots of people feel this claim too frightening. Not every fellow citizen does object to dictatorship, nor is democracy the highest ideal for everyone to strive for. Open societies are no societies for the anxious, for people who attach to security and predictability, for citizens whose world ends at the fence of their garden. Anxiety and fear of the unknown and strangers are likewise to be dreaded in the open society as closed ideologies and front line political groups wanting to establish so-called benign dictatorship.

Diversity

In talking about the open society one runs rather quickly into diversity, into social and cultural pluralism and into media diversity as a social and political end in itself. The epistemological impossibility of unquestionable truth constitutes the normative basis for diversity in knowledge, information and opinion. This applies to all knowledge, but it is especially applicable to knowledge of society and politics. In closed societies pretending to know the ultimate truth, be it the law of history, or the word of God and His prophets, there is no need to cater for diversity in information and opinion. Obviously, people, who say they exclusively own political and social truth in society themselves, can do without any diversity.

On Tolerance

Pluralism and Tolerance

There is a clear relationship between social and political pluralism and tolerance. In present-day multicultural and multi-ethnic societies tolerance in Europe, East and West, is a virtue not to be trivialised. Tolerance is the skill of standing behaviour and opinions from other people one actually does not agree to. Tolerance is to refrain from pressure and coercion on other people in order to repress deviant behaviour and opinions.

Intolerance is the opposite. Intolerant people quite the contrary do not tolerate what they reject, but try to stop this using pressure or coercion (Schuyt, 1995). An open, plural society leaves the question of the absolute moral correctness unanswered and underlines as a matter of principle the impossibility of final truth. It may be clear that such a society can only flourish in a social and cultural climate in which the other and the deviant are respected.

Pluralism and tolerance are not naturally linked: pluralism can only contribute to tolerance in society, if people are receptive in mind and prepared to face the fallibility of their own behaviour, opinions and ideas.

Permissiveness

Tolerance has sisters who take after her, even though they have very different effects on the open spirit of society. They are three: 'permissiveness', 'indifference' and 'appreciation'. Permissiveness is shutting one's eyes to something, is not preventing, not fighting behaviour one strictly speaking rejects. We might say that permissiveness is allowing something condemnable to happen because allowing it is a lesser evil than to fight it. Permissiveness lacks the respect that is characteristic of tolerance for other people. The permissive person hopes that one day his fellow citizen will change opinions and behaviour. In the meantime, however, he gives him a free hand to take his own divergent course.

Indifference

It is true, permissiveness may be a positive force in an open society, but it is not a very powerful one. A real big danger for an open society, however, is tolerance's second sister: indifference. In an indifferent society, individuals and groups do not take any interest in each other's behaviour, motives and opinions. Respect for the other is completely missing, let alone there is any affection for other people's culture, values and behaviour.

Appreciation

Indifference is nourished by an extreme relativisation of values and norms in society. In the end this boils down to a then broadly held view that one should leave everyone else his or her own private convictions, and above all, that one should not interfere in another person's business. Differences between people are of no importance at all, at least, in the indifferent person's outlook on life. Yet, what is left of pluralism if differences between people are in no way significant? It is here that we may meet tolerance's third sister: 'appreciation'.

Totally different to permissiveness and indifference, appreciation is an attitude of acknowledgement, admiration, recognition and receptiveness toward other individuals and groups in society that have different views and opinions. Appreciation is non-dualistic: appreciation is neither disapproving divergent opinions, nor convincing the fellow citizen of his or her being wrong. Appreciation is non-judgmental; appreciation is a joint search for synthesis, toward a new balance. An appreciating person lives up to a maxim like the simple one someday expressed by a well-known Hindu philosopher, Neem Karoli Baba: 'Don't throw anyone out of your heart.' (in Goldstein & Kornfield, 1987: 154).

Media for an Open and Receptive Society

Considering tolerance and appreciation as very strong democratic forces, I here want to make a plea for media responsibility for both an open and a receptive society. In my opinion, in studying media's political and social responsibility, it is not enough to focus on openness only. In a living democracy, media in addition to *open-mindedness* should contribute to *receptiveness* in their audiences. Heterodox people and minorities in terms of background, origin and descent should not only be permitted and tolerated in society. They should be appreciated and invited to social and political dialogue and to taking joint responsibility for society. This is not an easy task for media in an era in which we have hardly recovered from the post-modern '*anything goes*'.

Media operate in a cultural and economic environment. Addressing the theme of this book, we might wonder whether it is possible to indicate economic and cultural factors in media and media markets that are conducive to both open and receptive media performance? My provisional answer to this question is positive. There are at least two routes for media research that could give communication scientists and media policy-makers some more insight into the media's potentials for promoting democracy. The first route is an economic one; it is the route leading to uncover the economic basis of open diversity in media supply. The second route is a cultural one, a route bringing us to the cultural basis of what we might label as 'receptive journalism', that is, journalism enhancing capabilities of audiences to adapt receptively to the ever increasing pluralism in society.

Open Societies: Media Competition and Open-Minded Diversity

Today's information society did put an end to scarcity in the means of communication and made liberalisation and competition possible in communication markets, notably in telecommunications and broadcasting. This in it self may be applauded. However, that is not yet saying, that there are only positive and linear effects of the unprecedented informatisation of society on the kind of access to communications one would like to have in an truly open society. We may underline this in exploring the relationship between media competition and media diversity. What is the basic economic foundation of diversity? What kind of media competition is conducive to a truly open-minded diversity?

Reflective and Open Diversity

Media diversity refers, of course, to the variety of media products that are available to citizens and consumers. It is one of the major media performance indicators, next to *access*, *efficiency*, and *quality* (see also McQuail, 1992: 65 ff.). As Denis McQuail and I have argued in the early eighties, 'diversity' is an ambiguous concept, a concept with two faces. Being both a normative and empirical concept at the same time, media diversity gives rise to two diverging approaches, one more top-down, normative and qualitative, and one more bottom-up, empirical and quantitative.

First, diversity may be conceptualised from a normative point of view that lies outside the realm of actual media use. This approach reflects the notion that media are pervasive social phenomena that may influence people considerably. Thus, to prevent the emergence of biases in public opinion, media content should express as many different opinions as possible in an equal manner and in a sound way. This type of diversity is *open diversity*: the extent to which divergent preferences and opinions are *equally* (i.e., statistically uniformly) represented in the media (cf. Van Cuilenburg & McQuail, 1982: 40-41).[1] The objective of open diversity may be labelled as *equal access for ideas* to society's communication system.

The second way to define 'diversity' is in terms of the match between actual media users' preferences and the reflection of these preferences in media content (cf. Van Cuilenburg and McQuail, 1982: 40-41). *Reflective diversity* is the extent to which existing population preferences are *proportionally* represented in the media. From this perspective, diversity is *access for people*. If each individual or group has equal access to the media to express his or her preferences or to contribute to media content, we may say media to be reflectively diverse.

In discussing the open society, of course, open media diversity is far more attractive than reflective diversity. Open diversity gives space to

1 An overview of this study in English is presented in McQuail and Van Cuilenburg (1983).

cultural, social and political innovation and change, whereas reflective diversity has an inherent tendency toward the middle, toward the *status quo* in existing social and cultural structures.

Competition and Diversity

The last decade, media markets, and notably television markets, have been liberalised considerably. New media actors did enter the market and media competition has substantially increased in most countries. Liberalisation is often welcomed under the assumption that media competition is good, and that more media competition is even better for media innovation and diversity. In this train of thought, media competition is the economic basis par excellence for media diversity. We have argued before and elsewhere (e.g. Van Cuilenburg, 1999; and Van Cuilenburg, 1998), however, that this hypothesis does not take into account that different forms of media competition favour different types of media diversity. Media markets generally are far better in reflecting current preferences in society than in openness. Especially under conditions of *fierce competition*, media markets tend toward market conformity and diversity reflecting mainstream preferences and demand. It is only under conditions of *moderate competition* that markets offer media space to experiment and to serve niches and minority preferences. Moderate competition goes with market dynamics and open media diversity. Beyond mild and moderate competition, however, there is always the risk of *ruinous competition* only resulting in Hotelling's *excessive sameness* of media content.

In studying the role media can play to strengthen the open society, I would suggest to focus on economic media market factors that promote first and foremost moderate competition between media. For, it is this type of competition that seems most promising to media innovation and open-mindedness in media content. And thus, most promising to an open society.

Receptive Societies: Inclusive and Open-Hearted Journalism

The second route for research I want to propose is receptive journalism. No matter how important open media diversity is, it does not make an open society a receptive society yet. Where the open society as far as media are concerned is best being served by moderate competition and open diversity, a receptive society presupposes that journalism takes a new social responsibility. What does this mean? What kind of journalism promotes cultural and social receptiveness in audiences to the distinctiveness of different constituent groups in society? This question cannot be answered without new theories to be built, without old ones to be elaborated and a lot of empirical research still to be done. Even so, some tentative and a little bit provocative remarks may already be made.

Premise #1: Inclusive and Open-Hearted Journalism

Receptive journalism starts from two closely connected ethical premises. First, receptive journalism is inclusive and open-hearted journalism. Some years ago, Josina Makau and Ronald Arnett edited a reader titled *Communication Ethics in an Age of Diversity* (1997). Several contributions to this book may be relevant for elaborating and modernising the old, 1947 *social responsibility theory of the press* (Hutchins, 1947). One of these contributions is by Julia Wood (1997). She explains the genesis of cultural diversity from what she labels as *standpoint theory.* According to standpoint theory, differences among social groups are produced and reproduced by cultural structures and practices that designate criteria such as sex and race for assigning individuals to groups with unequal status and opportunity. 'Once distinct groups are constructed, a culture prescribes specific roles that involve and exclude particular activities, which further constrain members' perceptions, knowledge, and subjective consciousness.' (Wood, 1997: 9). Different cultural standpoints generate different communication cultures which primary function is the social inclusion and social exclusion of people. Exclusion and inclusion are based on the tendency to judge cultural differences in a hierarchical way: 'Within Western culture differences are not regarded as neutral – that is, as simply different. Instead, we view them as better or worse, and better is usually our way and worse the other person's way! [...] Typically, we don't realize how ethnocentric our standpoints are [...]' (Wood, 1997: 15). Wood suggests four ways to facilitate moving beyond judgement and toward an appreciation of the opportunities inspired by diversity in society: self-reflection, openness to others, curiosity toward differences, and a Both-And orientation, putting an end to thinking in terms of either-or, in terms of in-group and outgroup (Wood, 1997: 17-19). These are rather beautiful tasks for truly socially responsible media in an open society, are they not? Receptive journalism spreads the message that social diversity is not simple an obstacle to overcome. Receptive journalism is inclusive and promotes reversing perspectives. To quote Josina Makau, a communicative ethic in a plural society is based on 'response-ability': '[...] the capacity and desire to listen, to reach out to others, to "hear each other into speech"' (Makau, 1997: 55).

Premise #2: Weakening the Cultural Ego

The second ethical premise of receptive journalism is that journalism should teach cultural change as a way of life, and weaken *cultural egos*, that is, the cultural identities of groups in society as being ultimately an illusion. This ethical premise is a far more radical one than the first. The cultural self merely is a constructed self; it has no real existence outside our thinking, outside our opinions, and outside the mental pictures in our head. People desire security and grip. So they attach to what they consider to be their cultural identity. The steady nature of cultural egos, however, is a social illusion that, if mentally attached to, often produces more social trouble than solutions. The news bulletins every day are full of tragedies and disasters created by national or ethnic cultural egos. Cultural identities change all the time and are never fully fixed. Receptive journalism in an open society makes people aware of this irrefutable fact of life. Receptive journalism breaks down the cultural egos of its audiences, breaks down cultural dogmas and orthodox thought, and teaches cultural change and awareness of the fallibility of people's own opinions, values and norms.

Concluding Remark

The Expert Meeting on Media and Open Societies was a meeting of East and West, to be more precise, a meeting of Eastern and Western Europe. Though, the participants together form a truly international scientific community with nearly universal scientific values, it still was a meeting of different cultures and different historical backgrounds. Hopefully this fact brought along a diversity of scientific perspectives on media in open societies from with we all can benefit in our future research and teaching. Maybe, Western communication scientists could learn from our Russian colleagues, how one effectively builds an open society from scratch after decades of closed ideology, science, media and social life. What problems are societies in transition to democracy and openness confronted with? Can media indeed play an effective role in this transition toward political, social and cultural openness, or are other agents of change far more important? And, put forward in all modesty, perhaps our Russian colleagues could learn from the Western open society experience, that openness is only the first step toward sustainable democracy, an important step, but nevertheless only just one step. Openness and tolerance in society have to be complemented with receptiveness, appreciation and social inclusion, if we want to avoid that openness and tolerance deteriorate into social apathy and indifference. In one of the papers of this conference I read that recently in Moscow a new concept was introduced, that is, the concept of 'the new city generation': '"The new city generation" has its roots in the new urban culture with all its lively contradictions mixed with post-modern elan, [...] high self-esteem, creativity and vital energy. All those in their 20-ties, 30-ties and early 40-ties, almost everybody, whose identity was forged in the stormy nineties, can qualify.' (Zassoursky, 2000: 225). Though I am in my fifties and thus do not qualify merely on the basis of age, this concept of 'new city generation' brings me in a rather positive mood, especially because of the way it is defined: the 'new city generation' consists of those, who share an openness to the future, an interest in the other, and a quest for the new. Well, this is what an open and receptive society is all about. I could not say it myself more eloquently.

References

Goldstein, J. and Kornfield, J.
1987 *Seeking the Heart of Wisdom.* Boston/London: Shambala.

Hutchins, R.M.
1947 *A Free and Responsible Press.* Report by the Commission on Freedom of the Press. Chicago, Ill.: University of Chicago Press.

Makau, J.M.
1997 Embracing diversity in the classroom. In J.M. Makau and R.C. Arnett (eds.), *Communication Ethics in an Age of Diversity,* pp. 48-67. Urbana and Chicago: University of Illinois Press.

Makau, J.M. and Arnett, R.C. (eds.)
1997 *Communication Ethics in an Age of Diversity.* Urbana and Chicago: University of Illinois Press.

McQuail, D.
1992 *Media Performance. Mass Communication and the Public Interest.* London: Sage.

McQuail, D. and Van Cuilenburg, J.
1983 Diversity as a media policy goal: A strategy for evaluative research and a Netherlands case study. *Gazette* 31 (3): 145-162.

Popper, K.R.
1945 *The Open Society and its Enemies.* 2 volumes. New York: Harper & Row Publishers.

Schuyt, C.J.M.
1995 [1994] Het wankele evenwicht tussen tolerantie en intolerantie [The unstable balance between tolerance and intolerance]. In A.C. Zijderveld (ed.), *Kleine Geschiedenis van de Toekomst: 100 Thesen over de Westerse Samenleving op Weg naar de Eenentwintigste Eeuw* [A Small History of the Future], pp. 66-72. Kampen: Kok Agora.

Van Cuilenburg, J.
1998 New perspectives on media diversity: Toward a critical-rational approach to media performance. In Y.N. Zassoursky and E. Vartanova (eds.), *Changing Media and Communications*, pp. 71-85. Moscow: Faculty of Journalism/Publisher ICAR.

Van Cuilenburg, J.
1999 On competition, access and diversity in media, old and new: Some remarks for communications policy in the information age. *New Media & Society* 1(2): 183-207.

Van Cuilenburg, J. and McQuail, D.
1982 *Media en Pluriformiteit* [Media and Pluriformity]. Den Haag: Staatsdrukkerij.

Wood, J.T.
1997 Diversity in dialogue: Commonalities and differences between friends. In J.M. Makau and R.C. Arnett (eds.), *Communication Ethics in an Age of Diversity*, pp. 5-26. Urbana and Chicago: University of Illinois Press.

Zassoursky, I.
2000 The Open Society and the New Urban Culture as presented in public communication process. In J. van Cuilenburg and R. van der Wurff (eds.), *Media and Open Societies*, pp. 223-228. Amsterdam: Het Spinhuis.

Open Society

Freedom and Responsibility versus Etatism and Permissiveness

YASSEN N. ZASSOURSKY
Faculty of Journalism, Moscow State University, Russia

Introduction

It was more than ten years ago that President Mikhail Gorbachev started the movement towards democracy and market economy by promoting Glasnost, the opening up of society for its citizens and the world at large. Since then, freedom of the media has been firmly established in Russia.

The press played a major, if not a crucial role in defeating the authoritarian administrative command system of government and management, and thus contributed to the development of the 'open society' in Russia. Initially, media gained popularity and credibility by their independent, critical and responsible performance. They enjoyed growing support by audiences and skyrocketing daily circulations. For example, the dailies *Komsomolskaya Pravda* and *Trud* reached a circulation of 24 million copies. However, after the first years of this so-called 'golden age of the free press', the media lost their momentum. The distribution of the two dailies mentioned fell dramatically to 750 thousand copies each. Circulation of Moscow dailies dropped from more than 100 million copies to 6 million copies a day. And more importantly, the public became discontent and disappointed with the media.

Freedom of the Press as Instrument of Democracy

The Russian road to democracy and to civil society is really rocky. Disenchantment with unfulfilled promises is so strong, that the very notion of democracy has become a kind of swearword. It is characteristic that during the last Duma and Presidential electoral campaigns, the rhetoric has strikingly changed in comparison with earlier campaigns. Neither democracy nor freedom of the press, issues that carried the day during the early 1990s, were still among the slogans of either candidates or their programs. Much more fashionable have become clichés such as 'law and order', and 'state' and 'national interests'. Patriotic appeals rather than universal human values or human rights now dominate electoral campaigns.

In this changing climate, Russian newspapers and television broadcasters are often and commonly accused of being irresponsible and permissive; characteristics that in the minds of ordinary Russians are in many cases associated with the notion of 'freedom of the press'. Reacting to these public concerns, some federal and local government officials question the validity of the freedom of the press. They talk about the necessity to make the press more responsible and less permissive, expressing more concern for the interests of the state and local authorities. At the same time and at the other end of the spectrum, media owners promote their commercial interests at the expense of professional standards and objectivity.

Under these circumstances it is of crucial importance to define the true meaning of the 'responsibility' of the media. Responsibility of the media should not be equated with accountability to the government that tends to use media for its own interests. On the contrary, media should present a public evaluation of the performance of the government and the state. This makes the free press an indispensable instrument of democracy.

Responsible Media: Between the State and Advertisers

An etatist approach to the media is counter productive. It erodes the very essence of the freedom of the press. It turns media into tools of the government. It substitutes responsibility by accountability to government officials for whom society seems to mean the state; to government officials who tend to disregard the human rights of individuals, including the right that the government and the state are accountable to the individual citizens. Finally, an etatist approach discredits the very notion of the responsible and free press. It creates barriers to the free flow of information, to the openness of society.

At the same time, media owners and advertisers press for commercial gains. They treat the freedom of the press as a license to gain profits by attracting huge audiences with sensationalism and cheap entertainment, by presenting sexism and violence – with little regard for humanistic values, for the just requirements of morality. In this case, freedom of the press is substituted by 'permissiveness'. And 'permissiveness' becomes a barrier for the public to access knowledge about and to understand what is going on in society. Permissiveness, in its own way, interferes with the 'open society'.

As a result, media and journalists are caught in a no-man's land. They are in the crossfire between the state and the government on the one side, and the owners and advertisers on the other side. The losers in this case are not only journalists and the media, but also the public, society, the individual citizens.

Conclusion

The 'open society' requires free and responsible media. Both are threatened by etatism and permissiveness, by state control and by commercialism. Even Internet, which has seemed to become a most reliable source of objective information, is being threatened by attempts at government regulation and by permissiveness – to put it mildly – regarding the content of some of its sites. We should therefore work towards creating responsible, autonomous and objective media. We should work towards finding mechanisms to retain and develop open access; to retain and develop freedom of information and communication as a human right in the modern democratic society.

Part II

SOCIAL RESPONSIBILITIES OF MEDIA IN A CHANGING SOCIETY

Media and Democracy

What is Really Required?

KAARLE NORDENSTRENG
Department of Journalism and Mass Communication, University of Tampere, Finland

Abstract

This paper reviews contemporary theories of democracy and what they say about the mass media. Democracy today with all its problems presents a big challenge for the media, with clear requirements placed on media by the principles of democracy. The requirements related to elections, openness, knowledge/conversation, and citizen's responsibilities are discussed. The paper concludes that it is possible to arrive at a number of concrete guidelines for the media, while there are more principal questions and challenges which need to be kept on the professional and academic agenda.

Introduction

In their paper at the Media Beyond 2000 Conference in London, April 1998, Jan van Cuilenburg and Denis McQuail examined the media policy paradigms distinguishable in the post-World War II developments in communications policy-making in the USA and in Europe (Van Cuilenburg & McQuail, 1998). The second of their three paradigms placed democracy as the central value pursued at the level of ultimate goals, as shown in Figure 1.

The next and still emerging 'new communications policy paradigm' in their scenario no longer places democracy as the ultimate goal; instead the goal has been changed to three aspects of social policy: political welfare, social welfare, economic welfare. Still, it is obvious that welfare stands here as a way to materialise democracy.

In general, it is not difficult to see that today the concept of democracy looms around discussions of media policy not only in this circle, but practically in all platforms, both intellectual and political. A typical example is provided by the European Commission's report from the high level group on audiovisual policy chaired by Commissioner Marcelino Oreja. It begins with a premise:

that a modern democratic society cannot exist without communication media which:

– are widely available and accessible;
– reflect the pluralistic nature of such a society and are not dominated by any one viewpoint or controlled by any one interest group;
– make available the information necessary for citizens to make informed choices about their lives and their communities;
– provide the means whereby the public debate which underpins free and democratic societies can take place, means that the market will not necessarily deliver on its own. (Oreja et al., 1998: 9).

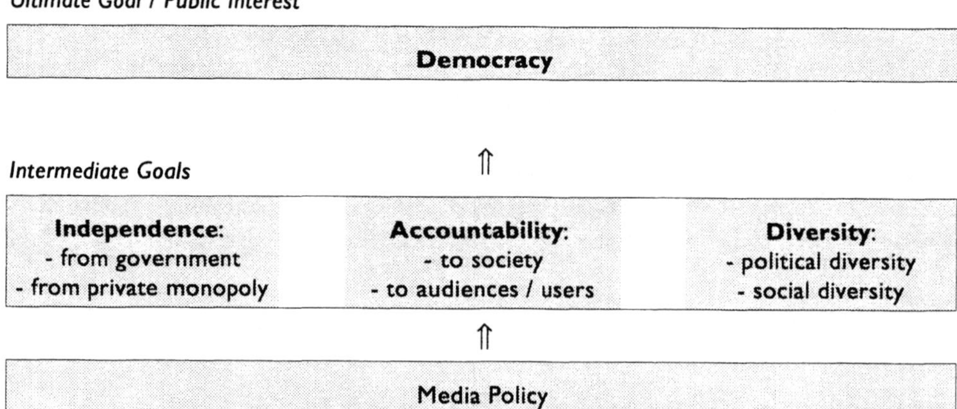

Figure 1 The second paradigm of public service media policy (1945 - 1980/ 1990) acccording to Van Cuilenburg & McQuail (1998: 67).

My own interest in democracy is based on personal involvement in media policy making, on national as well as international levels (for the latter, see Vincent et al., 1999). Its current focus comes from the project where Denis McQuail and three other colleagues have joined with me in trying to articulate the normative roles of the media, and to do it in a more satisfactory way than over 40 years ago in the *Four Theories of the Press* (Nordenstreng, 1997a). Democracy is naturally a cornerstone in this exercise, and, therefore, we have been led to take another look at what democracy is – from the traditions of its political philosophy to the structures and policies of arranging media in democratic society.

This paper reports some of that work in progress. Its focus is on reviews of relevant scholarship and it remains still sketchy as far as addressing the title's question is concerned.

Theories of Democracy and What They Say About Media

Democracy means rule by the people or popular power. It combines two Greek words, which already suggest a conceptual complex rather than a crystal clear meaning. *Demos* refers to a citizen body living in a *polis*, but it also refers to the lower classes, 'the mob'. *Kratos* for its part could mean either power or rule. Regardless of the fact that the majority of Greeks were women and slaves who were not considered to be free citizens at all, even the idea of all citizens introduced the problem of wealth, as highlighted by Aristotle: 'Whenever men rule by virtue of their wealth, be they few or many, there you have oligarchy; and where the poor rule, there you have democracy.' (in Arblaster, 1994: 13-14). No wonder, then, that democracy has always been a controversial and confusing concept. On the other hand, it has inspired much analytical reflection, beginning with the Greek classics and ending with the contemporary reviews (e.g. Soerensen, 1998).

An excellent guide for the history of ideas concerning democracy is *David Held* (Professor of Politics and Sociology at the Open University, UK). The second edition of his *Models of Democracy* (Held, 1996) is subdivided into four classic models and four 20th century models as displayed in Figure 2.

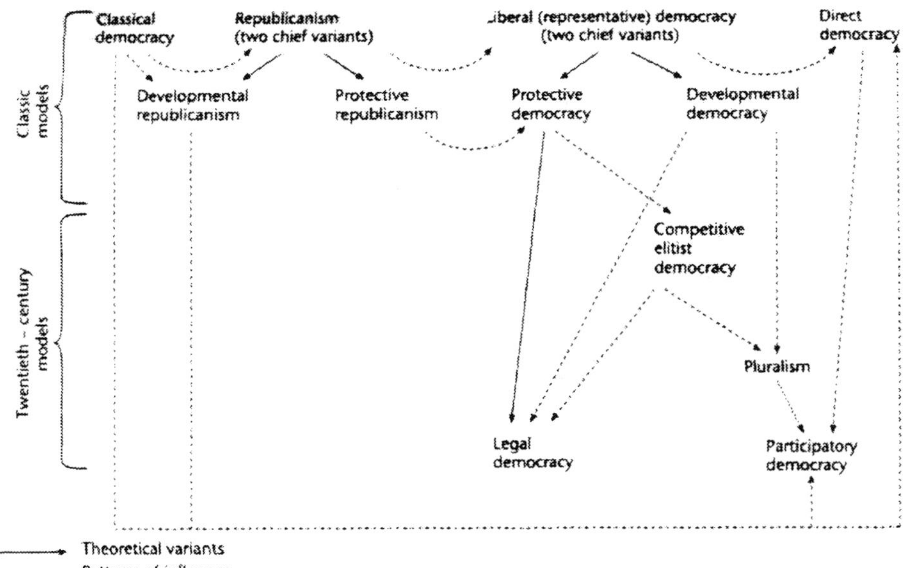

Figure 2 Variants of democracy according to Held (1996: 5)

This fairly complex map of models can be condensed into three basic variants of democracy:

1. direct or participatory democracy based on an active citizen and republican government,
2. liberal or representative democracy based on elected officers pursuing the interests of citizens, and
3. one-party democracy based on a pyramid structure of delegative relationships (Held, 1995: 5-16).

The third variant is obviously out of fashion after the upheavals of Soviet Communism (although Marxism remains as a vital intellectual resource), and Held's prospects of democracy today are geared around two emerging models: 'democratic autonomy' and 'cosmopolitan democracy' (Held, 1996: 274-360). The first approaches contemporary democracy in the context of a nation state, whereas the second explores how democracy extends to regional and global levels.

Mass Media and Democratic Autonomy

Held's models contain little – surprisingly little – that directly calls upon the mass media as elements of democracy. The subject index of his book has merely one reference to mass media: in connection with Marcuse's criticism of false consciousness, Held reminds how the media 'were shaped to a significant extent by the concerns of the advertising industry with its relentless drive to increase consumption' (Held, 1996: 239). Naturally, Habermas and the public sphere can be found, but they remain passing remarks rather than central constituents of the models.

Yet, a closer look at Held's contemporary models does open up media landscapes. While democratic autonomy involves 'the ability to deliberate, judge, choose and act upon different possible courses of action in private as well as public life' (Held, 1996: 300), the first of its five general conditions is 'open availability of information to help ensure informed decisions in public affairs' (idem: 324).

Held's reasoning here is based on criteria laid down by *Robert Dahl* (Professor Emeritus of Political Science at Yale University, USA), above all 'effective participation', 'exercising final control over the agenda' and 'gaining enlightened understanding' (e.g. Dahl, 1998: 37). The last-mentioned criterion makes a direct call for journalism and mass communication: 'Within reasonable limits as to time, each member must have equal and effective opportunities for learning about the relevant alternative policies and their likely consequences' (ibid.). Referring to new media developments including Internet, Dahl notes that:

> the sheer amount of information available on political matters, at all levels of complexity, has increased enormously. Yet this increased availability of information may not lead to greater competence or heightened understanding: scale, complexity, and the greater quantity of information impose even stronger demands on citizens' capacities.
>
> As a result, one of the imperative needs of democratic countries is to improve citizens' capacities to engage intelligently in political life. I don't mean to suggest that the institutions for civic education developed in the nineteenth and twentieth centuries should be abandoned. But I do believe that in the years to come these older institutions will need to be enhanced by new means for civic education, political participation, information, and deliberation that draw creatively on the array of techniques and technologies available in the twenty-first century. We have barely begun to think seriously about these possibilities, much less to test them out in small-scale experiments. (Dahl, 1998: 187-188).

One such experiment is no doubt the creation of citizen juries to deliberate over public issues, with eventual voter feedback mechanisms using interactive television, email, etc. (Held, 1996: 321-322). Variants of these are 'deliberative polling' (e.g. Fishkin, 1997) and naturally 'public journalism' (e.g. Glasser, 1999).

Strong Democracy

The model of contemporary democracy is often called 'deliberative democracy' and it can be seen as the third main historical stage following the 'direct' and 'representative' models. The same idea is conveyed by the concept of 'strong democracy' elaborated by *Benjamin Barber*, primarily with a view to the USA but fitting well also to the rest of the Western world. Barber (1998) suggests that the civil society should not be seen just as a synonym for the private sector (the libertarian perspective) or as synonym for community (the communitarian perspective, including reactionary tendencies from Patrick Buchanan to Jörg Haider) but as a domain between government and market – something that opens up a perspective to 'strong democratic civil society' and that can also be called 'civic republicanism',

> in that it has democratic virtues, encourages the habits and practices of democratic ways of living, and is defined by both publicness and liberty, egalitarianism and voluntarism. It is a model for an ideal democratic civil society: with citizens who are neither mere consumers of government services and right-bearers against government intru-

> sion, on the one hand, nor mere voters and passive watchdogs for whom representative governors are only vestigially accountable, on the other. Rather, its democratic citizens are active, responsible, engaged members of groups and communities that, while having different values and conflicting interests, are devoted to arbitrating those differences by exploring common ground, doing public work, and pursuing common relations. (Barber, 1998: 36-37).

Barber proposes to make such a civil society real through a number of practical strategies, beginning with 'enlarging and reinforcing public spaces' and followed by 'fostering civic uses of new telecommunications and information technologies, preventing commercialization from destroying their civic potentials: specifically, a civic Internet; public access cable television; a check on mass-media advertising (and commercial exploitation of) children' (Barber, 1998: 75). These proposals have a striking similarity with those made by critical media scholars beginning with *Herbert Schiller* in his systemic criticism (Schiller, 1969) and *George Gerbner* in his Cultural Environment Movement (Duncan, 1999). There are more and more of those who observe that the media are currently threatening rather than supporting democracy, but that there still is a margin of opportunity for remedy.

Cosmopolitan Democracy

Returning to Held's contemporary models, his second variant, cosmopolitan democracy is outlined through four areas where the regional and global systems are challenging the formal sovereign authority of democratic nation-states: (1) the world economy, (2) international organisations, (3) international law, (4) culture and environment (Held, 1996: 341-351). The media, both telecommunication and mass media with their multinational conglomerates, are part and parcel of the fourth area, although Held does not suggest them to 'imply the development of a single global media-led culture – far from it' (idem: 350). Still, they imply that:

> many new forms of communication and media range in and across borders, linking nations and peoples in new ways. Accordingly, the capacity of national political leaders to sustain a national culture has become more difficult. For example, China sought to restrict access to and use of the Internet, but it has found this virtually impossible to do. (Held, 1996: 351).

The prospects of cosmopolitan democracy are stimulating and offer welcome substance for the often shallow concept of globalization. However, this paper focuses on democracy in the more traditional context of a nation state, which still remains the main conceptual domain where media-democracy relationships are being discussed. The same context dominates even *The Changing Nature of Democracy* (Inoguchi et al., 1998), compiled by the United Nations University, which includes also chapters by *Elihu Katz* ('Mass media and participatory democracy' rehabilitating Gabriel de Tarde) and by *John Keane* ('The Philadelphia model' reconfigurating republicanism through his concepts of Micro, Meso and Macro public spheres).

Ideals and Practice

We can summarise the main contemporary models of democracy and the respective types of public sphere according to Nieminen (1998):
- direct democracy – popular public sphere
- representative democracy – elite public sphere
- deliberative democracy – pluralistic public sphere

Of these, the first one remains as a romantic ideal. The second one describes most of the contemporary reality despite its problematic character. The third one typically stands for practices that can remedy the defects of contemporary representative democracy. Actually, this typology, as useful as it may be in clarifying conceptual differences, does not only serve as an analytical tool but also operates as a normative instrument in suggesting what is the latest and best of the variants: the deliberative democracy and the pluralistic public sphere.

Such typologies and their perspectives are introduced at the level of models and theories. It is another matter how things are in reality; obviously there is a wide gap between everyday practice and theoretical models of democracy. It is worth noting that a similar theory/practice contradiction exists in the media field between the doctrines about the media in society and the actual operation of the media. As shown by Nordenstreng (1997b), doctrines are shifting towards more popular and participatory media theories, whereas reality is dominated by contrary tendencies with global market forces.

While we should not overlook reality, we should also observe what the history of ideas tells about our contemporary thinking on democracy. In this respect, it is not difficult to see that after the post-modern turn, accompanied by a lot of confusion, we are entering a new stage with a renaissance of Enlightenment. Obviously it is not the same old Enlightenment reborn but something new – with democracy and media closer to citizens and their full participation.

Democratic Pyramid

An instructive synthesis of the contemporary view of what is democracy is provided in a book commissioned by UNESCO from *David Beetham* and *Kevin Boyle* (Professors of Politics and Law at Universities of Leeds and Essex, UK, respectively). Starting with 'the twin principles of *popular control* over collective decision-making and *equality of rights* in the exercise of that control' (Beetham & Boyle, 1995: 1), they present four main components or building blocks of a functioning democracy: (1) free and fair elections, (2) open and accountable government, (3) civil and political rights, (4) a democratic or civil society (idem: 30-33). The four components constitute a pyramid as illustrated in Figure 3.

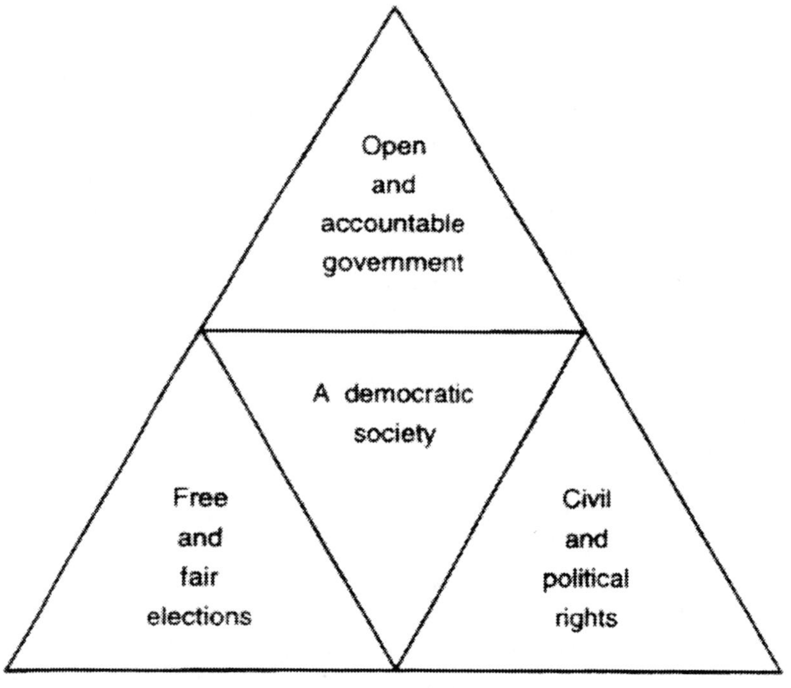

Figure 3 The democratic pyramid according to Beetham & Boyle (1995: 31)

The book elaborates these four components and also poses the question: Why are the media important to democracy? (Beetham & Boyle, 1995: 11-13). The answer begins with the most obvious – often overlooked when listing the functions of media in democracy – namely that all governments 'in every type of political system, seek to win for their policies the support or acquiescence of the population' and that therefore a legitimate function for the media in a democracy is 'simply to provide a channel for government propaganda' (idem: 11). But the main tasks listed are, first, the 'watchdog' role to inform the public and to investigate the government so as to 'offset the sheer weight of its public relations machine' (idem: 11), and second, the role of a forum for public debate which also provides 'a vehicle for the expression of public opinion to the government' (idem: 13). A separate point is made of the independence of the media, whereby

> the media can only perform these key democratic tasks if they are properly independent, and not dominated either by the government itself or by powerful private interests. The dominance of a government can be limited by making the publicly financed media accountable to an independent commission or to representatives of citizens' groups, and by allowing competition from privately financed media. The dominance of powerful private interests can be restrained by limiting concentrations of media ownership, and by other forms of regulation. None of these on their own, however, can guarantee that the media fulfill their democratic role impartially and effectively. Ultimately that depends upon the independence and professionalism of journalists, editors and producers and upon a widespread public acknowledgement of the vital contribution that the media make to the democratic process. (Beetham & Boyle, 1995: 13).

While such a statement by theorists of democracy sounds good to media scholars and educators, it remains easy theory against painful practice. In reality, the true face of democracy is exposed in the concrete ways by which public service and commercial media are run, and by which professionalism of journalists is materialised. Yet it is important to highlight the principles and repeat the theoretical positions – even if they may sound like trivialities – since only that effort will clarify the problems of democracy and the need to do something about them.

Problems of Democracy and Challenges to Media

The preceding review shows that the concept of democracy is not only open to different interpretations but also problematic because of a gap between what it means in theory and how it is being implemented in practice. Although democracy has become today – after the collapse of Communism in Eastern Europe – perhaps the main frame of reference for political development, its ideals are seldom materialised in everyday life. Rather the contrary: the more central democracy has become as a philosophical and political ideal, the more distant it often seems to be as a practical reality. Actually, the model of deliberative democracy, and

Barber's concept of strong democracy, can be seen as constructs attempting to overcome this contradiction between the theory and practice of democracy.

Paradoxes of Democracy and Media

The media are in the centre of this challenging contradiction. *Anthony Giddens* (President of the London School of Economics, UK) refers to it as 'the paradox of democracy' (Giddens, 1999):

> On the one hand, democracy is spreading over the world [...] Yet in the mature democracies, which the rest of the world is supposed to be copying, there is widespread disillusionment with democratic procedures. In most Western countries, levels of trust in politicians have dropped over past years. Fewer people turn out to vote than used to, particularly in the US. More and more people say that they are uninterested in parliamentary politics, especially among the younger generation. (Giddens, 1999: 3).

And Giddens continues about media as part of this equation:

> The media, particularly television, have a double relation to democracy. On the one hand, as I have stressed, the emergence of a global information society is a powerful democratising force. Yet television, and the other media, tend to destroy the very public space of dialogue they open up, through a relentless trivialising, and personalising, of political issues. Moreover, the growth of giant multinational media corporations means that unelected business tycoons can hold enormous power. (Giddens, 1999: 7).

Accordingly, Giddens joins *Robert McChesney* in contrasting the rich media with poor democracy. McChesney (1999) highlights the 'media/democracy paradox' of our time:

> On the one hand, it is an age of dazzling breakthroughs in communication and information technologies [...] provides a bounty of choices unimaginable a generation or two ago [...] On the other hand, our era is increasingly depoliticized; traditional notions of civic and political involvement have shriveled. Elementary understanding of social and political affairs have declined.... It is, to employ a phrase coined by Robert Entman, 'democracy without citizens'. (McChesney, 1999: 1-2).

The same kind of concern was raised by *Pierre Bourdieu* in a pamphlet (1998) where he claims that television is 'a threat [...] to democracy itself' (Bourdieu, 1998: 10). This threat to democracy comes from a lack of participation and trust in formal political systems – a disengagement of citizens, which is seen to be crucially fed by the media. The argument may be exaggerated, overlooking an emerging civic culture with 'lifestyle politics' (Dahlgren, 2000), but all the same such symptoms of malaise in democracy serve as fuel for examining the challenges faced by the media, or seen from the other side, the requirements placed to the media.

Democratic Challenges to Media

The EU report quoted in Introduction above (Oreja et al., 1998), singled out some characteristics of the media without which 'a modern democratic society cannot exist'. Those stand as a fairly representative sample of various lists on the tasks and roles of the media in society, to be found in official texts (from constitutions to committee reports) as well as in academic and professional literature. The most central of these points is no doubt the third one regarding 'information necessary for citizens to make informed choices about their lives and their communities'. The same classic point is quoted by Derek Edwards, Peter Golding et al. (1999: 40) with the words of former Director General of the BBC, Charles Curran, whereby broadcasters have a responsibility 'to provide a rationally based and balanced service of news which will enable adult people to make basic judgments about public policy in their capacity as voting citizens of a democracy'.

In one of the first academic contributions to reflections of communication and democracy in the 1990s, Slavko Splichal (1993: 5) lists four general assumptions regarding communication in all types of democracy:

1. Citizens are well informed.
2. Citizens are interested [...] in [...] politics.
3. Citizens have equal rights to speak and participate in decision making.
4. All decisions are submitted to public discussions.

Such lists lead us to examine and elaborate in greater detail the question of what is required from the media in a democracy. Obviously this question is implicit in a lot of contemporary media research, with even calls for action by reform movements (see e.g. Nordenstreng, 1999). Yet, an in-depth and systematic study of media and democracy remains rare – surprisingly rare given the popularity of democracy as a normative frame of reference. Among notable exceptions who offer serious food for thought on media and democracy are John Keane (1991), James Curran (1991) and Karol Jakubowicz (1998).

Requirements for Media

What, then, can be concluded and what answer given to the question posed by the title? Here we shall focus on four aspects: (1) elections, (2) openness, diversity and pluralism, (3) knowledge and/or conversation, and (4) citizen's responsibilities.

Elections

Free and fair elections is the first of the four building blocks in the 'democratic pyramid' displayed in Figure 3 above. The strategic importance of elections is often forgotten in Western democracies, where they tend to be routinised although they are typically surrounded by conflicts – not the least regarding media access and coverage.

Elections in so-called new democracies have brought the topic back to the agenda, with the media playing a central role. Human rights organisations such as Article 19 have prepared guidelines particularly for election broadcasting (Darbishire, 1998), and research bodies such as The European Institute for the Media have monitored the performance of media during election campaigns in Central and Eastern Europe (Lange, 1999). A particular case was provided by the first post-Apartheid elections in South Africa and the subsequent Truth Commission (Van Zyl & Kantor, 1999).

These materials provide us with both general principles and specific rules about how media should perform in a democracy in connection with elections. There is little doubt about what is required here; the question is whether the media perform as they are supposed to do. In this regard it is reassuring to see that media monitoring has become a natural part of the election supervising in new democracies around the world. But the same should be done in old democracies. What is needed is just an inventory of relevant requirements and the will to implement them.

Openness

The second building block of the 'democratic pyramid' is open and accountable government, which together with the fourth element – democratic civil society – places special requirements on the media. An open society in this respect means above all diversity and pluralism of media content, both in terms of the variety of topics and voices brought to the public sphere and in terms of the viewpoints and values displayed. And as reminded by Jan van Cuilenburg (1998), there are at least two different types of diversity regarding media coverage of the socio-political spectrum: on the one hand 'reflective diversity' whereby the distribution of opinion in the media is more or less the same as within the population at large, and on the other hand 'open diversity' whereby media give equal attention to all identifiable positions in society. Obviously democratic values speak for the open rather than reflective version of diversity, but in practice this might be difficult for the political majority to tolerate, because it would favour various minority opinions at the expense of the mainstream.

This is an area where a number of practical rules are to be found in the codes of professional ethics. However, more homework is needed to specify how diversity and pluralism should be applied in media. This is not a mission impossible, since there are no obstacles of principle to arrive at quite a detailed and concrete set of guidelines about how to ensure and maximise diversity and pluralism. The question is simply whether enough so-called political will can be found to enforce this homework and its implementation – whether media are interested in taking democracy seriously.

A particular aspect of openness is the question of minority rights and tolerance concerning orthodox groups. In general, liberal and democratic tradition has supported ethnic, religious and other minorities, which today constitute part and parcel of the human rights doctrine canonised in international instruments beginning with the Universal Declaration of Human Rights. This overall doctrine respects autonomy of minority groups and places an obligation to national and global majorities to allow the minorities to exist and even supports their exercise of own language, customs, etc., including the media. Meanwhile, minorities themselves are supposed to follow the same liberal values, as spelled out in the theory of minority rights by Will Kymlicka (1995). But what about minorities which do not subscribe to liberal values and which may even pursue opposing philosophies of intolerance, both regarding their own members and communities at large? This question was concretely faced some years ago in Algeria where democratic elections were aborted when fundamentalist Islamists seemed to gain majority, and it has recently become a big issue in the European Union where neo-Fascist political parties have gained significant popular support as shown in Austria.

What is required from the media in these situations should be easier to settle than the question of minority rights of intolerant and orthodox groups themselves. The latter question poses both philosophical and political problems which challenge the whole democratic tradition, but the media may approach the question as another aspect of diversity and pluralism. No doubt there are sensitive political issues involved, but that should not give an excuse for the media and its journalistic profession to give up the responsibility of determining what to do and performing in accordance with those requirements.

Knowledge/Conversation

This is a more problematic question in principle. What is at issue is the classic dispute known as the Dewey-Lippmann debate: whether the primary role of the media in democracy is to provide citizens with reliable information about the objective realities, or whether the media are supposed to serve as platforms of exchange of opinion and conversation between citizens (see chapters by Rosen, Carey and particularly Peters in Glasser, 1999). There is no question about the role of media as factual surveyors of the world, but there are different schools of thought regarding the importance of conversation between people and among communities.

A typical Habermasian mode of thinking has elevated the concept of rational debate into the centre of reasoning about what media should do in democracy, which has in practice stressed more conversation than knowledge. Post-modern and communitarian streams of thought for their part have also come to place conversation over and above knowledge. On the other hand, there are those who refuse to go with the trendy stream and instead question like Michael Schudson (1997), why conversation is *not* the soul of democracy. One of these sceptics, John Peters sides with Walter Lippmann of the 1920s 'that social complexity, speed, global warfare overstimulation, censorship, elite propaganda, mass inattention and stereotypes, the irrational character of human psychology, and an overworked and ill-disciplined news media all spelled the demise of popular sovereignty, or at least of its founding fiction of a well-informed public' (Peters, 1999: 103). Therefore Peters renounces the dream of dialogue as a pure form of democratic exercise and calls for caution in approaching public journalism.

A similar call for philosophical caution, particularly regarding television, is made by Jostein Gripsrud (1999). Karol Jakubowicz for his part, reminds us that the so-called information society does not offer magical solutions for democracy; rather the contrary since the electronic networks may support, instead of a direct civic discourse, a fragmentation of society: 'Accordingly, unless the information society develops other mechanisms for creating this sense of cohesion serving as a forum for public debate, the media are not likely to lose their importance in democracy in the foreseeable future' (Jakubowicz, 1998: 30).

Consequently, it is hard to arrive at a set of requirements for the media regarding the fundamental question of knowledge vs. conversation. Actually this is not an aspect that lends itself to concrete guidelines like in the cases of elections and openness above; this is rather a window which opens contextual perspectives for practical action. The perspectives opened are basically the same as those related to the classic issues of objectivity in journalism, and they call forth a philosophical examination of the kind of information which is being transmitted in news and other media messages. Such an epistemological as well as ethical consideration of media is vital for any serious media activity, because it is on this intellectual basis that the more tangible requirements are made.

Citizen's Responsibilities

One of the assumptions included in the above list by Splichal is that citizens are genuinely interested in politics – something that stands behind all the reasoning about media helping 'adult people to make basic judgments about public policy' (Curran, in Edwards et al, 1999: 40). Developments in Western democracies cast serious doubt on how this assumption is materialised in actual practice, given the distrust of political parties and public institutions, low voter turnout in elections, etc. On the other hand, we could also quote countertrends towards new 'lifestyle politics' and even conventional politics in cases such as the recent presidential elections in Finland (won by a woman from a Socialist party, not belonging to Church and living in open marriage – in a predominantly bourgeois and protestant country).

Schudson (1995: 223) points out to 'the reality that not all citizens are or ever will be rational, intelligent, active, and constant participants in the political process' and concludes that there are virtues of a schizophrenic situation of the news media 'to act as if classical democracy were within reach and simultaneously to work as if a large, informed, and involved electorate were not possible'.

In any case democratic theory places a responsibility on citizens to be interested and engaged in politics, including political messages provided by the media. It was symptomatic that Cees Hamelink (1994) included the following paragraph in the first draft for the People's Communication Charter:

> *People's Responsibilities*
> Article 26. In accordance with international law all people have the responsibility to strive towards the respect of human rights. In the light of this responsibility we urge all people to contribute to the implementation of the provision of this Charter. We recommend strongly that users of the media should form (national and international) coalitions to promote people's right to communicate. (Hamelink, 1994: 160).

This Article is no longer to be found in the final version of the Charter (Duncan, 1999: 175-181). Still, the idea of responsibilities built into citizenship is present, more or less explicitly, in all reasoning about media and democracy. It is particularly topical regarding the problems and paradoxes of democracy discussed above, whereby people are largely disillusioned with democratic procedures and the media seem to contribute to this malaise of democracy. Such a gloomy perspective poses a challenge to both the people and the media – they should become more responsible and begin to enforce democracy against the trends of the day.

Actually the previous sentence could be placed here as an overall conclusion of what was discussed above. Also, one could restate here that it is possible in principle to arrive at an extensive list of requirements for the media and that it is indeed important to do this – preferably as a joint project by media professionals and academics. Moreover, there are questions and challenges to media and democracy which cannot be turned into practical guidelines but which are equally important to elaborate and keep constantly on the professional and academic agenda.

References

Arblaster, A.
1994 *Democracy*. 2nd edition. Minneapolis, MN: University of Minnesota Press.

Barber, B.
1998 *A Place for Us: How to Make Society Civil and Democracy Strong.* New York: Hill and Wang.

Beetham, D. and Boyle, K.
1995 *Introducing Democracy: 80 Questions and Answers.* Cambridge: Polity Press.

Bourdieu, P.
1998 *On Television and Journalism.* London: Pluto.

Curran, J.
1991 Mass media and democracy: A reappraisal. In J. Curran and M. Gurevitch (eds.), *Mass Media and Society*, pp. 82-117. London: Edward Arnold. (2nd edition, 1996; 3rd edition, 2000.)

Dahl, R.
1998 *On Democracy.* New Haven: Yale University Press.

Dahlgren, P.
2000 Media, citizenship and civic culture. In J. Curran and M. Gurevitch (eds.), *Mass Media and Society.* 3rd edition. London: Edward Arnold.

Darbishire, H.
1998 Media and the electoral process. In *Media and Democracy*, pp. 79-102. Strasbourg: Council of Europe Publishing.

Duncan, K. (ed.)
1999 *Liberating Alternatives: The Founding Convention of the Cultural Environment Movement.* Cresskill, NJ: Hampton Press.

Edwards, D., Golding, P., Howitt, D., Mclachlan, S. and MacMillan, K.
1999 An audit of democracy: Media monitoring, citizenship, and public policy. In K. Nordenstreng and M. Griffin (eds.), *International Media Monitoring*, pp. 39-55. Cresskill, NJ: Hampton Press.

Fishkin, J.
1997 *The Voice of the People: Public Opinion and Democracy*. New Haven: Yale University Press.

Giddens, A.
1999 *Democracy*. In The Reith Lectures on the BBC World Service, 8 May.
<http://news.bbc.co.uk/hi/english/static/events/reith_99/week5>.

Glasser, Th. (ed.)
1999 *The Idea of Public Journalism*. New York/London: The Guilford Press.

Gripsrud, J. (ed.)
1999 *Television and Common Knowledge*. London and New York: Routledge.

Hamelink, C.
1994 *Trends in World Communication: On Disempowerment and Self-empowerment*. Penang: Southbound and Third World Network.

Held, D.
1995 *Democracy and the Global Order: From the Modern State to Cosmopolitan Governance*. Cambridge: Polity Press.

Held, D.
1996 *Models of Democracy*. 2nd edition. Stanford, CA: Stanford University Press.

Inoguchi, T., Newman, E. and Keane, J. (eds.)
1998 *The Changing Nature of Democracy*. Tokyo/New York/Paris: United Nations University Press.

Jakubowicz, K.
1998 Media and democracy. In *Media & Democracy*, pp. 9-33. Strasbourg: Council of Europe Publishing.

Keane, J.
1991 *The Media and Democracy*. Cambridge: Polity Press.

Kymlicka, W.
1995 *Multicultural Citizenship: A Liberal Theory of Minority Rights*. Oxford: Clarendon Press.

Lange, Y.
1999 Monitoring election coverage in CEE and the CIS. In K. Nordenstreng and M. Griffin (eds.), *International Media Monitoring*, pp. 387-406. Cresskill, NJ: Hampton Press.

McChesney, R.
1999 *Rich Media, Poor Democracy*. Urbana, Ill.: University of Illinois Press.

Nieminen, H.
1998 Media ja demokratia: Kohti pluralistista julkisuutta? [Media and democracy: Towards a pluralistic public sphere?]. In U. Kivikuru and R. Kunelius (eds.), *Viestinnän Jäljillä* [Tracing Communication], pp. 275-299. Helsinki: WSOY.

Nordenstreng, K.
1997a Beyond the four theories of the press. In J. Servaes and R. Lie (eds.), *Media and Politics in Transition. Cultural Identity in the Age of Globalization*, pp. 97-109. Leuven/Amersfoort: ACCO Publishers.

Nordenstreng, K.
1997b The citizen moves from the audience to the arena. *Nordicom Review* 18 (2): 13-20.

Nordenstreng, K.
1999 *Media and Democracy: Do We Know What to Do?* Paper presented at conference in honour of Herbert I. Schiller at the University of California, San Diego, 2-3 October.

Oreja, M. et al.
1998 *The Digital Age: European Audiovisual Policy*. Report from the High Level Group on Audiovisual Policy. Brussels: European Commission.

Peters, J.D.
1999 Public journalism and democratic theory: Four challenges. In Th. Glasser (ed.), *The Idea of Public Journalism*, pp. 99-117. New York: Guilford.

Schiller, H.
1969 *Mass Communications and American Empire*. New York: Augustus M. Kelley. (2nd edition, 1996, Boulder, CO: Westview Press.)

Schudson, M.
1995 *The Power of News*. Cambridge, MA: Harvard University Press.

Schudson, M.
1997 Why conversation is not the soul of democracy. *Critical Studies in Mass Communication* 14: 297-309.

Soerensen, G.
1998 *Democracy and Democratization: Processes and Prospects in a Changing World*. 2nd edition. Boulder, CO: Westview Press.

Splichal, S.
1993 Searching for new paradigms: An introduction. In S. Splichal and J. Wasko (eds.), *Communication and Democracy*, pp. 3-18. Norwood, NJ: Ablex.

Van Cuilenburg, J.
1998 Diversity revisited: Towards a critical rational model of media diversity. In K. Brants, J. Hermes and L. van Zoonen (eds.), *The Media in Question. Popular Cultures and Public Interests*, pp. 38-49. London: Sage.

Van Cuilenburg, J. and McQuail, D.
1998 Media policy paradigm shifts. In search of a new communications policy paradigm. In R.G. Picard (ed.), *Evolving Media Markets: Effects of Economic and Policy Changes*, pp. 57-80. Turku: The Economic Research Foundation for Mass Communication.

Van Zyl, J. and Kantor, L.
1999 Monitoring the South African media: The shift from Apartheid propaganda to the Truth Commission. In K. Nordenstreng and M. Griffin (eds.), *International Media Monitoring*, pp. 407-426. Cresskill, NJ: Hampton Press.

Vincent, R., Nordenstreng, K. and Traber, M. (eds.)
1999 *Towards Equity in Global Communication: MacBride Update.* Cresskill, NJ: Hampton Press.

The Social Responsibility of the Media as a Concept in Transition

YASSEN N. ZASSOURSKY
Faculty of Journalism, Moscow State University, Russia

Abstract

This paper argues that the concept of social responsibility itself is vague and ambiguous enough to allow its use for various and often conflicting purposes, as will be shown on the basis of various historic examples from the East and West. Therefore, we should rather accept and promote the responsibility of the media to the citizens, as a tool of human rights, rather than to the state. Especially with regard to the Internet, it is urgent to develop under the auspices of UN or UNESCO an international charter in co-operation between users, business, and governments which will make media organisations as well as individual providers of information to the Global Net accountable to the world community.

Introduction

The concept of the responsibility of the media has been undergoing substantial transformations and changes under the new circumstances created by the rapidly developing new information and communication technologies. The emergence of the Internet as a new global and universal communication and information sphere has dramatically changed ways of access to the media and information in several ways – media became accessible in electronic form extending their availability on the one hand and opening possibilities for direct use of information from various data banks on the Web on the other hand. Thus the media lost their monopoly for the delivery of information to the public, but they retained their key role as sources of content for the Internet.

Under these circumstances the role of the media undergoes dramatic changes – they are getting global audiences through their electronic versions and they are loosening their attachment to the territory of their terrestrial distribution and widen the scope of their influence beyond their media packaging as providers of content for the Internet. Thus their responsibility extends beyond their media format and involves new players:

besides traditional journalists, editors, owners, readers, listeners, and viewers, they include Internet providers, the telecommunications industry and their international and national regulators, and consumers of electronic data. Convergence and globalization provide new opportunities for developing the Open Society within and beyond national borders and impose new responsibilities and new roles upon the media.

Understanding changing and transforming responsibilities of the media in the Information and Knowledge Society requires an insight into the very concept of the responsibility of the media since its inception, its development in various countries under different circumstances in Europe, and in the United States.

The Development of the Concept of the Responsibility of the Press

The first documents proclaiming the freedom of the press do not mention any need for promoting special instruments for the accountability of the press. The first mentioning of this possibility is in the French Declaration of Human and Civic Rights of 26 August 1789. Its article 11 proclaims: 'La libre communication des pensées et des opinions est un des droits les plus précieux de l'homme; tout citoyen peut donc parler, écrire, imprimer librement, sauf à répondre de l'abus de cette liberté dans les cas déterminés par la Loi.'[1] (Duhamel et al., 1992: 11). In this way opposing the abuse of the freedom of the press, the Declaration thus sets up the first case for proper and improper use of the press which really involves the responsibility and accountability of the media in its liberal sense as different from the First Amendment to the Constitution of the United States which declares complete separation of the press from the State and the Government. The French media laws of the 19th and 20th centuries developed this concept in various legal provisions, providing laws regulating the rights and responsibilities of the press.

Etatist Conceptions of Social Responsibilities

The responsibility of the press concept got a new twist in Mussolini's Fascist Italy where it was manipulated to subordinate the media to the Fascist State. The responsibility to the Fascist State was seen as a substitute for

1 'Free communication of ideas and opinions is one of the most precious human rights; henceforth citizens may speak, write and print freely, though in cases defined by law they may be made to answer for their abuse of this right.' (Duhamel et al., 1992: 11)

the freedom of the press. Moreover, one of the theoreticians of Fascist journalism law put it bluntly: 'institutes of people's culture and propaganda, and first of all the newspaper are the spiritual militia of Fascism' (Iovane, 1939: 38; in translation). In this way, the responsibility of the press was seen as a part of Fascist education of the population in which journalism was turned into an instrument of closing the society, of separating it from the world.

That was an etatist totalitarian approach to the concept of the responsibility of the press which proves that there might be different interpretations of this idea. A crucial aspect of the notion of the responsibility depends on the interpretation of the role of the state, its relationship with the citizens and the character of the state itself. In the case of Fascist Italy the state was dictating the will of the Fascist rulers to the public deprived of the right to reject or elect the government, and the responsibility of the media was seen to serve the Fascist regime and to indoctrinate the population isolated by the closed society from the outside world.

The Soviet Union proclaimed its antifascist stand. Its media were overtly antifascist, but their role was prescribed by the Communist party. 'The Soviet journalist must co-ordinate each move with the Party Programme and statutes, with the norms of Party life, apply to himself the highest requirements not only while carrying out his duties, but in all other spheres of life.' (Prokhorov, 1978: 96; in translation). The Soviet system of the media and its responsibility was essentially based on authoritarian and at certain stages (as during notorious purges of the late thirties) on totalitarian concepts. 'The totalitarian model for explaining the structure and development of Soviet society presupposes a total control over communication. However, in practice this control was far from total, although it was the aim of the system.' (Nordenstreng & Pietilainen, 1999: 150).

The social responsibility of the media in the Soviet Union was seen as a responsibility to the society, to the people, but mostly through serving the Communist Party and the Soviet State. This approach led to the subordination of the media to the Communist party politics, with a heavy dependence on the role of the leaders of the Communist party from Stalin to Khrushchev in a straightforward authoritarian way. Finally Mikhail Gorbachev turned the tide against the party bureaucrats to restore democracy and free press. The free press remained during the Perestroika period an instrument of the Communist party used for changing the trend of the development of the Russian society towards openness and democracy. At this stage a new concept of civic responsibility of the media was evolved, which was seen as 'responsibility to the society for a measure of conformity of the position and its realisation to the objective needs of social development.' (Prokhorov, 1995: 270; in translation).

This concept is close to the social responsibility of the media approach of the Hutchins commission, although it does not specify the role of different actors in the media and communication process.

The Soviet pattern of the media was essentially an instrumental model, in which responsibility was referred to the Communist party leadership and first of all the Communist party leader himself, who in reality played a major role in determining the changes in media modes.

The social responsibility of the media in the Soviet Union was seen and presented as a responsibility to the society, to the people, but mostly through serving the Communist Party and the Soviet State or just the government. The corresponding colloquial formula was coined by the military – we serve the Party and the Government – though this obsession with the government used to be a part of traditional Russian mentality – for Tsar, God and Fatherland. However, being the servants of the party, journalists were expected to look for the interests of the society with a special reference to the people and ordinary men and women. This was an important part of the Soviet mass media and communication discourse.

The Theory of Social Responsibility

In 1947 the theory of the social responsibility of the press was presented and promoted in the United States by the Hutchins Commission to defend the public from the monopoly of the press corporations. It outlined six fundamental tasks of the press as servicing the political system, enlightening the public, serving as a watchdog over government, servicing the economic system, providing entertainment, and maintaining its own self-sufficiency (Peterson, 1956; Liebovich, 1995).

Critics of this theory objected to it on several grounds.

- First, it was argued that the theory implied 'a radical reconstruction of the relationship between individuals and communities, with a new emphasis on the latter. Social responsibility theory thus represents the triumph of community over the lone individual.' (Nerone, 1995: 78).
- Second, from a liberal perspective, responsibility was considered a nice word for authoritarian regulation aligned with the authoritarian and Soviet communist theories, as permutations of communism (Nerone, 1995).
- Third, from the left, social responsibility theory was considered to endorse the status quo, by making monopoly media look like the voice of the people (Nerone, 1995).

It is interesting to note that these criticisms mentioned by the authors of *Last Rights. Revisiting the Four Theories of the Press* are very close to the evaluation and critique of the American concept by Soviet media experts, who in reviewing the 'four theories of the press' saw the weakness of the American concept in that it made media responsible to the government, thus moving closer to the authoritarian concept. In this sense Nerone's criticism that the theory of social responsibility signals the triumph of the community over the lone individual, seems extremely pertinent and appropriate.

An analysis of different approaches to the concept of the responsibility on the basis of Italian, Soviet and American experiences demonstrates its broadness and adaptability to different political and social structures. It also demonstrates the real dangers of becoming trapped into an etatist, authoritarian or even totalitarian scheme, if the interests of the audiences are disregarded and discarded to the pressure of political or economic forces.

Social Responsibility Theory in Russia

In Russia the concept of responsibility of the media went at least through four stages:

- First, during the Perestroika period, responsibility meant responsibility to the Party, led by the reformist Mikhail Gorbachev, and responsibility to the public; opposing the state and party bureaucracy.
- Second, after the adoption of the media law, 'responsibility of the media' became responsibility to the journalists' teams and the public; opposing the intrusion of the state into media practices.
- Third, during the presidential campaign of 1996, 'responsibility of the media' lost its civic fervour and turned for many journalists into responsibility and almost subjugation to the coalition of banks and corporations that supported President Boris Yeltsin, with journalists being forced into a fight against pressures of the new owners of the media to defend their professional journalistic integrity.
- Fourthly, in the last three years, the notion of responsibility was losing momentum under the pressure of media tycoons and state officials involved in the so-called 'information wars' for economic and political gains. In this last period, journalists try to resist and to retain and regain from the owners and the state their rights, granted by media law.

Unfortunately, public institutions and self-regulation have not been developing in Russia. Practically there is no public television, and the channel bearing the name of Public Russian Television (ORT) is partly owned by the state and private corporations, with a nominal board of trustees that has no real power and whose opinion is disregarded by the management and administration of the ORT. Therefore, the ORT unfortunately is one of the most ardent and energetic information warriors in Russia today.

Responsibility in its Relation to Media, State, Public, and Human Rights

In each case the concept of the media responsibility involved the decisive regulatory role of the State, with varying degrees of its involvement: from totalitarianism and authoritarianism, to liberal constitutional and democratic regulation as presented by Article XIX of the Universal Declaration of Human Rights, and article 10 of the European Convention of Human Rights, which is a bit more restrictive than the Article XIX.

Media Law and Ethics

The Russian media law proclaims the freedom of the press, but provides for the State to register the media, to provide access to official information, and to distribute broadcasting frequencies. The law also envisages the right of the State and its institutions to own, set up and promote mass media. Therefore, the Russian State has practically a dual position of regulator and owner of a substantial part of the media, especially in broadcasting and in the rapidly developing sector of regional media dominated by local authorities. The state thus is a most important player in the mass communications sector in content and in organisational structures of the media. And this often puts constraints on the openness of the Russian society, though the access to information act has passed the first reading in the Duma.

Information wars waged by media corporations seem to reveal various aspects of criminal activities and corruption in various sectors of Russian society, but in most cases mutual accusations are based on gossip, leaks from unnamed sources and they finally lead to the loss of credibility of media and journalists and to complaints of the public to the effect that media are often irresponsible and unreliable.

The Union of Russian Journalists, the Foundation in Defence of Glasnost, human rights activists and other professional organisations are trying to promote professional standards of objectivity and public concern in the face of growing use of media as instruments of politicking. Under these circumstances promotion of the media ethics and of responsibility of the journalists to the public and to the citizens becomes a crucial issue.

Internet News and Information

With mass media losing credibility and with decreasing access to newspapers and magazines, which are often losing their circulation due to economic difficulties and low purchasing ability of the population more people are trying to get their news and information from alternative sources and most of all from the Internet.

The Internet penetration in Russia is comparatively small – 1.5 million Internet lines with about 6 million regular users for a population of about 140 million. Most of the users of the Internet are young and middle aged professionals, researchers, educators and especially students.

I believe that the Russian intellectual and business elite has been widely using the information resources of the Internet and has been in a way relying on them in an increasingly substantial way. Therefore the Web has become an extremely important factor in the Russian information infrastructure, promoting more open and immediate access to information and thus becoming a major catalyst of openness and consequently of the Open Society.

Unfortunately politicking came into Russian Internet bringing information wars into web sites. Special sites have been created to spread rumours and compromising data about various politicians and candidates in parliamentary and presidential elections.

The growing importance of the Internet also prompted speedy reaction from the Russian ministry of the Interior. In the latest case of State interference in public access to information, it created a special Department 'R' for combating crimes in the sphere of high technology. This unit is monitoring the Internet in Russia and has succeeded in removing from the Web the notorious site 'Kogot' (Claw), which was accused of spreading false and provocative information.

Responsibilities to Citizens

Russian officials and politicians, referring to the responsibility of the media, in fact mean responsibility to the State. The totalitarian and authoritarian heritage of the Soviet era is still exerting its influence. The development of the Open Society is decisively dependent upon abandoning etatist 'control' syndromes in Russia, especially in the information and media sphere. Responsibility is called upon, when the public starts complaining about pornography, and violence in the media, most of all on television. But numerous state institutions have not changed the climate of entertainment programmes. Often appeals to the responsibility of journalists on the part of various state institutions and officials are just a pretext for widening the bureaucratic machine and for interfering into the activities of the media, often with a political reason.

I believe that the concept of social responsibility itself is vague and ambiguous enough to allow its use for various and often conflicting purposes. It is my sincere concern and belief that we should rather accept and promote the responsibility of the media to the public, to the citizens. In any case, the essence of the problem is not in the name, but in understanding the mission of the media as a tool of human rights of individuals rather than of the State. The responsibility should be to individuals, to citizens, who after all comprise the society; they are the society. But it is most important to change the policies, rather than names. And this is especially true for the media based upon new information and communication technologies.

It is usual to ascribe responsibility to the journalists, and much more rarely to ascribe it to the editors and only in exceptional cases in Russia to owners. But taking into consideration the often crucial role of media proprietors in determining the policies of the media, it is extremely important to extend the notion of the responsibility to media holdings and corporations. The case of the Swedish Bonnier AB group is important. This group is actively promoting its ethic principles. Its web site puts its policies in the following way: 'We stand for freedom of speech and a feeling of responsibility for our readers, listeners, viewers, advertisers and employees, and for the society in which we live and operate.' (Braun, 1999). Certainly it is even more important to live up to these high ideals. But even this declaration of intent is a move in the right direction which might be a good example for Russian media industry. Education of media owners in the 'art of responsibility' may prove to be difficult, but in most cases their position is crucial for the behaviour of the media.

In any case, nowadays regulation of media can not be the monopoly of the State. It should involve organisations of journalists, editors, publishers and consumers of information and mass media products – readers, listeners, viewers, network users.

Responsibility in the Changing Information Milieu: The Internet and the Open Society

The Internet has been rapidly becoming a major source and vehicle of the Open Society. It undermines the monopoly of the media industry (its owners, publishers, editors, journalists) on the direct and immediate access to information. And it opens the way for the public, for the citizens, and what is especially important, for individuals to use, create and exchange information freely and openly in their own interests. Traffic rules for Internet information flows should be established on the basis of consensus of users, providers and the States in the spirit of public responsibility to the citizens of the world.

The above is the suggestion of the conference held recently in Kuala Lumpur. In this case, it was suggested that the Internet should be regulated jointly by public and private bodies. A two-day conference – the World Summit of Regulators of the Internet – is held in Paris on November 30, 1999. The United States seem unwilling to regulate the Internet, but the Federal Communications Commission announced that it would participate in the Paris conference. Certainly, Internet regulation is a very delicate matter; it should not interfere with the free flow information and with the openness of access and use of information.

Traffic regulation of communication flows under the new circumstances should take into consideration media laws, ethic and professional codes, agreements between journalist organisations and associations of media owners, and interests and concerns of media consumers as represented by media councils. Globalization of information activities makes it really urgent to develop under the auspices of UN or UNESCO an international charter in co-operation between users, business, and governments, which will make media organisations as well as individual providers of information to the Global Net accountable to the world community and to its citizens.

References

Braun, B.

1999 *Objective and vision.* <http://www.bonnier.se/eng/objective_vision.asp>.

Duhamel, O., De Moor, A., Pollmeier, C., Vilanova, P., Vernet, J. and Portelli, M.

1992 *La Constitution française. Français-anglais-allemand-espagnol-italien.* Paris: Presses Universitaires de France.

Iovane, E.

1939 *Diritto Giornalistico.* Milano.

Liebovich, L.W.

1995 Has the press become responsible? In J.C. Nerone (ed.), *Last Rights. Revisiting Four Theories of the Press*, pp. 100-104. Urbana, Ill.: University of Illinois Press.

Nerone, J.C.

1995 Introduction to 'Social responsibility theory'. In J.C. Nerone (ed.), *Last Rights. Revisiting Four Theories of the Press*, pp. 77-79. Urbana, Ill.: University of Illinois Press.

Nordenstreng, K. and Pietilainen, J.

1999 Normative theories of the media: Lessons from Russia. In Y.N. Zassoursky and E. Vartanova (eds.), *Media, Communications and the Open Society*, pp. 146-159. Moscow: Faculty of Journalism/IKAR Publisher.

Prokhorov, Y.

1978 *Vvedeniye v Zhurnalistiku.* [Introduction into Journalism]. Moscow.

Prokhorov, Y.
1995 *Vvedeniye v Teoriyu Zhurnalistiki.* [Introduction into the Theory of Journalism]. Moscow.
Peterson, Th.
1956 The social responsibility theory of the press. In F. Siebert, Th. Peterson and W. Schramm (eds.), *Four Theories of the Press,* pp. 73-103. Urbana, Ill.: University of Illinois Press.

Openness in States in Transition

The Role of the State and Journalists in South Africa

IRINA NETCHAEVA
Faculty of Journalism, Moscow State University, Russia

Abstract

This paper analyses whether South Africa is moving to the Open Society scene. The author discusses the social conditions that are required to provide all citizens with equal access to ICT, and to bring about an Open Society. She argues that at the moment these conditions do not yet exist in South Africa. Subsequently, she investigates the role of journalists in the transformation of South African society. The author argues the need for a more community centred interpretation of the social responsibilities of media and journalists in South Africa.

Introduction

According to studies of European scholars, states in transition have to undergo processes of marketisation and democratisation. The market economy existed already in South Africa in the *apartheid* age, but the market was closed for enterprises of blacks and barred for foreign companies. Now these barriers are disappearing. More and more foreign firms are entering the South African market. The numbers of black businessmen have rapidly grown thanks to the policy of affirmative action and black empowerment. These changes are especially obvious in the information and communications sector. Major global multinational corporations have already been operating on the South African market. Many black-owned or partly black-owned companies have been set up in the mass media sector. People from previously disadvantaged communities have got senior decision making positions in all South African media groups.

Democratisation processes are growing even more rapidly. After the democratic elections of 1994 political and administrative power structures on the institutional level were replaced by new democratic constitutional institutions. At present in South Africa all main democratic institutions exist: president, parliament, political parties, democratic elections, ombudsmen and a system of diverse mass media. The broad use of modern information and communication technology (ICT) in South Africa successfully contributes to this democratisation process. This became obvious during the last elections. Electronic media provided better, broader and quicker coverage of elections than traditional mass media. They were able to produce more detailed election coverage, such as party profiles and manifestos. They used discussion forums and graphics. One could visit three or four sites to get the complete picture of the elections. A special site constructed by 'iafrica.com online', <www.iafrica.com>, has allowed South African expatriates to participate in the elections and to vote for candidates in their former districts.

Unequal Access to ICT

However, the question whether South Africa is moving to the Open Society remains urgent. On the one hand contemporary South Africa is closely linked to the emerging global Information Society. It has more Internet users than any non-OECD country. The total number of Internet users is now estimated at 1.27 million and is expected to reach 1.4 million by the year 2000 and 2 million by the year 2002. The Media Africa organisation, <www.mafrica.org>, which studies Internet developments in Africa in general and in South Africa in particular, says that Internet usage in South Africa has been growing at a phenomenal speed since 1995. The annual growth rate reached a high of 86% in 1998 but is expected to decelerate to 50% in 1999 (Media Africa, 1999). South Africa has the best telecommunication systems in Sub-Sahara Africa. In 1998 the South African telecommunication company Telkom, controlled by the South African government, serviced 4.6 million telephone lines, reaching more than 50% of households. (There are 9 million households in South Africa excluding hotels and institutions.) There were 4.2 million telephone lines in 1997 and 3.9 million lines in 1996. Of the 4.6 million lines, 127,272 are payphones. 74% of Telkom's telephony network is digitised; and it was planned to complete the digitalisation by the end of 1999 (DoC, 1998). In March 1999 the first South African produced satellite was launched into orbit. Overall government support for R&D in South Africa is 5 times more than in the countries of Sub-Sahara Africa, which usually spend near 0.2% on these goals. South Africa spends near 1% of GNP (while most developed countries spend 2-3%) (UNESCO, 1999).

On the other hand, South Africa can not provide access to ICT for the majority of its population. Only few people, as a rule white and rich, have access to the new media, as South Africa does not have required social conditions to provide all citizens with equal access to ICT.

Polarisation and Exclusion

The South African society probably is one of the most polarised societies in the world. In the country one can see various processes of social differentiation such as inequality, polarisation, coexistence of wealth and poverty, social exclusion. It has highly inequitable income distribution. The poorest 40% of households (equivalent to 50% of the population) earn less than 11% of total national income. While the richest 10% of households (equivalent to only 7% of the population) receive over 40% of total income (May, 1998: section 2.2.). For a long time South Africa's Gini index (currently 59) was the highest in the world, and today only that of Brazil is higher.[1] Inequality of income distribution between race groups is considerable, and accounts for 37% of total income inequality. However, inequality within race groups is also substantial; African households, for example, have a Gini coefficient of 54, nearly as high as the national figure. Rural/urban inequality is also considerable (World Bank, 1999).

Manuel Castells in his well-known book *The Information Age: Economy, Society and Culture* argues that social exclusion is a process by which certain individuals and groups are systematically barred from access to certain basic standard of living and from participation in the main social and occupational opportunities of the society (Castells, 1996: 73). In contemporary South Africa one can easily find all these conditions that have caused the exclusion of a substantial part of the population: unemployment, conditions of migration, illegal status, inability to pay the rent, extreme poverty, lack of skills, functional illiteracy, illness, and so on. Social exclusion exists in the 'black cities' (in Johannesburg, which became a black town). And it is a general phenomenon in black rural regions of the country, where many schools have no electricity (SAIRR, 1999: 2), where a substantial part of people are still illiterate and until now have no access to telecommunications and mass media. All these result in the restriction of access not only to ICT, but also to 'knowledge'.

South Africa can move successfully to the Open Society only if universal access to information and telecommunications would be provided for all South Africans. This may be done only through improving social conditions and empowering rural and depressed communities. Like other states in transition South Africa together with its economic and social problems has to solve the problems of its national identity and citizen-

1 The Gini index or coefficient measures the extent to which the distribution of income among individuals or householders within an economy deviates from a perfect equality distribution. A Gini index of zero represents perfect equality, whereas an index of 100 implies perfect inequality.

ship. This decision is not characterised by rational choice but is mostly influenced by passions and emotions of patriotism, cultural affiliation and shared symbols of national history. The immediate neighbourhood, regional relationships and memories of a common past are crucial in constructing borders between 'we' and 'others' (Lauristin, 1997: 28). We have to add language and religion to these categories. South Africa does not have all these common symbols and emotions: its peoples have different histories, religions, languages, national passions and emotions of patriotism. And 'memories of the common past' can lead only to new conflicts. The responsibility for building the nation and especially for the education of individuals as independent, mature and responsible citizens remains on South African journalists, the government and NGOs.

The South African Government

The South African government plays a considerable role in economic, social and education policies and in developing the communication sphere. A lot of money is spent on electrification of the country. The reorganisation of education and telecommunication spheres was started in 1994. In June 1999 the new President Tabo Mbeky suggested a new plan for the South African renaissance. It includes reconstruction in some spheres, and first of all in telecommunications and the power industry. Recently the Department of Communications is conducting a study of the convergence of telecommunications, broadcasting and IT to ensure that South Africans are not left behind in these new developments.

In May 1999 a *Discussion Paper on Definition of Universal Service and Universal Access in Telecommunications in South Africa* (USA, 1999) was published. This document, prepared by South African Telecommunications Regulatory Authority (SATRA) together with the American Universal Service Agency, analyses how to provide universal access to telecommunication services in all areas and communities in the Republic (USA, 1999). The South African government promised that in the nearest future 75% of households would gain access to a telephone. The Government has also made a commitment to create online links for every university, high school and public library. In 1999 the government has already begun to install public information terminals at post offices across the country to give communities access to the Internet, e-mail and government services. Telecommunication centres (telecentres) have already been constructed in several communities to give citizens access to modern technological communication equipment such as telephones, faxes, copier services and the Internet. They also give opportunity for direct access to government departments, education and other public goods and services. The recent establishment by the Government Communication and

Information Services (GCIS) of a new site, 'Government Online', was an attempt to give the public access to current government information. The government is planning to incorporate e-mail services to allow the public greater access to the decision-making process.

It is clear that South African authorities pay much attention to the IC sector. However, the Universal Service – the long-term goal to provide telecommunications service to all households in South Africa – will not yet be implemented for many years. Universal Access is a goal that can be realised in a few years. But in the *Discussion paper* the general feeling was expressed that not earlier than in 5 years all communities in South Africa would have something like a telecentre (USA, 1999).

Social Responsibility of the Media in South African Transition Society and the New Paradigm of the South African Journalism

There are many discussions in the country about the role of South African journalists and their responsibility. Should journalists participate in political and public life or should they be free individuals and honest viewers and chroniclers? Should they take an active part in the nation building process which is sometimes also called by South Africans, rather cynically, 'sunshine journalism', or should they be watchdogs of society? Individual or community? Libertarianism or communitarianism?

During the *apartheid* age journalists usually were the guards of the Nationalist government, especially concerning state-controlled broadcasting. But at the same time several powerful and influential opposition publications appeared in South Africa in different times, especially in the English language press. Newspaper journalism in South African has very old and strong traditions. It is enough to remember such famous publications as *World*, *Rand Daily Mail*, *Mail* and *Guardian*. South African mass media had prepared the democratic changes in the country and played an important role in the victory of ANC in the democratic elections of 1994. Some specialists consider that South Africa has the best journalism school in Africa.

A New Journalistic Paradigm

At the present moment there exists a widely accepted opinion that professional standards of South African journalism are decreasing. Partly it is true. Like in any country in transition structural transformation of the mass media, broadening of audiences, and inside instability lead to a decrease in journalism quality. Media professionals often underline that the South African media are going to improve the situation through better journalism education, knowledge of new technologies, interaction between industry, professionals and journalism educators. Now there are nine schools of journalism in the country. Academic research of mass media is conducted in Natal, Rhodes, Stellenbosch and other universities. Each year the Journalism Faculty of Rhodes University organises conferences on problems of mass media, journalism training, and new technologies in Africa and holds meetings of media experts. Rhodes University has its New Media Laboratory, which specialises in research in the field of new ICT.

South African journalists and other media professionals understand the necessity of a new journalism ethics code in new South Africa. At the South African National Editors' Forum (SANEF) and Newspapers Consultative Conference on Journalism Training in 1997 a special group of media experts tried to define a new paradigm of the South African journalism. This paper suggested the following points for discussion:

Old paradigm features:

- Eurocentric.
- Authoritarian.
- Male-focused.
- Fragmented into content areas; no links between these areas for sense.
- No context to events.
- Reactive information not reflective (reflective in the sense of analysed, thought about, interpreted).
- The 'mirror' notion in which the media is just a reflection; non-ideological; it provides facts with no point of view; objectivity (the impossible task) is upheld.
- The notion of 'balance' which presents issues as having two sides only (pro and con); it denies the complexity of issues.
- It provides information alone which has low value, at the expense of contact and community. The focus is on information not audience, i.e.: not on what the information really means to people.
- Little recognition of different audiences.
- Stories without meaning and relevance.
- The manner of the telling ('storytelling') is absent.
- Stories dictated by sources and not receivers.
- Ownership: monopolies, the bottom line dictates.
- Adherence to party political views.

[...]

New paradigm features:

- As journalists, we have a role in society, we link the individual to the world. We need to give our audience a sense of what it is to be South African on the African continent and connected to the world.
- There needs to be a consciousness of diversity: not just in terms of race and gender but also class, rural/urban and youth/aged.
- Our audience is diverse and complex.
- We must emphasise context; interpretation; research; investigation; complete reporting and analysis.
- We must foreground the storyteller (the individual and the media organisation).
- We should use African voices (modes of communication rich in narrative).
- We should respect our audiences and engage in dialogue.
- In our use of sources we should move beyond 'the authorities'. Audiences are also sources. We must remember to foreground and situate who the sources are.
- The policy statement : 'In recognition of our role in society as storytellers; as the link between South African citizens and the world; we strive to promote:
- stories, told in a multiplicity of African voices, that are well researched; contextualised; analytical; interpretative; in dialogue with, and respectful of,
- an audience that is complex and diverse,
- through media that are owned:
  1 Symbolically by the audience and
  2 Economically by a diverse group of stakeholders,
- enabled by newsroom structures that empower storytellers.
  (Thloloe, 1998).

Between Sub-Saharan Africa and the Developed World

It has been already mentioned that South Africa is a unique country in many respects. It is a developing country but if we refer it to the developed world it will also be true. South Africa is the centre for Sub-Saharan Africa and the periphery for most developed countries. In this context the role of South African journalists is especially significant. They do not only link the information rich and information poor individuals and communities in their own country, but they also provide the connection between the world and Sub-Sahara Africa. It is well known that the gap between the information rich and the information poor regions widens daily. If this process is not to be stopped it can lead to complete marginalisation of

Africa. And the South African journalists' duty is to provide access to information to 'socially excluded people and territories'. From this point of view it is especially remarkable that in the first feature of the old paradigm the necessity of refusing Eurocentrism was underlined.

South African journalists need to give their audience a sense of what it is to be South African on the African continent and connected to the world. It is obvious that now the media and first of all the electronic media are West-orientated. The world takes the information about Southern countries from the news agencies of the North. This information brings Northern ideals and patterns. As a result, some people in South Africa consider that African moral values are being eroded. If Southern journalists empower themselves, this balance of information power could be radically shifted and equalised. Theoretically the Internet allows both journalists and newspaper organisations to become their own news agencies without having to rely on Western dominated news agencies like Reuters and Associated Press, etc. (Naidoo, 1998: 49). It is remarkable that not all South African professionals are of this opinion. During the discussion about African context of the media at the 'Highway African' Conference this year a staff member of South African Broadcasting Corporation (SABC) stated that since Europe and the US had led Africa all these years, why shouldn't they continue? 'Eurocentricity was not a big issue then'. Other South African participants underlined the need to make African information more African. Electronic media (and we remember that information agencies also use new technologies) should also express the African point of view more vividly. Africans have to provide information about Africa by themselves.

There are very few African political web-sites in the Internet until now. Thus, it is very important that South Africa's numerous web-sites provide democratic political Afrocentric viewpoints on their online websites to Sub-Sahara Africa and to the whole outside world.

Storytellers and Educators of Society

South-African journalists are storyteller of society. This thesis is repeated in the media experts' paper many times. The authors of the paper consider that in *apartheid* times mass media prepared stories without meaning and relevance. The manner of the telling ('storytelling') was absent. Stories were dictated by sources and not receivers. The authors of the paper stress that the new journalism model brings into focus the community values, what the information really means to people. Do we understand our society? Do we understand the people in our target areas or provinces? Their cultures? The social, political and economic dynamics? What are we doing to address this? Such questions are common for the journalists of post-*apartheid* South Africa. Their task now is to interact with their communities. It may be said that the new South African journalism paradigm is community-centred, while the old one was media-centred and society-centred. This community-centred approach requires from South African journalists to play many additional roles besides the roles usual for west countries.

The South African journalists have to educate people. This is especially important in the case of South Africa, where numerous previously disadvantaged groups began to participate in social and political life of the country. Media workers need to be at the forefront of the changes to help the new audience. Many journalists think they must be more dynamically involved in all aspects of life in Africa, especially in the area of consumer education and sustainable development. Neither the peasantry, the urban proletariat nor the middle classes have a culture of wanting to know and understand the issues that affect them directly. People who use media in their life not only have a better understanding of history, but they are also better informed about future scenarios. The absence of an educated and informed public can, in the long run, have its impact on the quality of democracy and the strength of the South African political system. The main task of journalists in this situation is to broaden the media audience in the country, to empower rural and depressed communities (first of all women's groups, school children and youth from the disadvantaged majority) by giving them access to ICT and the ability to use it.

The South African journalists have to disseminate knowledge for development. Knowledge gives people greater control over their life. Journalists can help South Africans to know more about AIDS and other diseases, how to use fresh water, about industrial pollution, health, survival in difficult conditions. There are various initiatives aimed at bringing connectivity and partnership programs to schools. 'The Newspapers in Education' program is one such effort. The Department of Journalism of Rhodes University runs a newspaper-training program with local disadvantaged teenagers. In an online newspaper pupils are writing about their social concerns and the problems they face, such as teenage pregnancy, smoking, drinking, etc. They receive e-mails from other teenagers around the world who experience similar problems in their communities. The program helps pupils to know the world better, which is sure to help them in the future. They will be more computer literate than other pupils. They will also be better producers and consumers of information.

Rhodes University students have published a series of photo booklets. This year it was called *Survivors. A guide to surviving the trauma of rape or abuse – and helping the police to get a conviction.* The first two booklets were entitled *Yes* and *POPS* and were published in 1997. *Yes* was linked to the Youth Empowerment Scheme and *POPS* was aimed at helping the police to create a new image among youngsters. I saw these booklets. They are professionally made and have a high educational value.

Consciousness of Diversity

There needs to be a consciousness of diversity: not just in terms of race and gender but also class, rural/urban and youth/aged. Our audience is diverse and complex. South Africa is indeed a multinational state in full sense of this word. We can not talk about South African journalism without mentioning the racial question. These are three main lines of racial and national contradiction, inherited from the past: polarisation between blacks and whites, differences between whites and whites (English and *Afrikaans* speaking), and often conflicts between blacks and blacks. All these separation lines exist in the mass media.

The differences between the *Afrikaner* press and the English liberal press are well known from the *apartheid* times. After the democratic elections the most remarkable contradiction between them was in 1997 when they became opponents in the discussion concerning their participation in hearings of the Truth Reconciliation Commission. Two major English-language media groups, Independent Newspapers and Times Media finally submitted to arbitration of the TRC. Both *Afrikaner*-controlled media groups, Nasionale Pers (Naspers) and Perskor, decided not to co-operate with the commission. But still there were different opinions inside both groups. These disagreements can be seen in all their publications and in their attitude to the role of the journalist in society. Surely the traditional division lines between the conservative *Afrikaner* press and the liberal English press are still vital.

But the new conflict between the white press and the new media force – the black journalism – is, in our opinion, more serious and deeper. Blacks are becoming a force, both in the business, political and media sectors. Even the most conservative editors of previously white newspapers have to count the realities of the day and not only now orient their publications to black readers, but also start taking black journalists in their staff. Black journalists speak as opponents to whites in different issues. They constantly criticise white journalists in different media for not supporting and developing the idea of African renaissance and for ignoring the idea of the nation building.

To overcome this dangerous gap between black and white media professionals such mixed organisations as South African National Editors' Forum (SANEF) were established. SANEF was formed on the basis of the merger of the Black Editors' Forum and the mainly white South African Editors' Conference to reunite black and white journalists. But until now they can not change the situation and liquidate the separation lines dividing the black and the white.

'*We should respect our audiences and engage in dialogue*', says the paper. It is again very important for South Africa as it is a true multinational country. There are a great number of nations, organisations, parties, religions and so on. Ryland Fisher, editor of the *Cape Times*, gave an interesting example. His newspaper published an article about the murder of Rashaad Staggie – a member of Muslim organisation Pagad. The Pagad quickly became known as a militant Muslim organisation. The danger of this is that the word militant becomes synonymous with Muslim, leading non-Muslims to suspect all Muslims as militants. After that the editorial staff began thinking about the ability or inability to report about a diverse community in a transitional society. Since then, wrote Ryland Fisher, the *Cape Times* has taken great pains trying to get closer to their community, to be objective, not to be quick to label people or organisations. They meet with as many community groups as possible and invite their criticism and ideas. 'We must, in the truest sense, become the pulse of our communities. We must be able to tell our readers what is going to happen, and not only record what has already happened' (Fisher, 1998).

The New Technology is the New Responsibility

Now it is interesting to analyse the role of South African journalists and their responsibility in the Information age. The development of new technology may contribute a lot to improving democracy and liberation, but for success it is necessary to improve education in the media sphere, too. The Internet can not and will not feed the starving masses nor will it educate children on its own. However, it is a powerful tool that can exacerbate change in Africa. African media have the resources, the power and the voice to provoke changes (Naidoo, 1998: 51).

Rural communities need most attention from the media professionals. There are a lot of community radio stations in the country. Indeed community radio offers until now the only opportunity to provide people in distant rural poor regions with access to media. These people can not yet benefit from using the new technology. But the majority of South Africans have access to radio. Radio is the media of poor people. In South Africa the number of listeners is growing in percentage more than audiences of other media, first of all thanks to an increase of rural listeners. It is not by chance that the coalition of 133 developing countries urged in May 1999 the UN to keep radio and other traditional media outlets as a means of disseminating information rather than relying only on the Internet (UN, 1999).

Still, much is done lately by journalists and NGOs to help people to get access to information and communication systems. The educational initiatives for schools are very interesting. In 1998 'Soweto Digital Village' was organised. A computer centre was set up near Johannesburg, with the aim of providing the community with opportunities to develop computer and entrepreneurial skills. The 'Thousand Schools Project', the initiative funded by the Independent Development Trust, supported by Microsoft, plans to develop 900 computer centres around the country. Another initiative was 'School-Net South Africa', a national NGO expanding the use of the Internet in South African schools. About 14 Grahamstown schools, a mixture of private, public and previously disadvantaged, participate in this project. The importance of these projects is clear. A study of the effective use of the Internet conducted in two provinces discovered that despite the enthusiasm of some co-ordinators, the lack of trainers and inadequate facilities prevent computer education from wide spreading among school graduates.

The Internet has allowed journalists easier access to the government. Journalists need to lobby governments to increase the amount of information on line. Journalists cannot battle the government alone, but together with NGOs and other organisations, and using the Net, they can make some progress. African journalists need to become masters of new technologies, to advertise new media through their own activity, especially among other stakeholders in Africa – governments, NGOs, businesses, etc. This can only be done when the journalists themselves begin to use and understand the new media. Journalists must be literate in Information Technology. Media people have to promote the African values in the Internet.

An idea is expressed sometimes that journalists in the information age have to filter the information on the World Wide Web to avoid information overload of the public. I think this question and others – Does the editors' responsibility extend beyond what is on the actual newspaper or does it include linked information via hypertext? Is journalism becoming a lazy profession where it is easier to take, than to create? Is the line between advertising and editorial blurring, a distinction that has long been held sacred in traditional journalism? – will be discussed among South African media professionals.

Conclusions

We think that the role of the State is becoming more important in the new South Africa. The role of the mass media and especially of the new media is also increasing. The role of the radio and the Internet in particular for the South African society as a dual society which has the most developed telecommunication infrastructure as well as a significant part of excluded people, should also be underlined. Disadvantaged communities can have access to the new technologies through the radio. And journalists are going to play a significant role in this process.

All discussions about the Open Society presuppose the behaviour of an intellectual, independent, mature and responsible citizen. In our case we do not have such a uniform citizen. And because of that, South African journalists have to play many additional roles besides the roles that are usual in Western countries. The role of journalist as a communicator among media and communities is underlined in South African theoretical papers and in mass media materials. Many South African journalists consider that their main task is to interact with their communities.

These are no fixed schools of media studies in South Africa. In the past media scholars and professionals chose between two main different theoretical approaches: functional and critical. Both of them suffered from a bias that was deeply embedded in their starting-point. Functionalism wishes to see the media as a conscious, stabilising element in a democratic society (media-centric approach), thus neglecting the hidden structures of societal development. On the other side, the critical perspective tries to reveal the overall structures that cause the media to function within certain frameworks (society-centric approach), thus denying the role of the media profession as an unaffected corrective to state and society. Each national system and individual media – even each individual journalist – shares more than one paradigm (Nordenstreng, 1997). We can find different approaches and the features of different paradigms in contemporary South African journalism. But it may be said that the new South African journalism paradigm is community-centred. While the old one was media-centred and society-centred, the new South African journalism paradigm mainly reflects the features of the communitarianism conception.

References

Castells, M.

1996 *The Information Age. Economy, Society and Culture.* Vol. 2. Cambridge, Mass.: Blackwell.

DoC

1998 *The State of the Telecommunications Industry in South Africa.* Department of Communications (DOC). <http://docweb.pwv.gov.za/docs/strategy/state98.html>.

Fisher, R.

1998 The challenges we face. *Rhodes Journalism Review* (15).

Lauristin, M.
1997 Context of transition. In M. Lauristin and P. Vihalemm (eds.), *Return to the Western World. Cultural and Political Perspectives on the Estonian Post-Communist Transition*, pp. 25-40. Tartu: Tartu University Press.

May, J. [ed.]
1998 *Summary Report on Poverty and Inequality in South Africa.* <http://www.polity.org.za/govdocs/reports/poverty.html>.

Media Africa
1999 *Second South African Web Commerce Survey.* Media Africa. <http://www.mafrica.co.za>.

Naidoo, K.
1998 *African Media Online. An Internet Handbook for AFRICAN Journalists.* Occasional paper No. 3, presented by the New Media Laboratory, Department of Journalism, Rhodes University. Paris Dakar: Panos Institute.

Nordenstreng, K.
1997 Beyond the four theories of the press. In J. Servaes and R. Lie (eds.), *Media and Politics in Transition. Cultural Identity in the Age of Globalization*, pp. 97-109. Leuven/Amersfoort: ACCO.

SAIRR
1999 *Some Interesting Facts about South Africa.* Pretoria: South African Institute of Race Relations (SAIRR).

Thloloe, J.
1998 A new paradigm for journalism in South Africa. *Rhodes Journalism Review* (15).

UN
1999 *Press Release PI/1134.* Despite new technologies, world still depends on radio, committee on information told as it concludes general debate. <http://www.un.org/News/Press/>.

UNESCO
1999 *UNESCO Statistical Yearbook 1999.* UNESCO. <http://unescostat.unesco.org/statsen/statistics/yearbook/YBIndexNew.htm>.

USA
1999 *Discussion Paper on Definition of Universal Service and Universal Access in Telecommunications in South Africa.* Universal Service Agency (USA). <http://www.usa.org.za/pdf's/discussion1.pdf>.

World Bank
1999 Distribution of income or consumption. In *World Development Indicators 1999.* World Bank. <http://www.worldbank.org/data/wdi/pdfs/tab2_8.pdf>.

Development of Global Information Exchange Principles

A Way to Prevent International and Non-International Armed Conflicts

ANDREI RASKIN
Faculty of Journalism, Moscow State University, Russia

Abstract

This paper argues that new information and communication technologies could provide a new and unique chance to prevent the escalation of international and non-international military fighting. Media coverage may act as impediment against human rights violation and can watch behaviour of armed forces in any conflict. Unfortunately, current examples also show that international media are used as way of propaganda, and that journalists' activities in a conflict zone are banned.

Introduction

New information and communication technologies could provide a new and unique chance to prevent the escalation of international and non-international military fighting, establishing the multinational watch of the human rights violation as well as the watch of armed forces usage attempts in any conflict.

Cross-cultural and cross-countries coverage of armed conflicts with help of satellite television equipment gives new opportunities for various countries' audiences to get live news from different parts of the world. This way a very powerful international public opinion can be formed. Such a new communication reality could lead to the creation of better conditions for the creation of a global Open Society.

But unfortunately new technologies, which are already world-wide adopted by major media companies, are not often used in the desirable way that would contribute to better policy making processes and social agenda setting principles from a global point of view.

The New Technology Paradox of Conflict Coverage

The prominent BBC World Service news program anchorman Nik Going, who is also involved in humanitarian analytical reporting, in his recent publication *Media Coverage: Help or Hindrance in Conflict Prevention?* (1997) pointed out a very important tendency in war conflicts observation.

> The Media's role in the new generation of regional conflict and substance violence is ambiguous, unclear and often misconstructed [...] It is regrettable, that more real-time technology to report from the world's zones of conflict has not necessarily been matched by a qualitative improvement in journalism or information flow. Instead, the trend is towards superficial, less-than-well-informed reporting, often based on second- or third-hand information as opposed to primary data (Going, 1997: 1).

Besides the political and military authorities in conflict zones, the conditions in the media marketplace also influence war coverage. The journalists, especially those who report for the big commercial news powers, have to play the rating-circulation revenue game. They have to pay more attention to the 'hot' sensational facts than to the dangers, from a humanitarian point of view, that follow from the war routine. Coverage by way of news or documentary is therefore increasingly rare. As a result, the public is presented with numerous examples of poor and inane reporting. There is also the problem of editors who have the power to decide what should be on the air or in a newspaper. Very often these editors and news directors try to represent their audience's choices and tastes. They believe that their audience doesn't want to see how Africans are killing Africans, just because these facts have become 'routine'.

Opportunities and Limitations of Media Coverage of Conflicts

We observe a big paradox when we study day-to-day media coverage of armed conflicts in various parts of the planet. The developed world has a lot of real-time technology. News organisations have highly mobile satellite TV transmission systems that can broadcast from anywhere. TV news pictures can now be broadcasted even on telephone lines. There is more ability and mobility to cover war crises. TV news coverage can be done with modern Hi-8 video cameras and low-cost digital video hand cameras (DVC) which are small, portable and easily hidden. All these new techniques allow even non-professionals who might be witnessing dramatic facts to report war news.

There is more video available from more conflicts, yet there is less editorial interest in transmitting it. More often video materials are presented on the screens only with ideological or propagandistic purposes, as happened many times during the recent conflict in Kosovo. Technology has facilitated the globalisation of the news. The situation could allow the comprehensive coverage of real global issues, which should include early warning of conflicts and any efforts at prevention. But globalisation rather promotes the limitation of conflicts' media coverage.

Edward Girardet, the editor of the *Crosslines Global Report*, a monthly publication on humanitarian reporting, criticises the new technology paradox. He stresses that

> [...] portable direct-link satellite units, cellular phones, lap-top computers, modems, fax machines, Internet – such technology does not necessarily mean that the quality of news reporting has improved. Nor does it mean that so-called 'new media' with all its remarkable forms of easy access has enabled us to be any better informed today about wars and humanitarian issues around the globe than in the 1970s or 1980s. Such technological facilities raise more than ever concerns about journalistic responsibility (Girardet, 1997).

A tendency for image searching instead of facts gathering and presenting is also a serious problem which stands between the new technological and communication opportunities and real 'infotainment' coverage.

The pressure to provide 'real-war' footage is often dominating a television crew's work in a conflict zone. Staff of freelance journalists and cameramen risk their lives in order to find such 'pictures' for producers sitting thousands kilometres away from a conflict zone waiting for 'hot' war images. Searching for 'real-war' footage puts journalists in real dangerous missions. Many combatants, terrorists, and other players in conflicts understand the nature of commercial television and kidnap, injure, or murder journalists.

Media Coverage and Propaganda

The example of the television coverage of the Kosovo conflict showed many positive and negative tendencies of the present-day role of media in war time, which puts the problems of fairness and objectivity at the centre of attention. The Kosovo crisis coverage presented attempts to use international media as way of propaganda. Attempts of the media to manipulate public opinion of the world audience under the pressure of media tycoons, politicians and military commanders, can be seen as part of a particular communication tendency that follows first of all the interests of wealthy power groups. If until recently just the television companies were the target of such interests groups, so nowadays step by step such a role is given to the Internet. During the Kosovo conflict both sides involved in the conflict from the beginning of the military actions opened their propaganda style information pages on the Net, <www.crisisweb.org> and <www.kosovo.net> for the NATO allies and <www.gov.yu> for the Belgrade authority.

The Dagestan-Chechnya Conflict

But the propagandists during the Dagestan-Chechnya conflict went even further. Using the Goebbels-style 'black radio station' experience, they opened the provocative information pages <www.chechnya.gamma.ru>, 'the Chechen opposition service' (more likely to be operated from the Russian Defence Information Department, by name of the Chechen opposition). This site published for instance the appeal made by Movlady Udugov, a key figure in the previous Chechen conflict (1994-1996) and a very skilled propagandist and member of the self-declared Chechen Government, to stop fighting with the Federal troops and support him as a new president of Chechnya. At the same time a lot of information is circulated on the official Chechen site, <www.kavkaz.org>. But if one would change the ending of this address from '.org' to '.ru', one would go to the site of one of the Caucasian travel agencies. The Internet 'information wars' could be the title of this new game.

The leading world television companies coverage of military conflicts also influence the world decision-making process by discussing the responsibilities of politicians and military commanders for their orders and politics. Such media participation during a conflict coverage may lead to unexpected results and consequences of a war.

Access to Information from Conflict Zones

The development of new information and communication technologies also affects the journalists' rights to get to conflict zones and gather information. Sometimes politicians and military commanders use a lot of different ways in order to ban journalists' activities in a conflict zone. The presence of a journalist with a portable video camera or even without it, can make that audiences are shown the neglected sides of a war, even war crimes. Understanding this, authorities try to limit as much as possible journalists' opportunities to report on a war. The rich experience collected by different PR agencies help them in controlling information.

Protection of Journalists by International Law

Gathering news during a war is a very dangerous mission. According to International Humanitarian Law,[1] a journalist is considered a person who attempts to obtain, comments on, or uses information for the press or for radio or television. A journalist can be any correspondent, reporter, photographer, or cameraman, or his film, radio or television technical assistant, habitually carrying out such activities as his/her main occupation. From 1899 to 1949 the only journalists especially protected by the law of armed conflicts were war correspondents; or in more accurate words, journalists duly authorised by a belligerent to follow its troops. Captured war correspondents were entitled to prisoner-of-war status. The Additional Protocols to the Geneva Convention of 1977 made no change in the rules relating to war correspondents, but Article 79 formally reiterated that journalists engaged in dangerous professional missions in areas of armed conflict have the status of civilian persons, on condition that they refrain from any combat activity. They may obtain identity cards attesting to their status as journalists and can be protected as civilians.

Journalists who are nationals of a non-belligerent State and who work during an international armed conflict are given the benefit of peacetime law; that is, if captured by a party to the conflict, they may not be detained save for serious reasons, in default of which they are generally released.

From the first glance journalists could benefit from the protection provided by International Humanitarian Law which regards them as civilians. Such a status allows them to work rather independently in a conflict zone maintaining their professional duties. But in fact the freedom to gather information, to interview responsible political or military figures as well as to visit some areas, are surely limited or even restricted. An authority in a conflict zone has a lot of ways to manipulate journalists giving them that sort of news that is more or less controlled by special information departments. And attempts of correspondents to go deeply into the details of a military operation are stopped by the request or even orders to follow the adopted rules in a particular area. When a journalist would feel the desire to overcome such rules, he would be met with strong measures including arrests and provocation. As a result, being more independent gives less opportunities to organise real news coverage of crisis events.

---

1 The Geneva Conventions with two Additional Protocols and the The Hague Conventions (see ICRC, 1983).

Who needs information from a conflict zone? First of all it is not the public. Donor institutions require high-quality data and analysis, including trends and comparative information. For quick and productive humanitarian operations, aid agencies need to know the exact number of refugees, wounded people, safety places for hospitals and food delivery stations settings. The role of the modern cellular and satellite communication technologies is highly important. The co-operation with the news media is also a key factor for the common humanitarian actions.

Humanitarian Reporting

A huge potential power to blow up the traditional media style of war reporting lays in the heart of new information technologies. The Internet and multimedia could present in the nearest future the real full scale coverage of humanitarian crises and military conflicts. Step by step more serious information services offer their resources to all computer possessors and the Internet subscribers.

But it is necessary as soon as possible to solve one of the most important problems of the news flow in cyberspace which is guaranteeing that facts are checked in the freely and independently operating virtual sphere. When reading a newspaper or watching most TV news programs, the average reader or viewer assumes that the output has been checked and verified by editors and skilled journalists.

The technological revolution which caused a lot of problems alongside with creating new communication opportunities, occurred in a very dramatic period in world history. The period of transition from the 'two-blocks' world to a new diverse global organisation was accompanied by some political and humanitarian catastrophes. During the rather calm 1970s, it would have been very difficult to assume that the world order would be completely reorganised with such dramatic circumstances as military conflicts in relative peaceful regions.

Roy Gutman and David Rieff, editors of the latest publication on humanitarian reporting, *Crimes of War: What the Public Should Know*, wrote in the preface to their book, which consists of 140 true war articles prepared by 90 journalists from 12 countries including Christiane Amanpour's articles on Bosnia and Jeremy Bowen on Chechnya:

> Less than two years after the fall of the Berlin Wall [...] it took a war in Europe – Croatia in 1991 – to stir public interest. The war in Bosnia-Herzegovina (1992), the Rwandan genocide (1994), and Chechnya (1995) amplified the alarm bell [...] Bosnia was the trigger. In the heart of 'civilised' Europe, Serbian forces had set up concen-

> tration camps, deported non-Serbs in cattle cars, destroyed towns and villages, organised the systematic rape of Croat and Muslim women, and targeted civilians in the name of ethnic cleansing. Western alliance watched passively, and were it not for the glare of media attention as had occurred more than decades earlier in Vietnam [...] (Gutman & Rieff, 1999: 9)

Unexpectedly the 1990s has become the war years for millions of people. According to the Department of Peace and Conflict Research (DPCR) of Uppsala University, Sweden, all regions of the world have witnessed at least one major armed conflict during the 1990s (see Table 1).[2] Asia and Africa – the largest regions in population and territory – consistently showed the greatest number of wars, although the number has declined in both regions. In Europe after reaching a peak in 1993 and 1994, the number of conflicts continues to fall. In the Americas a reduction in the intensity of conflicts means a considerable shift from wars to intermediate armed conflicts, the total number declining slightly. Unlike the other regions, the Middle East shows no significant decline in the number of armed conflicts.

Table 1 Number of major armed conflicts by region per year over seven years (1990-1996)

	1990	*1991*	*1992*	*1993*	*1994*	*1995*	*1996*
Europe	1	2	4	6	5	3	2
Middle East	5	7	5	6	6	6	6
Asia	15	12	13	11	11	12	11
Africa	11	11	7	7	7	6	6
America	4	4	3	3	3	3	3

Source: International Federation of Red Cross and Red Crescent Societies (1997: 135).

Conclusions

Taking these realities into consideration, it is the right time to start thinking again more thoroughly and deeply about how new technology and communication opportunities could positively influence the solving of humanitarian problems, could better promote peace in the world, could lead to better understanding of the Open Society principles.

2 An armed conflict is defined as 'major' when at least 1000 battle-related deaths have occurred since the beginning of conflict.

There are some first examples of how Internet projects can contribute to humanitarian reporting. 'The Memorial Group' from Ryazan carries out from the beginning of the war in Chechnya and Dagestan the action 'Stop the war' on its site <www.hro.org>. 'The Consultant Plus', the Moscow based Law Company started to publish the International Humanitarian Law documents on the site <www.consultant.ru>. Some productive projects could be found in the West, too. For instance, one of the best international Internet projects on humanitarian reporting is 'The Crosslines Global Report', <www.ichr.org>, as well as a new site 'The Crimes of War', <www.crimesofwar.org>.

The tragic events of Bosnia, Rwanda, Chechnya, and other conflicts proved the following truth: a campaign against war, for human principles and for a safer future can not be stopped, not even for one day. If recently the struggle for peace was made in a framework closed to other States, nowadays it is a real chance to construct the Open Society with the global vision and joint strong measures of collective security and stability.

References

Girardet, E.R. (ed.)
1997 *Somalia, Rwanda, and Beyond. The Role of the International Media in Wars and Humanitarian Crises.* Crosslines Global Report.

Going, N.
1997 *Media Coverage. Help or Hindrance in Conflict Prevention?* New York: Carnegie Corporation.

Gutman, R. and Rieff, D. (eds.)
1999 *Crimes of War: What the Public Should Know.* New York, London: W.W. Norton & Company.

ICRC
1983 *Basic Rules of the Geneva Conventions and their Additional Protocols.* Geneva: International Committee of the Red Cross.

International Federation of Red Cross and Red Crescent Societies
1998 *World Disasters Report 1997.* Oxford: Oxford University Press.

Responsible and Accountable

Broadcasting Policy between Public Obligation and Private Needs

JO BARDOEL, KEES BRANTS AND RENÉ PLUG
The Amsterdam School of Communications Research *ASCoR*,
University of Amsterdam, The Netherlands

Abstract

This paper argues that the coming of private, commercial broadcasting has put pressure on the financial position and the performing role of most West European public broadcasting organisations as guarantors of quality, diversity, reliability, access and affordability in public information provision. Public broadcasters still claim state support to realise their self-defined public function, yet governments and citizens tend to hold public and commercial broadcasters directly responsible for their performance. The paper will critically examine the assumptions and practices on which public broadcasters' claim for a monopoly on public functions is based.

Introduction

Public broadcasting, at the time when it was still bathing in its monopolistic glory, was characterised by a sense of social responsibility and of responsiveness to the public. The former meant that the organisations lived by a cultural-pedagogic obligation to society, in which quality, information, truthfulness, objectivity and independence from state and commerce were some of the keywords. The latter meant that broadcasting organisations both took account of and were accountable to the public. In practice however, it was either through political or administrative institutions that these public broadcasters were held accountable.

The coming of private, commercial broadcasting, and thus the breaking up of the public monopoly, has put pressure on both the financial position and the performing role of most West European public broadcasting organisations. The latter's reaction has been that they are necessary to guarantee a wide range of quality programs and a diversity of views and opinions aired. They thus claim state support because, where private stations are after the audience's money, they are after their well being; where the other emphasise television as a pleasure machine, they hail its meaning producing function; where the commercial stations give what the public wants, they give what it needs (Brants, 1999); where they are the embodiment of the Enlightenment ideal, the commercial stations are the epitaph of post-modern culture, et cetera.

At the same time several empirical trends make it more difficult for public broadcasters to claim a monopoly on public functions in the future. The recent policies of liberalisation and deregulation have caused a shift in realising social responsibility away from governments to media organisations, public as well as commercial. More and more critical citizens hold these organisations directly responsible for their performance, not making much difference between the public or private status of these actors, and as a result social responsibility becomes a relevant policy issue or even an asset not only for public but also for commercial broadcasting organisations. More in general the ideas about social responsibility and social ethics tend to shift towards more volatile and negotiable norms that are subject of continuous debate. Consequently the claim of public broadcasting institutions as the sole guardian of the public interest and the relation between governments and public institutions will become less exclusive over time.

Our research will look at the assumptions and practices on which the claim on a monopoly on certain public functions is based. How is the cultural-pedagogic logic operationalised under new circumstances? To what extent can public service broadcasters rightfully lay a claim to a monopoly or do commercial channels also perform in a social responsible way? Are they taking the public more seriously? Or are responsiveness to con sumers and to citizens two different things? And either way, what are the consequences for government policy vis-à-vis financing and program obligations of public broadcasting? Although this paper is a reflection of the first results of our research and draws mainly on examples from the changing broadcasting landscape in the Netherlands, it will at least try to formulate some preliminary answers to some of these questions.

The Context and Origin of an Ambiguous Concept

Despite all the attention for the subject matter there is no coherent theory on social responsibility of media in general, or of broadcast media in particular. Some of the notions of responsibility refer to *content*:

- information is not merely a commodity, but also a social or *'merit good'* (Collins, 1998; Picard, 1989) or 'merit programming' (Levin, 1980: 44-46, in Brown, 1996: 7);

- *content* should be accurate, diverse and of a high quality (BRU, 1985; McQuail, 1994: 127).

Other notions of responsibility refer to the media's function for *society*:
- apart from an economic role, media have political and cultural functions (Van Cuilenburg & Slaa, 1993: 168);
- so that individuals can fulfil their role as good *citizens* (Dahlgren & Sparks, 1991; Dahlgren, 1995; Nordenstreng, 1997b);
- and society has sufficient *forums* for the expression of opinions and identities (Hutchins, 1947; Council of Europe, 1994; also Porter, 1995).

And again other notions of social responsibility refer to their *organisational* status:
- media ownership is a *public trust* (Hutchins, 1947; Smith, 1989);
- content producers should therefore be *independent* from both state and market forces (Siune & Hulten, 1998);
- to avoid a situation of power without responsibility, communication media and professionals should be held *accountable* to the public (Blumler & McQuail, 1965: 186; Brants & Siune, 1992: 102; Blumler & Hoffmann-Riem, 1992) .

To complicate things, the word 'responsibility' (as an obligation to society and its citizens) is sometimes used interchangeably with 'responsiveness' (as listening to, taking account of the public). For one, social responsibility clearly is a normative notion, grounded in mostly implicit and often contested conceptions of 'the public interest'. It is linked to a belief in a 'makeable society' to which communication in the public sphere can and should contribute. It assumes that broadcast media are an instrument of social orientation and confirmation for citizens and of social cohesion for society as a whole. And it believes human nature to be positive, open minded and social, and the state (within the continental West European context at least) in the end to be benevolent and to act in that public interest.

A Practical Concept

There are a number of reasons for the ambiguity of the concept. In the first place, the roots of the notion of social responsibility do not so much lie in theory as in communications practice and policy (Hellman, 1999: 58). In fact the most relevant reflections on the matter do not stem from purely academic research but from policy advisory commissions such as the Hutchins Commission in the US (Hutchins, 1947) and the British Royal Commission on the Press (Royal Commission, 1977). In the UK the development of the doctrine can, according to Scannel (1980), be traced through the reports of successive committees on broadcasting. Consequently the concept tends to be practical, orientated towards problem solving and – as we will see – it has a highly legitimating value. As such this notion or concept is, as all policy (relevant) concepts, a 'negotiated' concept (Burgelman, 1995; also see McQuail, 1994) and indeed a social construct that results from a process of political struggle, social debate and academic reflection. As a result the definitions of this concept differ from country to country and from period to period (see McQuail, 1992; Smith, 1989; Syvertsen, 1992), reflecting national media policies and research traditions. Only with the benefit of hindsight have communication scholars tried to formulate more general theoretical frameworks for media performance norms (see McQuail, 1992: 71-78) or criteria for the responsiveness of television (cf. Mitchell & Blumler, 1994: 237).

In the second place, this diagnosis on the modest conceptualisation of social responsibility in the media in general is even more true for broadcast media. Being responsible was an almost self-evident part of the notion of public service. It is no coincidence that the examples just given originate from press policy. Not only because this is the older medium, but social responsibility as a concept was formulated explicitly only to the extent that the so-called free, market driven press behaved in an 'irresponsible' way (see Wieten, 1998: 105) by threatening the freedom of expression. Thus (self)regulation was considered necessary. In broadcasting the situation was quite different. For reasons of frequency scarcity government interference was considered inevitable and therefore – at least in Europe – any explicit legitimation of public policy in this domain was unnecessary. In fact, during most of broadcasting history the distribution of radio frequencies and thus access to broadcasting was a responsibility of the Ministry of Transport, like other public utilities as roads and waterways.

After a first, long period of *lacking* legitimation, we notice a new, *ritual* legitimation, in which an interfering welfare state paid attention to the subject more explicitly since the 1970s. It did so through extensive white papers, without much practical regulation however, since the public monopoly in broadcasting was not contested seriously at the time. The third phase of a more *explicit* legitimation in terms of social responsibility within broadcasting started only recently, in the late 1980s. Competition had become a reality and social responsibility became an asset in the discursive struggle between 'public' and 'commercial' broadcasting.

A Common European Framework

At present we notice that national policies and specificities are being replaced by a kind of common European framework of broadcast policy.

In fact, the EC Directive 'Television without Frontiers', issued over ten years ago, marks the end of the public broadcasting monopoly and the beginning of broadcast 'dual systems' in most continental European countries. At the same time, the EU cannot escape the question of how the cultural interest in content production should be safeguarded (cf. Blackman, 1998; Paterson, 1997). For the coming years it is clear that a cultural policy cannot longer be formulated in negative or 'exceptional' terms only (as a separate paragraph in the Maastricht Treaty or as an additional protocol to the Amsterdam Treaty). A deliberate cultural policy for the old continent needs new and fresh reflection on the social responsibility of communications media in the information society. Recent documents on converging communications policies (European Communications Council, 1997; European Commission, 1997; Soete et al., 1997; Oreja et al., 1998) begin to reflect the relevance of communication content's own merit, and not as a mere affiliate of economic and infrastructural (i.e. telecommunications) policies. In fact, we see here the same learning process that national governments went through over the last half-century.

At the same time it seems clear that the circumstances have changed so profoundly that a rethinking of social responsibility of broadcast media 'from scratch' is imperative. The recent shift of public hegemony to dualistic competition in broadcasting in a way makes it more difficult to safeguard a certain standard of social responsibility and public moral. Even more so because, as a result of liberalisation, deregulation and self-regulation, the power to materialise this has shifted from the state to social institutions and commercial enterprises. Moreover, it is not yet clear what the predominant broadcasting policy model of the future will be. Will there be a continuation of the present situation of highly regulated public broadcasters and less regulated commercial broadcasters, or will a new policy be introduced in which both public and commercial broadcasters share social responsibility and public duties (see Achille & Miege, 1994: 44)?

Partly as a result of this 'dual' media exposure, citizens have become more critical towards the social performance of enterprises and organisations. Valuing social responsibility becomes an asset even for multinational companies, as Shell has experienced (Brent Spar, Nigeria). In the non-profit sphere, this trend towards direct accountability to the public forces organisations to redefine general legitimating goals more concretely and 'measurably'. Redefining goals and criteria has also been necessitated since old paternalistic imperatives, in terms of the cultural-pedagogic logic, are not taken for granted anymore. Social ethics have become more flexible, negotiable and individual, reflecting the changing social composition of (post) modern society (cf. Bardoel, 1996). More in general, this raises the question what media responsibilities are 'left' in a society in which individuals seem to be self-sufficient and the fulfilling of individual needs by market mechanisms seems to have become the ultimate criterion.

All these trends together require a more deliberate strategic policy of broadcast organisations in the future, in which public organisations no longer hold an exclusive claim on public duties, privileges and resources. After the first deluge of commercial broadcasting, this is also an important reason why there is a new political interest and backing for the subject of social responsibility in broadcast media (see Sondergaard, 1996: 108).

Researching Social Responsibility Requirements

The way in and extent to which social responsibility (SR) notions are elaborated in theory and practice tend to vary from country to country and from period to period. Even the vocabulary of the discourse differs according to time and place; where the notion of 'social responsibility' is very much an Anglo-Saxon invention (McQuail, 1994: 123), in German-speaking countries the notion of the 'public sphere' is more common. The popularity of Habermas' work though has made this terminology more popular in – critical – Anglo-American discourse during the last decade, too (see Calhoun, 1992; Garnham, 1993; Thompson, 1995; Nordenstreng, 1997a).

We focus our research on the question, which SR-requirements have been imposed by society (i.e. governments) on broadcast media over time, and to what extent these requirements have changed recently and will change in the future.[1] Unlike the normative frameworks presented in recent academic literature (McQuail, 1992; Mitchel & Blumler, 1994) or political (advisory) documents (Broadcasting Research Unit, 1985; Council of Europe, 1994; Dries & Woldt, 1996), in this paper we prefer to follow a somewhat more empirical and inductive approach by reconstructing the evolution of the concept of social responsibility of (public) broadcasting as it can be traced back in policy papers, *in casu* of the Dutch government.

In this examination we will use the concept of social responsibility in a way as a *sensitising concept* (Blumer, 1969). This implies that the relevant

1 In later research we will focus on the obligations imposed on private, commercial broadcasters. Next we will take a look at the way in which both public and private broadcast organisations operationalise and implement all these requirements, either imposed by society governments or self-imposed, into their policies and practices of their respective organisations. Our research object is therefore firstly national government(s) and next public and commercial broadcasters. In our

concept remains open and ill-defined at the beginning of the (re)search, serving as a general guideline for analysing the policy documents, and gradually getting a more empirically based content. Our starting point was the assumption that there is a growing concern about the (absence of) social responsibility of (public) broadcasting over time, and even more so since the advent of commercial competition. Following this grounded theory approach, the first phase of the analysis will be explorative, in which indeed the exploration of the material and the finding of 'field-related' terms and concepts are crucial. In later phases of the analysis, specification and reduction gain importance and the empirical findings are combined with theoretical notions again. The aim of this qualitative research procedure is to go through the process of data collection, analysis and reflection over and over again.

In the *explorative phase*, a comprehensive list of SR-norms was composed stemming from academic research and various policy notions. Initially we made up a list of keywords in order to find first notions of SR-norms in policy documents. These keywords originated from literature that gave an overview of SR-notions in other countries (e.g. McQuail, 1992; Mitchell & Blumler, 1994; McQuail, 1998). The list was merely meant as a first tool to bridge the gap between abstract SR-theories, as referred to before, and the more concrete and practical notions to be found in the selected policy documents. With this list, the content of the above mentioned policy documents and their explanatory memoranda were analysed for the appearance of notions regarding social responsibility.

In the *reflective phase*, the various specific concepts were linked to a more general background by putting the complete list of SR-norms again into theoretical perspective. Furthermore, the SR-norms were categorised in order to position them within a theoretical framework and to search for general tendencies in the development of social responsibility in broadcasting policy. McQuail's (1992: 65-80) framework for media per-

---

research project we have chosen for a comparative perspective in both a geographical and a chronological sense. Concerning the geographical aspect we start with the Dutch situation and subsequently we will compare this case with a selection of other European countries and finally with EU-policies. Referring to the time frame we compare SR-policies over a quite long period (1965-1999), subdivided in – for reasons to be explained later – the 'old public order', a 'transition period' and the 'new dual order'. The main research methods are literature study, content analysis of policy documents, and (at a later stage) interviews. In this contribution – which is the first part of a larger *ASCoR*-research project – we focus on an inventory of notions of social responsibility (and related concepts) of Dutch governments vis-à-vis public broadcasting as reflected in the most relevant policy documents (laws, white papers) in the period 1965-1999.

formance assessment offered a valuable instrument for classifying the great variety of SR-norms and for assessing their relevance within a wider context. Also, it created a bridge between the categorised norms and some basic principles of media policy, such as freedom, equality and order (idem: 67-68). Most SR-norms could be clustered in selected categories of the framework; some were organised in separate categories beyond the scope of the model.

Finally, in the *interpretative phase* the use of social responsibility norms in the relevant policy documents was analysed and interpreted, as to their saliency, their range and diversity, and to potential shifts in emphasis and discourse over time. The analysis also focused on the interpretation of SR-norms with respect to their technological, social, political and cultural contexts. Moreover, the role of broadcaster responsiveness to citizens and the government was analysed, and the extent to which answerability is considered to be related to social responsible behaviour.

The Case of the Netherlands

Within the last few decades, the Dutch broadcasting system has gone through some radical organisational changes. During the *old public order*, the system was organised along the lines of the religious and ideological divisions within Dutch society, which was renowned for its 'segmented pluralism' (Brants & McQuail, 1998). The various homogeneous segments of society, also referred to as 'pillars' or 'societal streams', found equal representation in the Dutch media system. In a way, the media system was considered a cultural reinforcement of the existing political order, in which pillarised media were used as a platform to inform rank and file of the political elite, substantiating their role while creating consensus and stability (Bardoel, 1997: 13). The organisation of the broadcasting system in this period is characterised by non-commercialism, representation of the pillarised structure of Dutch society, and, from the end of the 1960s, controlled access for new broadcasting institutions. The most relevant policy documents of this period of time are the 1965 *Broadcasting White Paper* and the 1967 *Broadcasting Act.*

In the early 1980s a new period of time dawned in which the focus of broadcasting policy shifted from a national towards a more international perspective (Bardoel, 1994). The Dutch broadcasting system was challenged by the rapid development of new transmission technologies, such as satellite and cable, enabling foreign commercial institutions to access the system without complying with national regulations. The government responded with the 1983 *Media White Paper* and the resulting 1987 *Media Act*, which were designed to maintain the current system and protect it from external influences. However, in the light of the European regulatory developments, this defensive approach proved non-sustainable, resulting in a forced unconditional opening of the system to foreign commercial broadcasters in 1991 (Van den Heuvel, 1995: 198). This period of time, characterised by the preservation of the public monopoly and the protection of the existing broadcasting system, is regarded as the *transitional period.*

In the early 1990s a *new dual order* was formed in which commercial broadcasters were admitted to the Dutch broadcasting system. The number of national television and radio channels rose from 2 respectively 4 in 1987 to more than 10 respectively 14 ten years later. As a result of this expansion, the audience fragmented over the different channels. The share of public channels in national broadcasting dropped from approximately 80% (TV) and 88% (radio) in 1988 to 38% (both) in 1996 (Bardoel, 1997: 25; Bakker & Scholten, 1997: 74 and 124). The most important policy papers of this time are the 1995 *Liberalisation White Paper*, the 1996 *Liberalisation Act*, and various other amendments to the 1987 *Media Act*. Important is also the most recently introduced 1999 *Concession Bill* amending the 1987 *Media Act*, which reorganises the public broadcasting system and separately defines its public task.

Compared to the Anglo-Saxon or even the Anglo-American situation, it seems that the legitimation of communication policies in terms of social responsibility came relatively late to the Netherlands and remained limited until recently. One reason could be that the country has a tradition of a decentralised, consensual political system, in which the (nation) state was weak and civil society (as self-organisation of social groups) was strong (see Lijphart, 1975). Another reason could well be that in the adversarial two-party systems of the US and the UK the role of the state in media matters is permanently contested and therefore explicit legitimisation is required. The circumstance that both countries have a long tradition of commercial broadcasting marks also an important difference; McQuail (1998: 109) speaks even about the 'British exception' to the rest of Europe.[2]

Old and New Notions of Social Responsibility

In the first, explorative phase, the analysis of the development of social responsibility in Dutch broadcasting policy focuses on the use of SR-requirements that are imposed by the government on broadcasting media

2 The relative lack of overt legitimisation in the Netherlands can also be noticed in other countries, notably in Scandinavia (see Hellman, 1999: 58), where public broadcasting remained uncontested for a long time.

and institutions from the old public until the new dual order. Our starting point was the drawing up of a catalogue of keywords and notions related to social responsibility that we found in the literature. We assumed these terms to be related to the following normative considerations:

- the role media should play in/for *society* (in terms of functions for individuals and of social goals to be reached);
- the requirements that media *content* should meet;
- the contribution media should deliver to the principal *social sectors*;
- and, last but not least, the functions media of communication should serve in the interest of the individual *citizen*.

When looking at the different keywords, possible synonyms and related operationalisations in the different policy papers, we see under the *old public order* most of the four normative considerations reflected, be it not necessarily with the same emphasis (see Table 1). As to the role media should play in society (in terms of the functions for individuals), there is mentioning of information, education and entertainment. In terms of social goals to be reached, there is equality, freedom of speech, openness, co-operation and unity, communication between groups, public order, and more in general: democracy. As to the media content requirements we see the most elaborate and considered list. It is a whole range which is partly overlapping and which seems to stress the overcoming of the potential ideological power of the medium: fairness, diversity, variety, comprehensiveness, representativity, balance, independence, decency and security. As to the contribution to social sectors we see really only culture and, may be, religion; politics, which might be found as a social sector in other countries, is obviously well served by the pillarised system. And finally the interest of the individual citizen is reflected in the different notions of access, choice and right to reply.

Three notions disappear in the *transition period*: decency, access to intelligence, and a fair distribution of broadcasting time of the organisations. The first two can possibly be explained by the effect that the sexual revolution has had on the Netherlands, respectively by the emphasis that is put on education in a welfare state. The last notion disappeared as a result of the de-pillarisation of the broadcasting system and the end of scarcity of broadcasting time. At the same time, the number of references to social responsibility notions grows. Individualisation, de-pillarisation and immigration in Dutch society are reflected in emphasis on social cohesion, identity, cultural integration and minorities. The audience appears for the first time as an independent category. With the appearance of more entertainment focused public channels (TROS and Veronica), likely to buy American popular programmes, internal competition demands emphasis on quality, authenticity and creativity.

Table 1 Social responsibility norms in broadcasting policy

SR-norms	*Old public order*	*Transition period*	*New dual order*	
	Broadcasting White Paper & Broadcasting Act '65-'67	*Media White Paper & Media Act '83-'87*	*Liberalisation White Paper/ Act & Media Act '95-'99*	*Concession/ Bill '99*
Equality	✓	✓	✓	
Freedom of speech	✓	✓	✓	✓
Fairness (freq. division)	✓	✓		
Openness (access to broadcasting system)	✓	✓		✓
Diversity	✓	✓	✓	✓
Co-operation, Unity	✓	✓	✓	✓
Variety	✓	✓	✓	✓
Fair distribution (of airtime)	✓			
Culture	✓	✓	✓	✓
Education	✓	✓	✓	✓
Information	✓	✓	✓	✓
Entertainment	✓	✓	✓	✓
Forum/ Communication between groups	✓	✓		✓
Access to intelligence	✓			
Comprehensiveness	✓	✓	✓	✓
Religion	✓	✓	✓	✓
Representativity	✓	✓	✓	✓
Balance (programming)	✓	✓	✓	✓
Choice	✓	✓	✓	✓
Independence	✓	✓	✓	✓
Public order	✓		✓	
Decency	✓			
Security (state)	✓	✓	✓	
Right of reply	✓	✓		
Democracy	✓	✓	✓	✓
Pluriformity		✓	✓	✓
Communication within groups/ Social cohesion		✓		✓
Audience research		✓	✓	✓
Access to audience		✓	✓	✓
Individual preferences		✓		

Table I Continued

SR-norms	*Old public order*	*Transition period*	*New dual order*	
	Broadcasting White Paper & Broadcasting Act '65-'67	*Media White Paper & Media Act '83-'87*	*Liberalisation White Paper/ Act & Media Act '95-'99*	*Concession/ Bill '99*
National identity		✓	✓	✓
Minority groups/ Sub-cultural groups		✓	✓	✓
Local/regional identity		✓	✓	✓
Continuity		✓	✓	✓
Differentiation		✓	✓	✓
Cultural integration		✓	✓	✓
Authenticity		✓		✓
Creativity		✓		✓
Quality		✓	✓	✓
Policy consistency		✓		
Access of Audience			✓	✓
Balance (public vs. commercial)			✓	
Reach			✓	✓
Non-commercialism			✓	✓
Art			✓	✓
Availability			✓	✓
Innovation				✓
Ideology				✓
Anti-discriminatory				✓
Audience maximisation				✓
Audience optimisation				✓
Information selection				✓
Information processing				✓
Commentary				✓
Craftsmanship				✓
Interest				✓
Attractiveness				✓
Autonomy				✓
Answerability				✓
Publicness				✓
Public testing				✓
Self regulation				✓

Under the *new dual order* the right of reply, which has always been a contested and delicate notion for journalists, disappears. With the multitude of media outlets, there are apparently enough forums to voice opinions. New are specific functions for society like publicness, reach, innovation, ideology (surprising with the end of ideology in sight!), and information selection and processing. New content requirements are non-commercialism, art, commentary, anti-discrimination, craftsmanship and attractiveness. Access and choice for the citizen are further detailed with reach, availability and answerability. The effect of competition is seen in the (renewed) emphasis on the public/audience and on public testing. The need for policy – in the intermediate period only in need of consistency – is now best performed by self-regulation.

Increasing Awareness for Social Responsibility

In the second, 'reflective' phase of our analysis we have looked at the *quantity* of SR-norms used in the various policy documents. Here a tendency can be noted towards an increasing awareness for social responsibility. However, at the same time the number and volume of policy papers has grown as well. Since this simultaneous growth might merely show an increasing repetition of comparable issues instead of an actual growth of attention for the subject matter, we have operationalised its saliency not only by looking at the intensification over the three distinguished periods, but also by following McQuail (1992) in using a different categorisation. We can then locate also changes in range and diversity over time.

McQuail (1992) distinguishes three basic communication values which not surprisingly coincide with the core values of liberal democracies: freedom, justice/equality and order/solidarity. With his freedom of communication McQuail makes a connection between 'structural conditions (legal freedom to publish); operating conditions (real independence from economic and political pressures and relative autonomy for journalists and other "communicators" within media organisations); opportunities for "voices" in society to gain access to channels; benefits of quality of provision for "receivers", according to criteria of relevance, diversity, reliability, interest, originality and personal satisfaction.' (McQuail, 1992: 70). Equality refers first to an absence of discrimination or bias in the amount and kind of access available to senders or receivers, secondly, to diversity of access and content and, thirdly, to notions of neutrality, fairness and truth. Order, finally, refers to cohesion and harmony, which the media are expected to safeguard or enhance through promoting 'education and traditionally valued culture, [...] cultural autonomy and authenticity for social groupings' (McQuail, 1992: 74).

Table 2 Social responsibility norms (categorisation)

Access to channels (audience)	Access to intelligence Reach Availability
Access for senders (institutions)	Equality Fairness Fair distribution (airtime) Representativity Openness Access to audience
Independence (political)	Freedom of speech Independence from government Self-regulation
Independence (economic)	Independence from market forces Balance public vs. commercial Non-commercialism Autonomy
Quality	Authenticity Creativity Quality Innovation Anti-discriminatory content Commentary, criticism Craftsmanship Attractiveness
Identity (individualism)	Minority & sub-cultural groups Individualism/Individual choice
Identity (cohesion)	National identity Local/regional identity Social cohesion/Communication within groups Cultural integration/Communication between groups
Diversity (channels/institutions)	Pluralism/Pluriformity Differentiation Democracy Religion Ideology Choice
Diversity (programming/content)	Unity (co-operation) Comprehensiveness Variety Differentiation Balance Culture Information Education Entertainment Art

Table 2 Continued

Order	Public order Decency Security (state)
Responsiveness	Representativity Audience research Right of reply Answerability Publicness

Using this threefold classification and further specification, we see that diversity as a content requirement, quality (as aimed for in content) and access for senders have the widest range of references in the policy documents in all three periods (see Table 2). Looking at each period separately (see Table 3), there is a clear increase in the range of notions per category. While in government papers of the old public order 27 different notions were distinguished, the subsequent periods reveal 36, respectively 51 distinct SR-norms.

Table 3 The range of SR-norms in Dutch broadcasting policy documents

Basic values	*Categorised SR-norms*	*Old public order*	*Transitional period*	*New dual order*
Freedom	Independence (political)	2	2	3
Freedom	Access to channels	1	-	4
Freedom	Diversity (channels)	4	6	7
Equality	Access for senders	5	5	3
Equality	Diversity (programming)	8	8	10
Order	Quality	-	3	8
Order	Identity (individualism)	-	2	1
Order	Identity (cohesion)	1	5	5
Order	Un-cultural	3	1	2
	Independence (economic)	1	1	3
	Responsiveness	2	3	5
	Total	27	36	51

Another remarkable tendency is the vast expansion of notions referring to quality, and to a lesser extent also to social cohesion, diversity, independence from economic influences, and responsiveness. McQuail (1992: 77) places these first two categories in the cultural domain of a basic value he defines as 'order'. Following his framework, the developments regarding quality and cohesion indicate that the most significant growth of terms regarding social responsibility are in the cultural sphere, while other categories with a more modest growth or even a decline in the SR-norms used are of a political or economical nature.

A further noticeable development is the increasing attention for citizens as opposed to broadcasting institutions. Although this process is not apparent in the Table above – only the diversity of terms is depicted – the policy documents show a tendency in which the government keeps a greater distance from broadcasting institutions, while it focuses increasingly on the availability of and access to broadcast media for citizens. The liberalisation of the broadcasting system seems to play a notable part in this process. With the coming of the dual system, the policy papers show an increasing concern for the access of all segments of society to both public and commercial broadcasting systems. This indicates on the one hand a distrust of government in the market, and on the other hand a belief that the market (i.e. a commercial system) enhances certain SR-notions and is of some public importance.

Finally, a remarkable tendency is the increasing attention of Dutch policy makers for minority and sub-cultural groups. Although the diversity of terms regarding the preservation of individual identity (e.g. individualism, minority programming) even declines, the frequency and saliency of these terms have grown considerably over time.

Conclusions

Interpreting the use of social responsibility norms in Dutch broadcasting policy – as part of the third and last phase of our analysis – and drawing some general conclusions, the policy documents studied clearly show a growing attention and concern for social responsibility. However, the general policy principles originating from the old public order have changed not dramatically over time. Since the 1960s, (public) broadcasters have been obliged to carry a comprehensive and balanced programme, containing information, culture, education and entertainment in order to provide for the social, cultural, religious and ideological needs of society.

Three concurrent tendencies can be noticed. First, there is an increase in the diversity of SR-norms used in the various policy documents. A growing awareness of the importance of national programme production indicates an increase in the concern for national identity. There is also growing attention for the exchange of European culture, for the quality of programming and the independence of the broadcasting system from governmental and economic influences. In addition, different social groups cross-cutting traditional segments, such as minority groups, the elderly and the unemployed, are being addressed separately.

The second noticeable tendency is the growing refinement of SR-norm specifications. An indication for this development is the quantification of requirements concerning programme comprehensiveness, which was realised through the designation of quotas to several programming categories. The increasing norm refinement is also indicated by the allocation of specific amounts of airtime to nationally produced programmes. Finally, with the coming of the new dual order, the government papers show a further increase and refinement of the social responsibility concept in light of social (individualisation) and economic (competition) changes affecting public broadcasting. There is clearly more attention for the audience as consumers, and programmes should thus not only have quality but also attractiveness.

In interpreting these changes we can detect four tendencies and shifts.

1 From political to cultural motives. The analysis of Dutch broadcasting policy legitimation reveals a shift from predominantly political motives (related to basic values as communication freedom and democracy) towards mainly cultural motives (related to preserving national culture and identity).

In the old public order, the main reason for government regulation was a fair division of the scarce frequency spectrum between the traditional 'streams' segmenting Dutch society. When in the 1960s the cohesion within the traditional pillars started eroding and new societal groups appeared, the government was pressured to grant these 'new segments' equal representation within the broadcasting system. During the transitional period, the political motives mentioned above remained an important part of policy legitimisation, but also cultural motives appeared in policy documents. There was more attention for cultural production and greater concern for choice, authenticity, creativity and quality of programming. With the arrival of commercial broadcasting in the new dual order, the legitimation of broadcasting policy shifted more towards cultural motives.

2 From collectivism to individualism. Our research shows that Dutch broadcasting policy in the new dual order is primarily individualist and citizen-centred, while in previous periods it was more collectivist and state-oriented.

In the old public order the Dutch broadcasting system was organised along the lines of social segmentation. Most issues regarding social responsibility were approached in a collectivist manner and applied particularly to broadcasting institutions. In the transitional period new social groups, distinguished by age, ethnic origin and life-style, fuelled the need for a more individualistic policy approach. The liberalisation process in the beginning of the new dual order-period induced another individualist policy approach: citizen and consumer protection. After the admittance of commercial broadcasters, there was great concern for access of citizens to the entire broadcasting system, and maintenance of a pluralist and independent programming for an increasingly diversifying society. Through more audience research and greater obligations regarding the responsiveness to its results, the answerability of the broadcasting institutions towards citizens increased.

3 From ambiguous to positive assessment of economic forces. The government policy assessment of economic and market forces on the broadcasting system were found to vary for many aspects and for different periods of time. Some economic forces had been assessed positively since the old public order, while others had always been assessed negatively, and again other forces were gradually considered less harmful to the broadcasting system.

In each relevant policy document of the last three decades, the free market was considered an insufficient tool to assure the various policy goals regarding social responsibility of the broadcasting system. The liberalisation of the media sector and the creation of the new dual order suggest an increasing confidence in economic and market forces. The market mechanism is considered to induce a more efficient use of resources and an expansion of choice. Many policy documents however, stress the importance of consumer protection from market failure.

4 From purely national to also minority cultures. The attention for minority groups and different cultures in Dutch government policy has increased significantly since the 1960s. Whereas minorities were not or only scarcely mentioned during the old public order, minority groups have now become a considerable part of Dutch broadcasting policy.

That may sound like a paradox, as the pillars themselves were the organisational structures for the emancipation of religious (particularly catholic) and ideological (notably socialist) groups. As they started to erode, diversity of new societal groups, segmented along other lines than religion and class, increased. Because of the growing number of citizens of foreign origin, non-traditional cultures received more attention. Also, through the expansion of daytime broadcasts, the unemployed and elderly were catered for. It was also felt that the public system had to be more attractive to the young who seemed to be more interested in commercial than public channels.

Discussion

Our case study has demonstrated that the overall awareness of social responsibility, as reflected in the broadcasting policies of subsequent Dutch governments, has increased over time. It reflects both the increasing (discursive) struggle over public broadcasting in a dual and competitive system and the more critical stance of citizens and society towards the performance of social institutions and organisations in general. The shift towards cultural motives in broadcast policies seems a reaction to trends as the influx of cross-border television, the need to reposition public broadcasting vis-à-vis commercial broadcasting and, last but not least, the changing social composition of society.

In a sense, it seems that in broadcast policies the old, modernist paradigm – with freedom and equality as the core values – is being replaced by a more postmodernist approach. There is more room for individual cultures, styles, and tastes and less for paternalistic policies, at least in a rhetorical sense. More in general, our impression is that the specificities of Dutch broadcasting policies and their legitimation erode and are being replaced by more common, perhaps 'European' policy motives.

The social consequences of the information society and the realisation of social responsibility in old and new communications media have been reinvented frequently in recent years. Debates used to emphasise the so-called 'network' characteristics of the new technology and the new society. As a result – focusing on the social consequences and the political reaction required – the need of equal *access* for citizens, in line with the tradition of telecommunications or common carrier policy, was stressed. For some time it even seemed that converging communication policy would be just a new version of the good old telecommunications policy, stressing norms as universal service and access for all (Bardoel & Frissen, 1999). Broadcasting policy was considered outdated, since content policies were seen as a remnant of an era in which communication content was still a scarce commodity.

More recently the situation seems to be changing or even reversing again. Telecommunications policy is seen as 'merely' the exploitation of network and the carriage of communication services, that can be left to private enterprise and a public supervisor quite simply, whereas the production and delivery of content are considered as crucial again, for which a public domain is still needed. As a result the debate seems to shift from an emphasis on convergence of these policies to stressing the difference of both types of policy again, of separate distribution and content-related policies (see Plug, 1999).

References

Achille, Y. and Miege, B.
1994 The limits to the adaptation strategies of European public service television. *Media, Culture & Society* 16 (1): 31-46.

Bakker, P. and Scholten, O.
1997 *Communicatiekaart van Nederland* [Communication Map of the Netherlands]. Houten/Diegem: Bohn Stafleu Van Loghum.

Bardoel, J.
1994 'Om Hilversum valt geen hek te plaatsen.' De moeizame modernisering van de Nederlandse omroep ['It is impossible to build dykes around Hilversum.' The troublesome modernisation of Dutch broadcasting]. In H. Wijfjes (ed.), *Omroep in Nederland. Vijfenzeventig Jaar Medium en Maatschappij 1919-1994* [Broadcasting in the Netherlands. Seventy-five Years of Medium and Society 1919-1994], pp. 338-372. Zwolle: Waanders Uitgevers.

Bardoel, J.
1996 Beyond journalism. A profession between Information Society and Civil Society. *European Journal of Communication* 11 (3): 283-302.

Bardoel, J.
1997 Tussen lering en vermaak. De ontwikkelingsgang van de Nederlandse omroep [Between education and entertainment. The evolution of the Dutch broadcasting system]. In J. Bardoel and J. Bierhoff (eds.), *Media in Nederland. Feiten en Structuren* [Media in the Netherlands. Facts and Structures], pp. 10-32. Groningen: Wolters-Noordhoff.

Bardoel, J. and Frissen, V.
1999 Policing participation: New forms of participation and citizenship and their implications for a social communications policy. *Communications & Strategies* (34): 203-228.

Blackman, C.R.
1998 Convergence between telecommunications and other media. How should regulation adapt? *Telecommunications Policy* 22 (3) pp. 163-170.

Blumer, H.
1969 *Symbolic Interactionism. Perspective and Method.* Englewood Cliffs: Prentice Hall.

Blumler, J.G. and McQuail, D.
1965 British broadcasting: Its purposes, structure and control. *Gazette* 11 (2/3): 166-191.
Blumler, J.G. and Hoffmann-Riem, W.
1992 Toward renewed public accountability in broadcasting. In J. G. Blumler (ed.), *Television and the Public Interest. Vulnerable Values in West European Broadcasting*, pp. 218-228. London: Sage.
Brants, K.
1999 Public broadcasting and Open Society. A marriage under threat? In Y.N. Zassoursky and E. Vartanova (eds.), *Media, Communications and the Open Society*, pp. 228-243. Moscow: Faculty of Journalism/Publisher IKAR.
Brants, K. and McQuail, D.
1997 The Netherlands. In Østergaard/Euromedia Research Group (ed.), *The Media in Western Europe*, pp. 153-165. London: Sage.
Brants, K. and Siune, K.
1992 Public broadcasting in a state of flux. In K. Siune and W. Truetzschler (eds.), *Dynamics of Media Politics*, pp. 101-116. London: Sage.
Broadcasting Research Unit
1985 *The Public Service Idea in British Broadcasting*. London: BRU.
Brown, A.
1996 Economics, public service broadcasting and social values. *The Journal of Media Economics* 9 (1): 3-15.
Burgelman, J.C.
1995 Toekomstige uitdagingen van het communicatiebeleid [New challenges for communications policy]. In I. Baten and J. Ubacht (eds.), *Een Kwestie van Toegang. Bijdragen aan het Debat over het Publieke Domein van de Informatievoorziening* [A Matter of Access. Contributions to the Debate about the Public Domain in Information Provision], pp. 63-76. Amsterdam: Otto Cramwinckel.
Calhoun, C.
1992 *Habermas and the Public Sphere*. Cambridge, Mass.: MIT Press.
Collins, R.
1998 Public service and the media economy. European trends in the late 1990's. *Gazette* (60) 5: 363-376.
Council of Europe
1994 *The Media in a Democratic Society. Political Declaration, Resolutions and Statement.* 4th European Ministerial Conference on Mass Media Policy, Prague, 7-8 December 1994. Strassbourg: Council of Europe.
Dahlgren, P. and Sparks, C. (eds.)
1991 *Communication and Citizenship. Journalism and the Public Sphere in the New Media.* New York: Routledge.

Dahlgren, P.
1995 *Television and the Public Sphere. Citizenship, Democracy and the Media.* London: Sage.
Dries, J. and Woldt, R.
1996 *The Role of Public Service Broadcasting in the Information Society.* Düsseldorf: European Institute for the Media.
European Commission
1997 *Green Paper on the Convergence of Telecommunications, Media and Information Technology Sectors, and the Implications for Regulation. Towards an Information Society Approach.* (COM(97)623). Brussels, December 3 1997. <http:/www.ispo.cec.be/convergencegp/>.
European Communication Council
1997 *Exploring the Limits. Europe's Changing Communication Environment.* Berlin: Springer Verlag.
Garnham, N.
1993 The media and the public sphere. In Calhoun C. (ed.), *Habermas and the Public Sphere*, pp. 359-377. Cambridge, Mass.: MIT Press.
Hellman, H.
1999 *From Companions to Competitors. The Changing Broadcasting Markets and Television Programming in Finland.* Tampere: University of Tampere.
Hutchins, R.M.
1947 *A Free and Responsible Press.* Report of the Commission on Freedom of the Press. Chicago, Ill.: University of Chicago Press.
Lijphart, A.
1975 *The Politics of Accommodation: Pluralism and Democracy in the Netherlands.* 2nd edition. Berkeley: University of California Press.
McQuail, D.
1992 *Media Performance. Mass Communication and the Public Interest.* London: Sage.
McQuail, D.
1994 *Mass Communication Theory. An Introduction.* 3rd edition. London: Sage.
McQuail, D.
1998 Commercialisation and beyond. In D. McQuail and K. Siune (eds.), *Media Policy. Convergence, Concentration and Commerce*, pp.107-128. London: Sage/Euromedia Research Group.
Mitchell, J. and Blumler, J.G. (eds.)
1994 *Television and the Viewer Interest. Exploration in the Responsiveness of European Broadcasters.* London: Libbey.

Nordenstreng, K.
1997a Beyond the four theories of the press. In J. Servaes and R. Lie (eds.), *Media and Politics in Transition. Cultural Identity in the Age of Globalization*, pp. 97-109. Leuven/Amersfoort: ACCO Publishers.
Nordenstreng, K.
1997b The citizen moves from the audience to the arena. *Nordicom Review* 18 (2): 13-20.
Oreja, M. et al.
1998 *The Digital Age. European Audiovisual Policy*. Report from the High Level Group on Audiovisual Policy. Brussels: European Commission.
Paterson, R.
1997 Policy implications of economic and cultural value chains. In European Communication Council (ed.), *Exploring the Limits. Europe's Changing Communication Environment*, pp. 169-186. Berlin: Springer Verlag.
Picard, R.
1989 *Media Economics. Concepts and Issues*. London: Sage.
Plug, R.
1999 *Convergentie: Op Weg naar een Nieuwe Generatie Informatie- en Communicatiebeleid. Een Onderzoek naar het Convergentieproces in Nederland en de Implicaties voor Overheidsbeleid* [Convergence: On the Road towards a New Generation of Information and Communications Policy. A Study on the Convergence Process in the Netherlands and the Implications for Government Policies]. MA thesis. Amsterdam: University of Amsterdam.
Porter, V.
1995 Public service broadcasting and European regulation. *Mediaforum* (3): 30-34.
Royal Commission on the Press
1977 *Report*. London: HMSO.
Scannel, P.
1980 Public service: The history of a concept. In A. Goodwin and G. Whannel (eds.), *Understanding Television*, pp. 11 -29. London: Routledge.
Soete, L. et al.
1997 *Building the European Information Society for Us All*. Final Policy Report of the High Level Expert Group. Brussels: European Commission. <http://www.ispo.cec.be/hleg/Building.html>.
Smith, A.
1989 The public interest. *Intermedia* 17 (2): 10-24.

Siune, K. and Hulten, O.
1998 Changes in broadcasting: Is public service still alive? In D. McQuail and K. Siune (eds.), *Media Policy. Convergence, Concentration and Commerce*, pp. 23-38). London: Sage/Euromedia Research Group.

Sondergaard, H.
1996 Public service after the crisis. *Nordicom Review* 1: 107-120.

Syvertsen, T.
1992 *Public Service Broadcasting in Transition.* Oslo: University of Oslo.

Thompson, J. B.
1995 *The Media and Modernity. A Social Theory of the Media.* Cambridge: Polity Press.

Van Cuilenburg, J. and Slaa, P.
1993 From media policy towards a national communications policy: Broadening the scope. *European Journal of Communication* (8): 149-176.

Van den Heuvel, J.H.J.
1995 De ontwikkeling van de zorgfunctie van de overheid op het gebied van de omroep [The development of the care function of government in the area of broadcasting]. In Rathenau Instituut (ed.), *Toeval of Noodzaak? Geschiedenis van de Overheidsbemoeienis met de Informatievoorziening* [Chance or Necessity? History of Governmental Involvement in Information Provision], pp. 175-222. Amsterdam: Otto Cramwinckel.

Wieten, J.
1998 Reality television and social responsibility theory. In K. Brants, J. Hermes and L. van Zoonen (eds.), *The Media in Question. Popular Cultures and Public Interests*, pp. 101-112. London: Sage.

Part III

COMPETITION, MEDIA INNOVATION AND DIVERSITY

Diversity at Media Markets in Transition

Threats to Openness

ELENA VARTANOVA
Faculty of Journalism, Moscow State University, Russia

Abstract

This paper analyses the development and present state of the Russian media market in terms of media diversity. The author assesses the concept of diversity from economic, political and technological perspectives. She suggests that two major trends of Russian media development, e.g. growing commercialism and expansive politicisation, are in fact serious threats to openness and media diversity. New threats to diversity are emerging as a result of the rapid technological progress of the media, which deprives the majority of population of new means of communication and new diverse content products.

Implications of Diversity and the Case of Russia

As applied to media markets, the notion of diversity has several implications such as a relatively high number of media titles, a variety of products targeted at different social groups, designed for numerous social and/or political tastes of general public, for audiences grouped on the basis of specific interests, etc. From this point of view the Russian media of the post-Soviet period have made great progress. The diversity of the newspaper market in terms of political representation, contents' colourfulness and opinions' reflection, novelty of design and layout modes has obviously increased. Russian regional and local press has obviously benefited from the decrease in circulation and distribution of former all-Russian national dailies. An essential amount of newspapers which have been set up at Russian local markets as a result of the post-Soviet transformations definitely supported a new understanding of the market diversity which was accepted in Russia as an equivalent term of democracy and glasnost, e.g. a specific Russian vision of openness. The same was especially true for the broadcast media. Television and radio historically remained of particular concern to Soviet authorities. Because of the limited number of broadcast channels available for general audiences and poor programmes supply in the Soviet Union, a shift to 'more' market diversity turns out to become a real breakthrough in the broadcast media.

Radical moves to media diversity have created a fundamentally different media landscape in Russia. From the first glance, modern Russian media today demonstrate more common features with the Western media than with the Soviet, despite the fact that Soviet media system actually preceded and gave birth to the modern Russian media. Comparing Western and Russia media some Russian scholars underline their similarity and even conclude that the contemporary Russian 'information industry has become a profitable and attractive business for investments' (Gourevitch, 1999: 29). But the reality proves to be more complicated.

The emerging similarity occurs to become more mimicry than an analogy. In one of his profound but rather discouraging essays, *The End of Millennium or the Countdown*, Baudrillard (1998: 1) states that 'we are turning away from the history "in progress", with none of the problems it poses having been resolved [...]'. And later he continues by following:

> Everywhere we see a paradoxical logic which puts an end to an idea by its very realisation, its excessiveness (Baudrillard, 1998: 6).

The Russian context of media diversity perfectly illustrates this idea. The media diversity, which has emerged at the Russian media market, happened to present itself through an increased number of content products and media companies. However, a critical examination of the Russian media may lead to rather discouraging conclusions. The formal diversity in fact does not respond to the cultural, informational or political needs of the Russian audience. Stemming from Baudrillard's logic, one might state that the Russian media market only imitates diversity lacking the substance of the idea itself. The reasons for this are numerous.

Diversity as Market Performance and Democratic Value

By many Western scholars the concept of media diversity is considered to be of crucial value. As McQuail (1994: 143) says, 'the principle of diversity [...] is especially important because it underpins the normal processes of progressive change in society [...] which pluralistic forms of democracy are supposed to deliver'. In the context of Western traditions of democracy this concept implies at least two important dimensions which correspond to a market economy and social participation.

From the point of view of the market, media provide audiences with content products thus meeting their demands in news and entertainment (Picard, 1989: 17-18). Ideally, the diversity of media content supply should respond to the content demand of consumers. However, in many cases profit-oriented strategies of media companies prevent media from perfect satisfaction of consumers' demands. Various circumstances cause negative effects that badly influence diversity in terms of media products and their quality. Some of them are obvious. Concentration of ownership results in fewer numbers of competitive companies on the market and as a result in a declining amount of media outlets. Consequently this process leads to a subsequent decrease in diversity of contents. As Picard concludes, this kind of development has important implications in terms of diversity of information available to the public and the ability of the media to serve the functions ascribed to them in a democratic society (Picard, 1989: 34). Severin and Tankard directly point to the negative consequences of joint ownership of media companies that often means less diversity of coverage (Severin & Tankard, 1979: 240).

A traditional perspective in policy studies equates content diversity with the number of voices in the market or the community. However only recently a new focus has been put on the link between the sheer number of voices (multiplicity) and the number of different voices (diversity). Starting from another perspective, critical studies bring a new dimension to the concept of media diversity. The latter is viewed as not a substantial issue because information and entertainment are *polysemic* or subject to multiple reading and interpretations that create their own diversity, whatever the number of formal producers and distributors (Mosco, 1996: 258).

The development of media markets and structures has brought about new confusions and more complexity to the traditional understanding of diversity at the media markets. Van Cuilenburg argues that media diversity refers to heterogeneous media content, variety of news, genres, topics, cultural traditions, etc. This definition puts much emphasis on media content, and Van Cuilenburg underlines that a connection between media market structures, competition and media diversity is not simply linear and positive (Van Cuilenburg, 1999: 189). Moreover, there exist new dimensions of the concept of diversity. Using the concept of the intellectual market as the second market for media to operate, an idea suggested by Lacy and Simon (1993: 5), Van Cuilenburg underlines the significance of social dimensions of diversity. For modern societies diversity has become an important vehicle to make politicians hear voices of different social, political, cultural groups and categories in societies (Van Cuilenburg, 1999: 192).

These considerations are extremely valuable for further examination of media markets in their more advanced and developed structures. In an economically sophisticated context, media diversity has to be understood as a complex and multifold definition. The case of post-Socialist societies and especially of Russia proves to be different and therefore approaches to media diversity along with contemporary policy visions and outcomes of debates on limited social participation should also integrate some earlier observations. For instance, the importance of the quantity aspect of the diversity concept needs to be stressed as well.

Diversity at the Russian Media Market: A Delusive Hypothesis

The concept of media diversity has got a particular popularity among media practitioners and scholars in the post-Socialist region because it implied a lot of illusions inspired by changes in the media. At early stages of transition there existed a strong belief that such phenomena like pluralism, media diversity, equal participation in economic and political life were intrinsic features of the market-based economy. Some authors expressed this view by stating that only the development of private ownership, sale of media content for extracting profits and effective use of information as a market good would create conditions for the normal functioning of the media market (Androunas, 1993: 114).

Only recently a critical assessment of previous delusions has been made with an attempt to explain transformations of the Russian society and media within the overall context of the global development. By defining some of early approaches to the media market as the transformation utopia, Ivan Zassoursky (1999: 30) argues that uncritically positive attitudes to the market, neglect of state influences over the media and underestimation of the role of politicised capital have become the most general attitudes among Russian media scholars. The complexity of the post-Soviet development in Russia has been seriously distorted by the use of a sheer market approach in media studies.

In these circumstances the concept of media diversity seems very significant since it helps to throw more light on more complicated moments of developments which took place in Russia during the last decade. Whatever elementary the direct link between the number of media products and media diversity may appear, this link became the most important achievement of the first stages of Glasnost. Variety of content products appeared within the old framework of Soviet media that used to be economically controlled by the State and Communist party and started their movement to liberation from authoritarian control.

The first stages of media diversity in Russia have produced a visible growth within the media industry. In terms of number of media outlets media diversity was characterised by remarkable progress. In 1993–1997, the Russian media market has shown a 45%-growth in number of publications, a rapid expansion of private TV and the emergence of numerous commercial radio stations.

McNair (1994) defines the period of stable growth of media in terms of circulation and number of titles (1990-1992) as the golden age of the Russian press. Despite the fact that the number of broadcasting channels still remained rather limited, programming formats of major channels became more diverse bringing a variety of new genres and contents. As many scholars agree, the golden age of the Russian media brought about the highest level of plurality and diversity of content products (see Ivan Zassoursky, 1999: 81-82).

However, the Russian media reached maximum diversity at the time when the basics of the market had not yet been created in the country's economy including the media business. The first years of transformation showed a specific form of media diversity, which was not supported economically. Media diversity was still secured by the state and party economic resources, although the shift to less control over the media and more openness in media coverage obviously had already begun.

The creation of the present media system (1992-1996) encountered numerous problems. Paradoxically the evolvement of the media market has brought about the decrease in diversity in many respects. The emergence of previously non-existent types of publications – non-political, entertainment, popular and sensational papers – altered the old political press. The surface diversity – more newspapers concentrating on celebrities, private life, and sex – in fact has become an obstacle for the development of a serious analytical press. Resnyanskaya and Fomicheva argue that while the positioning of new quality newspapers at the national market has faced a number of serious problems, various 'yellow' publications such as women's or men's monthlies, weekly TV magazines and even Moscow tabloid-type dailies (Moskovsky Komsomolets) have increased their popularity (Resnyanskaya & Fomicheva, 1999: 76-77). Thus, the emerged diversity tended to become an indicator of growing tabloidisation, the trend which could be described by the revision of a traditional newspaper format by readers preferences and commercial requirements (Esser, 1999: 293).

The Broadcasting Market

Commercial interests have challenged the broadcast media even to a greater degree. As result, the first extensions of programmes' diversity such as the emergence of new genres (talk and quiz shows, soap operas, foreign serials and cinemas) and the introduction of advertising, have gradually eroded and destroyed old Soviet programming schemes. Educational programmes, documentaries, TV and radio production for different religious, cultural interests little by little disappeared from broadcast channels. The only channel that proclaimed the public service obligation, at least in its name as a dominant doctrine, remained the ORT channel. Owned partly by the state and partly by private companies, this channel is increasingly blamed for growing commercialisation and political servility. Even to a lesser degree ORT responds to major goals of public service broadcasting, which were defined by McQuail as diversity, ideals of 'the public interest' and 'quality of service' (McQuail, 1994: 127). Though with the limited share of viewers (not more than 5% of the Russian audience) a unique experience of the Kultura (Culture) channel opens up at least some new perspectives for TV diversity.

As a result, the subordination to 'the government of the day', as Sparks (1998: 176) describes it, reflected especially in news and current affair programmes, has become the major reason why the political and cultural diversity of the ORT programmes remains as limited as in the Soviet time.

Media Diversity as Reflection of Struggle for Power

The high degree of politicisation and partisanship is a typical feature of the bulk of media outlets in Russia. Although this might be a common observation for media systems in various post-Socialist countries, the dynamics and even nature of developments in different national contexts appear to be very different. For many Russian media companies 'governments of the day' are still associated with several powerful political and economic elites, very limited in number at the national level and restricted by one or two groups at local levels.

From the political point of view, media diversity is also regarded as an essential attribute of a democratic and open society. McQuail points to a direct link between a number of politically engaged media outlets and pluralism of political views in a society:

> A typical diversity question might be the degree to which news gave equal or proportionate attention to the views of several different political parties or candidates [...] There is more diversity where we find more categories (a wide range of opinion) and less diversity where there is very unequal attention to different categories (one opinion tends to dominate news coverage) (McQuail, 1994: 250).

By suggesting normative frameworks for media diversity Van Cuilenburg points to the significance of reflective diversity according to which 'media content proportionally reflects differences in politics, religion, culture and social conditions in the society in a more or less proportional way' (Van Cuilenburg, 1999: 190). The case of Russian media establishes a kind of negative modification for a suggested definition in a form of power reflection. While the struggle for power among few elites is widely covered by the national media directly owned or controlled by these groups, voices of smaller sections of society remain almost soundless.

The press, which is in nature more reflective, certainly provides Russians with more diversity in political views but the level of access to them is very low. The circulation and distribution scale for opposite or different views is very limited thus making the political scope in media rather narrow. As for the national TV channels, they remain totally dependent upon those who control them and reflect more the distribution of power than the distribution of political opinions among the population. The information war between the Moscow mayor Luzhkov and the former President's team including media mogul Berezovsky and the President's administration during the last Parliamentary Election Campaign in fact followed major border lines in media ownership. Other evidence of power reflection in terms of media diversity might be found in the present structure of media ownership. Major media companies are grouped around the most influential politicians. Their market activities are secured by the financial and/or industrial capital, which uses its media subsidiaries primarily in political goals (Vartanova, 1996; Vartanova, 1997).

Some Western scholars have pointed to political reasons of investing in the media business. Thus Bates argues that

> Media properties can be useful in ways other than in their capacity to generate economic returns. Many media owners perceive a value in their properties related more to the prestige of being a publisher or broadcaster, and in the potential to exert political or social influence through their media (Bates, 1993: 100).

This point may be of less importance for advanced and sophisticated media markets which are characterised by sustained economic development at the macro-level and by existence of at least some accepted rules by economic players. However, taking into account the variety of national particular media markets one could suggest that in some cases media are becoming much more dependent upon exceptional and abnormal but actually existing sources of value. In light of a fair market value concept, considerations of a political nature may become relatively important, but still they are not regarded as conditions under which market value is determined.

Political Capital and Control

However, in post-Socialist societies with transitional economies, considerations of political nature become extremely important. This is especially true of Russia, and the reasons for this are numerous. First, the long-standing Russian tradition of the state respectively Communist party control over the media has been inherited and successfully evolved by a new generation of media moguls and oligarchs, that emerged as an integrated political and financial elite. The essence of media diversity has been traditionally missing because in the Soviet Union there existed no advertising market at all. The news market was very limited and the opinion market in practice was dominated only by one ideology and by one system of philosophical views.

Second, the rise of a new post-Soviet etatist philosophy as the dominant political paradigm has dramatically reduced possibilities for alternative or marginal views to be reflected by the national TV channels which at present remain the only factor to maintain and consolidate the information space of Russia (Zassoursky, 1998: 16). Yassen Zassoursky also points to 'the growing tendency to turn media and first of all television again into instruments, tools, sources of power for the Government and private corporations, close to the Government' (Zassoursky, 1997: 221).

Third, there exists one more obvious explanation, which is also important from the economic point of view. Russian media still lack sufficient advertising, which could guarantee economic profit and some extent of political independence. Picard states that media industries operate in a dual product market. He continues:

> The second market in which many media participate is the advertising market [...] A more precise and descriptive explanation is that media sell access to audiences to advertisers (Picard, 1989: 18).

This point is crucial whatever the state of the advertising market is. However, poor, undeveloped or ineffectively managed advertising markets do not produce enough revenues to sustain media development. In Russia the advertising market still remains very vulnerable, thus reacting to various changes in economic situation. The Russian market of political advertising has on the contrary demonstrated a constant growth and a relatively good financial performance. Russian media in a greater degree than many other media industries in the world are dependent on the political advertising market. This trend reveals itself both during and between election campaigns, creating a serious deviation from 'normal' media economics.

Consequently one might say that in Russia the only profitable sector in the advertising market is political advertising. Therefore in pursuit of economic profit Russian media are selling access to audiences to politicians and political elites instead of advertisers of commodities and consumer services. Seeking for revenues at markets in depression media get increasingly dependent on politics and as a result reflective media diversity substantially decreases.

Diversity and Access

Among the negative consequences of reducing media diversity, access by Russians to media content should be mentioned among the first. Access to content products has been obviously worsened by a crucial decline in circulation of the all-national press, a crisis in distribution and increased state monopolism in paper and printing production. The most dramatic outcome of this trend revealed itself during the period from 1993 to 1997 when the circulation of all Russian dailies dropped by about 32% (Pankin, 1999: 12). Ineffectiveness and ill-management of the media economy have constituted another serious threat to the openness and diversity of the Russian media market.

In the media economy several factors have worsened the development of the media infrastructure which in fact would support diversity and openness of the media system. They are:

- an outstanding position of the Russian state as one of the major proprietors of media companies;
- a slightly eroded and transformed, but still monopolist control of the Russian state or municipal bodies over printing and distribution sectors;
- an existence of the broadcast transmission system and telecommunications still operated by the state;
- a lack of free and fair competition at the media market, which results into the neglect of audiences, needs and interests.

Access to the media by their audiences has recently emerged as a crucial characteristic to assess the level of openness and diversity of the media. Several factors such as the demand for media products including the demand for political participation through the media use, the level of income, dominant attitudes towards the media are important to estimate what are the interests of people and how the process of media openness is achieved.

Equal and universal access to the media is getting especially important in the era of the Internet and convergence, thus involving into realisation of diversity and openness new groups like operators, providers of access, services, creators of content products and users. An undeveloped technological infrastructure, on the one hand, and education and training, on the other, appeared to become major concerns for public policy and government actions in the field of the new media.

New threats to media diversity expand existing economic uncertainties, especially at the new media markets that diminish access to modern technologies by the poorest and uneducated groups of society. The gate-keeping control over the technological infrastructure by the state or telecommunications monopolies in practice decreases new opportunities for diversity brought about by the technological progress (Vartanova, 1998: 176-177). Russia is a perfect illustration of this development. The bad economic situation and political instability negatively influence the development of modern technologies. Information poverty in Russia is a rather widespread phenomenon. Like in other countries, including the most developed, the Russian situation is very uneven in terms of developing new information and communication technologies today. New information discrepancies coincide with the economic division of Russian society. In addition, there exists an increasing inequality between the geographic regions and economic areas that is also an important characteristic of the situation (Zassoursky & Vartanova, 1999).

Under present Russian conditions, policy-making in the area of new information and communications technologies should draw particular attention of the state, private business and especially the public to various aspects of access. Russia obviously needs the precise design of a balanced communications policy, which is to be positively understood and widely accepted by politicians, theoreticians and ordinary users. Obviously the focus of this policy should be public, universal and open access by Russians to the new media.

As we could see, media diversity in Russia today faces numerous threats. It challenges economic and political realities, restructuring of the media system, changes in dominant social, political and philosophical paradigms. There exist various approaches to a critical assessment of media diversity in Western media studies. McQuail suggests a manifold and divergent scheme to examine various aspects of the problem:

> In accounting for diversity of provision, the extent to which real alternatives are on offer can be registered according to several alternative yardsticks:
>
> – type of media (such as press, radio or television);
> – function or type (such as entertainment or information);
> – the level of operation (national, regional, local, etc.);
> – the audience aimed at and reached (differentiated by income, age, etc.);
> – language, ethnic or cultural identity;
> – and the politics or ideology.
>
> In general, a media system is more equal in character the more diverse the provision according to the criteria mentioned (McQuail, 1994: 143).

The case of Russia proves that standards should be found and developed to escape threats of illusive transitional markets.

References

Androunas, E.
1993 *Soviet Media in Transition. Structural and Economic Alternatives.* Westport: Preager.

Baudrillard, J.
1998 The end of millennium or the countdown. *Theory, Culture and Society* 15 (1): 1-9.

Bates, B.
1993 Valuation of media properties. In A. Alexander, J. Owers and R. Carverth (eds.), *Media Economics. Theory and Practice*, pp. 73-94. Hillsdale: Lawrence Erlbaum Associates.

Esser, F.
1999 'Tabloidization' of news. A comparative analysis of Anglo-American and German press journalism. *European Journal of Communication* 14 (3): 219-324.

Gourevitch, S.
1999 *Ekonomika Sredstv Massovoi Informatsii* [Economics of Mass Media]. Moscow: Izdatel'stvo Sabashnikovikh.

Lacy, S. and Simon, T.
1993 *The Economics and Regulation of US Newspapers.* Norwood, NJ: Ablex.

McNair, B.
1994 Media in post-Soviet Russia: An Overview. *European Journal of Communication* 9 (2): 115-135.

McQuail, D.
1994 *Mass Communication Theory. An Introduction.* 3rd edition. London: Sage.

Mosco, V.
1996 *The Political Economy of Communications. Rethinking and Renewal.* London: Sage.

Pankin, A.
1998 Krisis kak simptom vizdorovlenija [Crisis as the way of recovering]. In *God 1998: Chto Proiskhodit s Nezavisimost'uy Pressy v Rossii* [Year 1998: What Happens to Press Freedom in Russia?], pp. 12-15. Moscow.

Picard, R.
1989 *Media Economics. Concepts and Issues.* London: Sage.

Severin, W. and Tankard, J.
1979 *Communication Theories. Origins. Methods. Users.* New York: Hasting House.

Resnyanskaya, L. and Fomicheva, I.
1999 *Gazeta dl'a Vsei Rossii* [Newspaper for Whole Russia]. Moscow: Publisher ICAR.

Sparks, C. with Reading, A.
1998 *Capitalism, Communism and the Mass Media.* London: Sage.

Van Cuilenburg, J.

1999 On competition, access and diversity in media, old and new. Some remarks for communications policy in the information age. *New Media & Society* 1 (2): 183-207.

Vartanova, E.

1996 Corporate transformation of the Russian media. In *Media in Transition*, pp. 16-27. Moscow: Faculty of Journalism.

Vartanova, E.

1997 *Russian Financial Elite as Media Moguls.* Paper presented at the International Conference on Media and Politics. Brussels, 1997, 27.2-1.3.

Vartanova, E.

1998 National infrastructure for the new media in Russia. In Y.N. Zassoursky and E. Vartanova (eds.), *Changing Media and Communications*, pp. 174-188. Moscow: Faculty of Journalism/Publisher ICAR.

Zassoursky, I.

1999 *Mass Media Vtoroi Respubliki* [Mass Media of the Second Republic]. Moscow: Izdatelstvo Moskovskogo Universiteta.

Zassoursky, Y.N.

1997 Media in transition and politics in Russia. In J. Servaes and R. Lie (eds.), *Media and Politics in Transition. Cultural Identity in the Age of Globalization*, pp. 213-221. Leuven/Amersfoort: ACCO.

Zassoursky, Y.N.

1998 Changing media and communications. In Y.N. Zassoursky and E. Vartanova (eds.), *Changing Media and Communications*, pp. 174-188. Moscow: Faculty of Journalism/Publisher ICAR.

Zassoursky, Y.N. and Vartanova, E.

1999 Transformation in the context of transition: Development of new information and communication technologies within professional, legal and political frameworks. In *Information Societies: Crises in Making? Diagnostics and Strategies for Intervention in 7 World Regions*, pp. 284-330. Montreal: ORBICOM.

Competition, Media Innovation and Diversity in Broadcasting

A Case Study of the TV Market in the Netherlands

RICHARD VAN DER WURFF, JAN VAN CUILENBURG AND GENEVION KEUNE
The Amsterdam School of Communications Research *ASCoR*,
University of Amsterdam, The Netherlands

Abstract

This paper analyses how competition in broadcasting influences diversity of programme supply. We will argue that competition in oligopolistic broadcasting markets can take various forms, depending on the strategies adopted by broadcasters. We will distinguish between moderate competition and ruinous competition and discuss under what conditions these types of competition will emerge. We will hypothesise that moderate competition improves diversity whereas ruinous competition will lead to excessive sameness. And we will test these hypotheses for the television market in the Netherlands in the period 1988-1999.[1]

Introduction

Since the 1980s governments increasingly rely on competition and other economic mechanisms to govern information and communication industries. This 'economic turn' in policy making is justified on the basis of three assumptions. First, that competition will force suppliers of informa-

---

1 The data presented in the final section of this paper are part of a larger set of data that are continuously collected by Intomart, for the NOS (representing all Dutch public broadcasters), the STER (the organisation that sells advertising time on behalf of all Dutch public broadcasters), and IP (that sells advertising time for, and in this case also represents, RTL and Veronica). The help of Intomart (and more specifically Lex van Meurs) in providing the data, and of the NOS (more specifically Marjan Hammersma) in granting us permission to use the data for our analyses, is gratefully acknowledged. Of course, neither these organisations nor these persons can be held responsible for any errors or omissions in our analysis, nor does their co-operation imply that they would either agree or disagree with our conclusions.

tion and communication services to respond to demand as quickly and efficiently as possible. Second, that this necessity to respond quickly to demand is the best guarantee that not only economic, but also political and social welfare are maximised. And third, that a combination of technological, social-cultural and political developments removed the impediments to competition that long characterised the telecommunications and broadcasting industries. Consequently, competition is presented as the best way to protect the public interest in telecommunications and broadcasting, next to the press sector where competition has been the dominant mode of organisation for a much longer period of time.

This economic turn in communication policies is not uncontested. Especially in broadcasting it is feared that competition will induce companies to offer 'more of the same'. If this would be the case and competition would indeed result into reduced diversity, then competition would reduce rather than increase political and social welfare. Depending on one's theoretical and normative background, this argument can be phrased in economic terms of how markets for public goods such as broadcasting produce less than optimal outcomes (market failure) and thus require regulation; or in political-cultural terms of how economics is at odds with the cultural logic of broadcasting (Brown, 1996).

This paper will discuss the consequences of competition in broadcasting for diversity from an economic perspective. It will argue that competition is not only a market structure but also involves competitive behaviour. Competition as behaviour may either be moderate, prompting a combination of differentiation and low costs strategies, that will stimulate product and process innovation and will increase diversity; or it may be intense, resulting in short term, cut-throat price competition that will reduce innovation and diversity. The latter we label as 'ruinous competition' (Van Cuilenburg, 1999).

In the next sections, we will discuss diversity as criterion for media performance; present a theoretical framework for the analysis of competition and diversity in media markets; formulate several hypotheses on competition, media innovation and diversity; and provide a first empirical test of these hypotheses on the basis of developments in the Dutch television market since 1988.

Diversity in Media

Diversity refers to the variety of media products that are available to media users. It is one of the major media performance indicators, next to *access* (i.e. the opportunity for actors to share society's information and communication resources), *efficiency*, and *quality* (see also McQuail, 1992: 65 ff.). In formal terms, diversity can be defined as "the extent to which media content [...] differs according to one or more criteria." (Van Cuilenburg & McQuail, 1982: 36; in translation).[2] For a less formal, and more substantial and operational definition, we need (1) to formulate a normative yardstick that we can use to measure whether the variation observed is sufficient; (2) to define the level at which diversity will be assessed; and we need (3) to select one or more relevant dimensions on which media content could and should vary (e.g. political orientation).

Reflective and Open Diversity

Diversity can be measured and evaluated from at least two different perspectives, giving rise to two diverging but complementary approaches. Firstly, we can assess diversity by comparing variety in media content with variety in media users' preferences. Optimal diversity from this perspective exists when existing population preferences are *proportionally* reflected in the media. Following Van Cuilenburg and McQuail (1982: 40-41) we will call this type of optimal variety *reflective diversity*.

The relevance of reflective diversity follows from the normative principle that the media should fulfil needs of users in a fair way (criterion: representativeness). Each user should be treated equally, or – the other way round – media should pay equal attention to (the needs of) each user. Reflective diversity thus is related to the objective that users have *equal access to society's communication* systems (Van Cuilenburg, 1998; see Van Cuilenburg & Verhoest, 1998 for a discussion of 'access' as communications policy objective). If each individual has equal access to the media to express its preferences or to contribute to media content, one may expect media content to be reflectively diverse.

However, media that 'only' reflect existing opinions in proportion to their actual occurrence in society will reinforce the status quo, and will not match up to the media performance *quality* criteria of objectivity, creativity, innovativeness and provocativeness. A second option therefore would be to define that optimal variety or diversity exists when media pay equal attention to all 'reasonably thinkable' ideas, preferences and opinions, regardless of variations in public support for any of these ideas, preferences and opinions. We then adopt a criterion for diversity that lies outside the realm of actual media use. When divergent preferences and opinions are *equally* (i.e. statistically uniformly) represented in the media,

2 An overview of this study in English is presented in McQuail & Van Cuilenburg (1983).

we have a situation of *open diversity* (Van Cuilenburg & McQuail, 1982: 40-41). Open diversity implies *equal access for ideas* to society's communication systems.

Open diversity appears to be the more 'neutral' or objective norm of the two norms discussed. After all, all possible preferences and opinions (e.g. political opinions) are treated equally. Yet, measuring whether there is open diversity or 'equal access for ideas' in itself is a normative activity. There are so many different 'ideas' conceivable, that it is impossible to make a complete overview of all preferences and opinions that could and should be expressed in a situation of open diversity. Assessing whether all 'ideas' have equal access thus requires that an (ultimately normative) selection is made of all 'reasonably thinkable' ideas in society. Moreover, these 'reasonably thinkable' ideas should be grouped into internally cohesive and externally exclusive sets of ideas that deserve equal access to the media, based on the assumption that these sets of ideas are relevant, different, and comparable.[3] Measuring open diversity or 'equal access of ideas' in the end thus presupposes a top-down approach where one professional or political elite or another prescribes what perspectives should be taken into account and what not.

Measuring reflective diversity is in comparison a less normative activity. Of course, also determining whether the preferences of the relevant social groups are adequately reflected in media content, involves certain intersubjective decisions as to which type of preferences will be taken into account. Yet, a closer and more quantitative comparison of existing and reflected preferences is in principle feasible. After all, the criterion is not arbitrary chosen by the reviewer, but is based on the preferences of the users themselves. That is why we consider this a bottom-up, and more quantitative and empirical approach.

We therefore conclude that open and reflective diversity are at the same time complementary and incompatible objectives (as long as we assume that preferences and ideas are statistically normally rather than uniformly distributed in a society). Both objectives and related approaches have a role to play in media performance analysis and policy (Van Cuilenburg, 1998).

---

3 For example, whereas one observer might consider a news programme balanced when representatives of all major parties can have a say, a more radical observer might criticize the absence of a 'real' alternative perspective. For our study, this problem presents itself when we have decide which (categories of) programme types 'deserve' equal access to audiences, given a limited number of channels. In more specific terms, is there more or less open diversity when three channels broadcast information, sports and movies, or when they broadcast news, mainstream Hollywood movies, and *avant-garde* theatre?

Levels and Focus of Diversity Analysis

Both reflective and open diversity can be studied at different levels of analysis (Van Cuilenburg & McQuail, 1982: 37-38; McQuail, 1994: 157-158). Traditionally a distinction is made between four medium-related levels of analysis:

- the level of individual *units* of information (e.g. a television programme, or a newspaper article);
- the level of information service *bundles* offered by senders (e.g. an individual broadcasting channel, or an individual newspaper);
- the level of a specific medium *type* (either broadcasting or newspapers); or
- the level of society's information and communication *system* as a whole (broadcasting and newspapers and Internet and ...).

To these four, we may add two additional levels of analysis, that reflect ongoing convergence and concentration in the media industry, and that take suppliers and users rather than media as point of departure. These two additional levels of analysis are:

- the level of information supplying *corporations* (e.g. the collections of information services provided by Bertelsmann and Time Warner, respectively); and
- the level of information services fulfilling a particular *function* (e.g. news services, as provided by television, radio, newspapers, Internet services, and/or videotext).

The choice of the most appropriate level of analysis, of course, depends on the issue that is investigated. In our project we address the question whether competition has improved or reduced diversity for consumers. We take the choices that consumers make as our point of departure. Our level of analysis therefore should correspond with the full set of information packages that users usually choose, buy or obtain a particular package from. For the daily press, the level of diversity analysis should be the full set of all newspapers that people can choose a particular newspaper from. For television viewers, the appropriate level of analysis is either the set of all individual programmes broadcasted or the set of broadcasting channels, depending on viewers' viewing patterns.

Focusing on diversity from the perspective and at the level of consumers' choice, we have to make yet another distinction. We can either focus on diversity *within* a specific (combination of) information package(s), or on diversity *between* similar (combinations of) information packages. The former we will call *intra* diversity, the latter *inter* diversity. *Intra* diversity is important from a societal point of view. *Intra* diversity will guarantee that users will be confronted with different ideas and opinions. From the perspective of the individual user, *inter* diversity is important. *Inter* diversity will enable users to choose between qualitatively different information packages that match the users' preferences in varying degrees. Like open and reflective diversity, *intra* and *inter* diversity are complementary and incompatible. The more *intra* diverse information packages are, the less *inter* diverse they can be – and vice versa.

Dimensions of Diversity

Finally, analysing diversity requires that we identify the dimensions upon which media content can (or should) vary. Here we may consider countless possible dimensions, ranging from very general to very specific. Following up on the notions that media (should) fulfil an information, an opinion formation and a critical function, and that media (should) play a role in social-cultural, political-economic and social-economic issues (cf. Van Cuilenburg & McQuail, 1982: 13-23), a very general and basic assessment of diversity would be to assess whether media accomplish these roles and functions in a balanced way (open diversity) or conform consumers' preferences (reflective diversity). In our research project we study a more specific and restricted dimension of diversity, namely the extent to which different types of television programmes are being offered. This choice stems from the ongoing discussion whether growing competition has improved consumers' choice or on the contrary has led to increasing trivialisation of television content (less quality, more soaps, sports, shows, and sex; cf. Schoonhoven, 1995).

Media Competition, Innovation and Diversity

The argument that competition is the best way to bring about a diverse supply of television programmes builds upon the *Structure-Conduct-Performance* (*SCP*) model in economics. This SCP model can be summarised in two basic propositions.

First, the SCP model maintains that market performance is determined by firm behaviour, or market conduct, which in turn is determined by market structure. More sophisticated variants of the basic SCP model introduce feedback loops, and may even include policy as a separate explanatory variable, but nevertheless essentially focus on the same three key categories: market structure, market conduct and market performance (see Figure 1). (Ferguson, 1988; Scherer, 1996; also McQuail, 1992: 87 ff. and Wirth & Bloch, 1995).

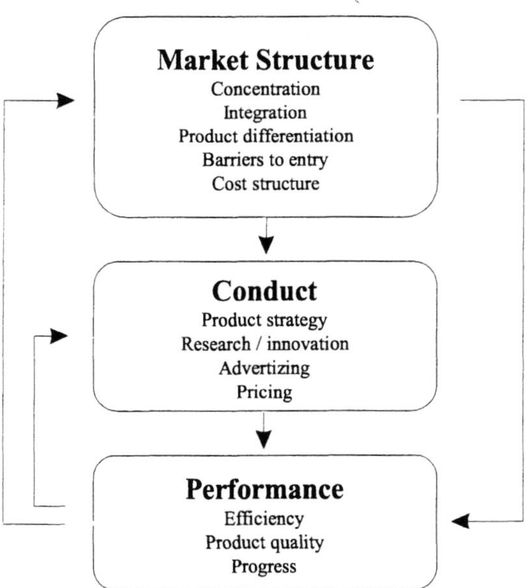

Figure 1 The Structure-Conduct-Performance model (McQuail, 1992: 87)

Second, the SCP model argues that optimal performance, including optimal diversity, can only be realised in fully (or in economic terms, perfectly) competitive markets. In these fully competitive markets, firms are forced to accept market-determined prices and to serve consumer demand as optimally as possible. Otherwise they will be competed out of the market. These fully competitive markets are contrasted with monopolised markets. Monopolists do have opportunities to increase profits by charging higher prices than competitive firms could, and/or by offering products that are less optimal from a consumer point of view. Monopolised markets thus perform less optimal.

Perfect Competition and Optimal Diversity in Media Markets

When we apply these models to media markets to argue that optimal diversity would only be realised by perfectly competitive media markets, we encounter several problems. From a normative point of view, we have to acknowledge that perfect competition, according to the model, would lead to a supply that optimally fits users' demand, i.e. to reflective diversity. Perfect competition is however less proficient in realising open diversity, which – as we argued above – is another important ingredient of media market performance.

In addition, and from a more pragmatic point of view, we have to acknowledge that media markets are a long way from being perfectly competitive. One reason is that perfect competition by definition implies the absence of product differentiation. Yet optimal reflective diversity can only exist without product differentiation in the exceptional case that audience preferences are homogeneous. In the more likely scenario that audience preferences are heterogeneous, diversity will imply product differentiation whereas perfect competition will not. In these cases, perfect competition and reflective diversity can only exist together when each different preference is served by a separate, perfectly competitive submarket. It goes without saying that such a situation would require an unrealistically large number of media companies.

An alternative and more realistic option, from an economic point of view, would be a situation of perfectly contestable monopolistic competition. Monopolistic competition implies competition between suppliers of heterogeneous, thus diverse, products. When these suppliers constantly face the risk that new competitors will enter the market when the latter see any opportunity to outcompete the former, markets can be said to be perfectly contestable (Baumol & Sidak, 1994: 42 ff.). Because of this threat, providers operating in perfectly contestable markets have to operate as efficiently as possible, even if they are monopolists in their own market segment. Perfectly contestable monopolistic markets thus theoretically could lead to optimal reflective diversity. Yet, also a situation of perfectly contestable monopolistic competition would require an unrealistically large number of suppliers, given the many dimensions on which diversity can vary.

Yet another reason why perfect competition in media markets is rather unlikely can be found in the particular cost structure of media products. Media content production, organisation and distribution typically entail high first copy costs of creating or acquiring media content, but very low or even negligible duplication and distribution costs (Hendriks, 1995). Media content production, organisation and distribution consequently show increasing returns to scale. This implies that profitability in media industries increases with market share, all other factors held equal. In addition, media content productions, as cultural products *per se*, show a high risk of failure (Hendriks, 1995). Large companies that can produce or acquire various media products and finance failures out of profits of successful productions, therefore have a strong competitive advantage. Size pays in media industries.

In sum, we can expect media markets to be heterogeneous oligopolies. Existing television market structures confirm this expectation. Conclusions that are based on the ideal-type model(s) of perfect competition (and monopoly) will not necessarily hold under these conditions. In order to understand competition in media markets, we therefore have to turn to models of oligopolistic rivalry.

Oligopolistic Rivalry in Media Markets

Starting point for our discussion of oligopolistic rivalry is Hotelling's Law of 'excessive sameness'. Hotelling (1929) argued that when demand is normally distributed, two competing firms tend to offer similar, mainstream products rather than to cater for the range of expressed preferences in a collaborative fashion. His argument shows similarities with a dilemma game. Suppose there are two media companies offering political news, and political preferences are distributed as displayed in Figure 2. The socially optimal solution would be that company *A* offers left-of-centre news programmes (best serving preferences *a*, *b*, *c*, *d* and *e* in Figure 2) while company *B* offers right-of centre programmes (best serving preferences *f*, *g*, *h*, *i* and *j*). However, when company *A* indeed offers left-of-centre news programmes, he runs the risk that company *B* moves to the centre, gaining audience from company *A*. In response or anticipation, company *A* moves to the centre as well. The end result will be that both media companies offer the same mainstream programme. Diversity offered will then not reflect diversity demanded, let alone that open diversity will be realised. If both companies could reach a market division agreement, on the other hand, existing preferences would be better catered for.

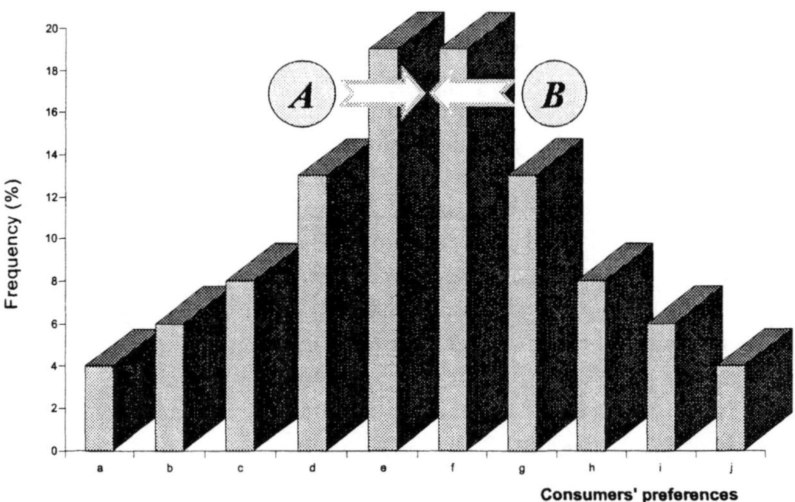

Figure 2 Hotelling's Law: Oligopolistic rivalry and excessive sameness

This basic insight has been elaborated into more sophisticated models of (broadcasting) competition (e.g. the Steiner and Beebe models; cf. Owen and Wildman, 1992: 64-100). These models all confirm that, given (1) a normal distribution of distinct consumer preferences that are independent from supply, (2) the inability of consumers to express the intensity of their preferences, (3) a shortage of suppliers relative to the number of preferences, and (4) a single programme period, competing suppliers tend to offer more of the same, at the expense of diversity. The other way around, the more preferences are statistically uniformly distributed, the better consumers are able to express the intensity of their preferences (for example, because broadcasters switch from advertised based to pay TV), and the more the number of suppliers matches the number of distinct preferences, the better competition performs.[4] This is of course a familiar picture, which we already discussed above. After all, the more the number of suppliers matches the number of expressed preferences, the closer we get to monopolistic competition.

The major question, however, is whether oligopolists would not be able to solve the original dilemma game. The argument of Hotelling and his successors seem to take for granted that competitors aim for head-on competition. This might be the case under the conditions that are implicitly and explicitly assumed in the models. Then indeed a static situation of intense price competition will occur, in which costs, profits and open diversity are minimised. Yet, when we relax the assumptions that preferences are independent of supply, that preferences can be classified in a finite number of distinctive categories, that differences in intensities of preferences can not be expressed, that we analyse a single programme period only, and/or more generally that companies do not co-operate in any way, other solutions become feasible. Hotelling himself, for example, already argued that when demand is considered elastic, "the tendency for *B* to establish his business excessively close to *A* will be less marked" (1929: 56). In such a situation, extra gains made 'in the centre' will be counteracted by reduced demand at the extremes. A similar outcome would occur when prices could be set equal to consumers' willingness to pay (i.e. when price discrimination becomes possible). Then the possibility arises that suppliers could make as large a profit by catering for "broad but shallow" markets as by catering for "narrow but deep" markets (Chae & Flores, 1998). Noam (1991: 45-57), finally, shows that when viewers are assumed to watch "programmes in a general range of their first preference [...] at a declining rate" rather than according to "unrealistic, binary yes-no decision rules" (1991: 47), competitors again tend to offer dissimilar programmes.

---

4 Waterman (1989/90) even argues that price competition can lead to a relative overproduction of product diversity, if preferences of viewers are assumed to be distributed uniformly along the circumference of a circle.

More generally, SCP theorists argue that market conduct of oligopolists, and hence performance of oligopolistic markets, is largely undetermined by market structures (Scherer & Ross, in Wirth & Bloch, 1995: 18; Gong & Srinagesh, 1997: 65). Perfect competition implies product homogeneity and intense price competition. Monopoly in general leads to higher prices and is compatible with product heterogeneity. Monopolistic competition implies product heterogeneity and will also lead to higher prices. In comparison, media companies in oligopolistic markets can either engage in intensive rivalry, which will lead to excessive sameness but also will reduce prices; or they can engage in more 'colluding' forms of rivalry that may promote diversity but also will lead to increased prices. In order to understand performance of media markets, we therefore have to leave SCP-based models that focus on competition as market structure, and turn towards other approaches that can help us to understand market conduct of oligopolists. Porter's model of competitive strategy is such an approach.

Three Competitive Strategies for Media Companies

Porter argues that under realistic conditions competitors can pursue three different generic strategies to develop a long term, sustainable competitive position and earn 'above-average' profits (1985: 11; also 1980/98: 35 ff.). They can decide to compete on costs, they can decide to compete on quality, or they can decide to focus on a particular niche market in which they can develop more easily a cost or quality advantage. Implicit in Porter's argument is that companies can only be successful when they follow a strategy that is not imitated by their competitors. Otherwise, a situation of intensive price competition and reduced diversity would result. Each of Porter's three strategies thus offers an alternative for the head-on competition that is considered to be the standard response in the Hotelling, Steiner and Beebe models.

The first strategy is the *strategy of cost leadership* (Porter, 1985: 12). Firms adopting a cost leadership or low cost strategy aim to acquire a structural cost advantage compared to their competitors. This implies a continuous focus on cost reduction and, we would like to add, investment in process innovations. Frequently, a low cost strategy includes capitalising upon learning effects and economies of scale and scope. Large and long existing firms therefore may have an advantage here. Media companies following a *low cost strategy* would aim to offer content to maximum audiences and/or as many viewers as possible to advertisers at the lowest possible cost, e.g. by realising economies of scale, concluding lucrative deals with content owners, and/or excelling in programming strategies.

As indicated above, a low cost strategy will be only sustainable "if the sources of a firm's cost advantage are difficult for competitors to replicate or imitate" (Porter, 1985: 97). In addition, Porter argues that such a low cost strategy will only lead to "superior performance if the firm provides an acceptable level of value to the buyer so that its cost advantage is not nullified by the need to charge a lower price than competitors" (1985: 97). A cost leadership strategy should therefore not be confused with a short-term price competitive strategy that is the standard response in the Hotelling-like models.

The second strategy presented by Porter is the *differentiation strategy.* By offering a differentiated product, firms aim to carve out their own sub-market where they are the preferred suppliers and where consumers get 'locked in'. Thus firms can aim to protect themselves against (price) competition. They can even aim to strengthen their position further by erecting mobility barriers; barriers that make it more difficult for competitors to imitate their strategies (cf. Chan-Olmsted, 1997). Examples of mobility barriers include the legal protection of product innovations under copyright law and the development of exclusive relations with suppliers or with distributors.[5] Media companies following a *differentiation strategy* would aim to attract as large an audience as possible with a distinct type of content and/or to offer a particular quality of attention to advertisers at reasonable costs.

Porter's third generic strategy is the *focus strategy.* Firms adopting a focus strategy target niche markets, where they can either gain a low cost or quality advantage, for similar reasons as the ones outlined above with respect to low cost and differentiation strategies. Media organisations following a *focus strategy* would offer a particular type of content to a particular audience segment and/or a particular audience segment to advertisers, because these companies believe they have a particular advantage in reaching that segment. Depending on whether competitors can realise substantial economies of scale, media companies aiming at smaller audiences might need to target these audiences in relatively large geographic areas. An example would be broadcasters like MTV and National Geographic that follow a focus strategy in many countries at the same time.

5 The success of low cost and differentiation strategies thus partly depends on opportunities to appropriate innovations. When innovations can not be appropriated but easily diffuse to competitors, no long-term advantage can be created, competition will be more stringent, profits will be low, and incentives to innovate will be reduced. On the other hand, when innovations can be appropriated, long-term advantages but also long-term dominant market positions can be created, profits will be higher, and incentives to innovate will increase (Soete & Ter Weel, 1999).

Moderate and Ruinous Competition and Media Market Performance

From a diversity point of view, low cost, differentiation and focus strategies are all to be preferred to short term price competitive strategies. Differentiation (focus) strategies by definition will improve *inter* channel diversity. These strategies imply that media organisations aim to present exclusive content that can not be easily reproduced by others; and – in addition – that these organisations will be forced to continuously improve their product quality. This tendency to offer exclusive content will contribute to *open diversity.*

The drawback of differentiation (focus) strategies, on the other hand, might be that production processes will be not as efficient as possible because of the relative lack of competition. Low cost (focus) strategies, in comparison, imply an emphasis on process innovations, and hence tend to result in reduced costs, also for customers. At the same time, low cost strategies will produce less (open) *inter* channel diversity than differentiation strategies because there is less impetus to supply exclusive content. Yet, low cost strategies will neither result into excessive sameness, because an 'acceptable level of quality' has to be maintained and strategy replication has to be prevented. Low cost (focus) strategies will therefore contribute to reflective diversity between channels; the offering of programmes that match consumer wants at relatively low costs. In addition, low cost strategies will contribute to *intra* diversity because large and consequently heterogeneous audiences are targeted. Differentiation and especially differentiation focus strategies will contribute to *intra* channel homogeneity (see Table 1).

Table 1 Generic strategies and diversity

	low cost	*differentiation*
general	- inter channel reflective diversity - intra channel diversity	- inter channel open diversity - intra channel homogeneity or diversity
focus	- inter channel reflective diversity - intra channel diversity or homogeneity	- inter channel open diversity - intra channel homogeneity

There seems to exist a trade-off, then, between *inter channel* open diversity, product innovation and relatively high costs, on the one hand, and *inter channel* reflective diversity, process innovation and relatively low costs, on the other hand. If (too) many companies would follow a low cost strategy and thus initiate a price war, at the short term costs could really be pushed down to marginal (i.e. almost negligible) levels. Companies could realise short term cost savings by re-selling content, by selling marginally changed content that can be produced very cheaply, and by selling content that is both a proven success and is already written down in other markets. Intensive price competition in the short term thus would lead to excessive sameness in media content supply. In the longer term, intensive price competition would lead the media industry in a particular market to bankruptcy. Income that approaches marginal cost levels in media markets will by far be not sufficient to recover investments, let alone to pay for innovations. Besides, consumers can be expected to turn away to other media or other activities because content quality and choice are declining. That way a vicious cycle of reducing profits, fewer investments, cheaper content, and diminishing audiences will occur. That is why we may call this type of short-term focused, intense price competition *ruinous competition* (Van Cuilenburg, 1999).

On the other hand, if many companies would follow a differentiation strategy, an increase in (open) diversity can be expected at the short term. At the longer term, however, prices will start to increase. This may cause customers to reduce demand or switch to substitutes, which will reduce income and hence negatively affect innovation opportunities for firms, again starting a negative cycle. Rising costs, however, may also create opportunities for new entrants that follow a low cost strategy. Such a new entrant, as long as it will not engage in too intense price competition, will offer relatively cheap content to maximum audiences, thereby contributing to reflective diversity. The resulting market situation, in which a 'healthy' mix of differentiation and low costs strategies exists, and in which process and product innovations can gradually diffuse to companies following a differentiation and low cost strategy respectively, would be of interest to both customers and firms. A major question therefore is under what conditions such a process of *moderate competition* will emerge. In the next section, we will discuss two approaches that may shed some light on this question, namely Porter's theory of competitive forces and the dynamic market theory.[6]

---

6 In our argument, we will limit ourselves to economic factors that may explain why ruinous or moderate competition will occur. Yet, next to these economic factors, also institutional factors will play a role in determining the intensity of competition. These include the role of governments as actors that might change competitive relations, as discussed by Porter and adherents of the SCP paradigm; and the role of organizational, professional and societal norms concerning 'good' content and 'proper' competitive conduct that will be reflected in the actual objectives companies aim for (see also McQuail, 1992: 87 ff). These institutional factors will not be taken into account in this paper.

Conditions for Moderate and Ruinous Competition

In his discussion of competitive forces and advantages, Porter (1980/98: 3 ff.; 1985: 4 ff.) mentions about 45 factors, classified into five categories, that may increase or reduce competition. For our argument, the following factors are the most important and relevant conditions under which competition in media markets will intensify.[7]

First, Porter's theory suggests that competition in broadcasting will intensity when *suppliers* (content owners or producers) *offer undifferentiated content* to broadcasters. When broadcasters cannot buy differentiated content, they can not adopt differentiation strategies. Hence, they will be more inclined to compete on prices.

Second, competition will become more intense when *advertisers (and users) can easily switch from one media company to another.* This factor underlines the importance of stability in media markets for moderate competition to emerge. One way in which media companies might reduce the ease with which advertisers and viewers switch from service provider would be by attempting to lock in viewers by offering niche programming. Another way would be to attempt to conclude long term contracts with advertisers or content suppliers.[8]

Third, attempts to lock in suppliers and advertisers will be more successful when content owners and advertisers are not highly concentrated and thus will not be able to exert much power over media companies. When *content owners and/or advertisers are highly concentrated,* on the other hand, competition can be expected to intensify again.

A fourth factor mentioned by Porter, but especially by Soete and Ter Weel (1999), as a factor that determines market stability and competition intensity is the extent to which innovations can be appropriated (i.e. patented, kept secret). When *innovations can not be appropriated* companies can not make long term R&D investments under the reassuring expectation that potential gains can fully be kept for themselves and that investments can be recouped. Instead, innovations will diffuse rapidly and competition will increase.

---

7 Other factors mentioned by Porter are important determinants of competition but will vary more between rather than within particular media markets (e.g. the existence of economies of scale); or are not relevant for the argument in this article (e.g. the threat of forward integration of content suppliers, the dependency on cable network owners, the attractiveness of substitutes; or the threat of backward integration of buyers).

8 It would be interesting to investigate in this respect whether the tradition of readers to subscribe to newspapers rather than to buy them on a daily basis contributed to diversity in the Dutch newspaper market.

Fifth, competition will intensify when *new entrants enter the market*, because the number of firms will increase, new entrants have to gain market share, and incumbents will defend their market position.

Sixth, the impact of new entrants on competition intensity will be larger, when *the number of firms is large, firms are of equal size*, and *firms have different backgrounds*. All else being equal, the number, size and differences between companies can in themselves also be expected to influence competition. Firms with different backgrounds (e.g. in terms of national origin, the extent of product diversification or vertical integration, or between commercial and public broadcasters) can be expected to respond differently to market changes. This will increase uncertainty in the market and intensify competition. The impact of competitors will also be larger when they are about equally powerful. The other way round, when one or more firms dominate the market, smaller competitors will have less impact and competition intensity will decline.

Finally, competition will get more intense, and new entry will have a larger impact on competition intensity, when *the market is growing slowly*.

In sum, competition can be expected to intensify when:

- content supplied by content owners is undifferentiated,
- advertisers and viewers can easily switch between media companies,
- content owners and/or advertisers are highly concentrated,
- innovations can not be appropriated,
- new entrants enter the market,
- the number of firms is large, firms are of equal size, and firms have different backgrounds, and/or when
- the market is growing slowly.

This latter factor, market growth and its impact on competition, is dealt with more extensively in the *dynamic market theory* (De Jong, 1993). According to the dynamic market theory, competition is essentially a function of the product life cycle. Each product's life cycle starts with a phase in which the product is introduced. The original model assumes that in that situation there is only one supplier and hence no competition. An alternative model, more adapted to the present reality of the information and communication industry, would acknowledge that innovations can also be introduced by an alliance of (would-be) competitors. Either way, in both cases the innovator(s) for a short while can earn a monopolist's profit, recovering his (their) R&D expenses.[9] Following the intro-

9 In some industries, e.g. pharmaceuticals, the monopolistic phase is 'artificially' extended by patent law.

duction phase, a phase of rapid growth will occur in which new entrants enter the market (or the initial collaborators start to compete). Given high levels of market growth, there will be few incentives for either product or process innovation. Still, learning curves and emerging economies of scale will contribute to cost reductions. In any case, competition will be moderate because of market growth. Then, after some time, markets will get mature and saturated. Concentration in the sector will increase. Firms need to decide whether they adopt a differentiation or a low cost strategy. It is this phase in which moderate competition can easily develop into ruinous competition. When oligopolists co-operate, moderate competition and the maturity phase will be prolonged. Increasing oligopolistic rivalry, on the other hand, will give a go-ahead to the phase of product decline. In this last phase in the product life cycle, concentration will increase further, and firms will follow low costs strategies, but generally will not succeed in generating extra profits. Consequently, one firm after the other will exit the market. This is the phase where ruinous competition will have its toll.

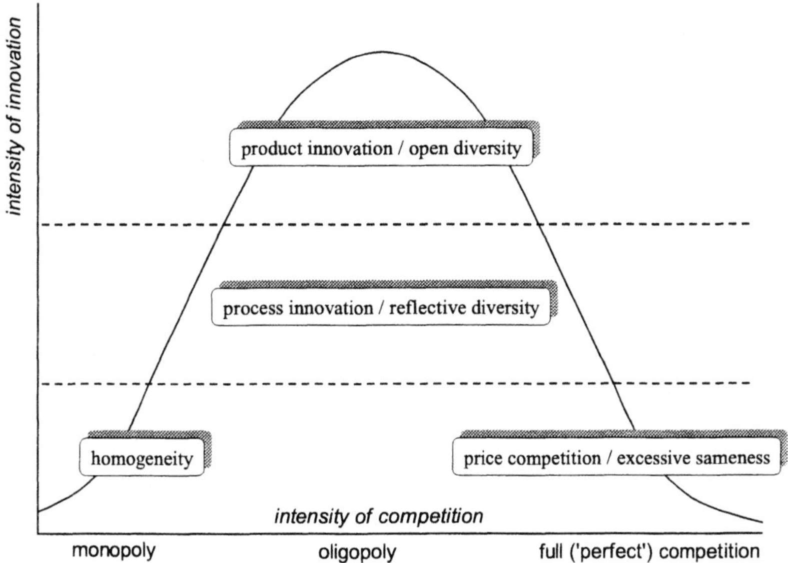

Figure 3 Media competition, innovation and diversity

In sum, and following both Porter's competition theory and the dynamic market theory, we postulate that a non-linear relationship exists between media competition, innovation and diversity (see Figure 3). Starting from a situation of monopoly, increasing competition will first stimulate process innovation and subsequently product innovation. However, when competition gets too intense, first product innovation and in the end even process innovation will be discarded. Then, when we end up in the situation of full ('perfect') competition in classic economic theory, only price competition will remain.

Hypotheses on Media Competition, Innovation and Diversity

In conclusion, we will formalise our argument in a number of definitions and hypotheses.

Firstly, we define *moderate media competition* and *ruinous media competition* as follows:
- A media market with moderate competition is a market in which media companies pursue a dynamic balance between differentiation, low cost and focus strategies.
- A media market with ruinous competition is a market in which media companies pursue intense, short-term price competition.

Secondly, we assume the following interrelations between corporate strategies and media diversity:
- Differentiation and focus strategies involve media product innovation and therefore tend towards open diversity of media products.
- Low cost strategies involve media process innovation and therefore tend to reflective diversity of media products.
- Intense price competition between media companies prevents both process and product innovation and therefore tends towards excessive sameness of media products.

Combining our definitions and assumptions, we thirdly formulate the following hypotheses:
- Moderate media competition will result in a dynamic balance of open and reflective diversity of media products.
- Ruinous media competition will produce excessive sameness of media products.

These hypotheses and the underlying argument are graphically presented in Figure 4.

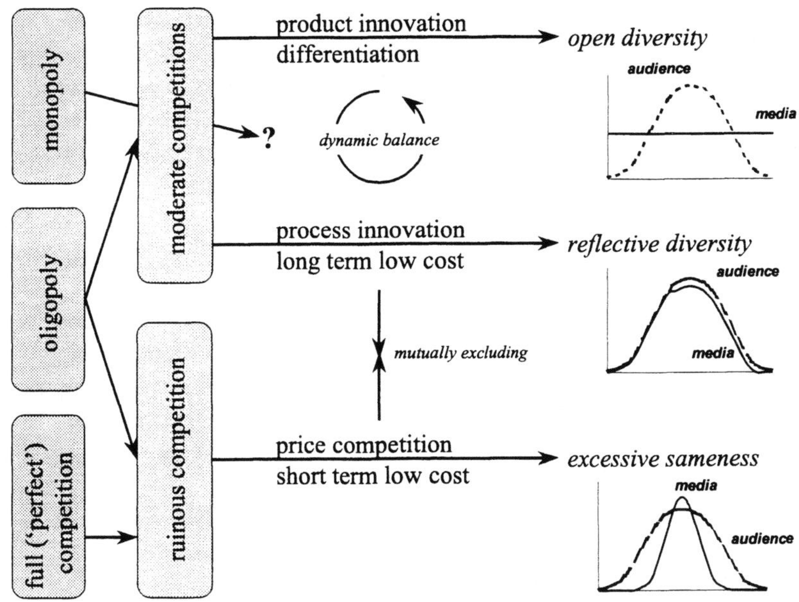

Figure 4 An economic media diversity model

Finally, focussing more directly on the effects of new entry on competition and diversity, we formulate the following additional hypotheses:

- New entrants that aim for approximately the same market share as incumbents intensify competition, and thus will cause a shift towards excessive sameness of media products.
- New entrants that aim for a considerable smaller market share (focus strategy) do not intensify competition and thus will contribute to diversity of media products.
- New entry in a situation of market growth will not increase competition intensity and hence will contribute to diversity of media products.
- New entry in a situation of market maturity will increase competition intensity and hence will reduce diversity of media products.

Competition and Diversity in the Dutch Television Market

In this final section, we present a first test of our model of media competition, innovation and diversity using data on the Dutch television market.

Commercial broadcasters entered the Dutch market in 1989. Since then, their number has steadily increased. At present, there are three public service broadcasting channels and six general commercial channels. Three of these channels are owned by the Holland Media Groep, a subsidiary of by CLT-UFA and Veronica,[10] two are owned by SBS SA and De Telegraaf (a major Dutch newspaper publisher) and one by Fox (Rutten & Buijs, 1999: 71-74). In addition, there are tens of new thematic channels. Thus, whereas in 1980 people on average were able to receive 3.8 channels with fairly good reception, in 1998 this number had risen to 23.5 (Van Meurs, 1999: Appendix 2).

Data, Variables and Hypotheses

For our analysis of the relationships between competition and diversity in the Dutch television market, we made use of data on television broadcasting and viewing patterns that are collected on a regular basis by Intomart (see Intomart, 1998). This dataset consists of quarterly estimates of:

- the amount of total time that is spend on each major channel to any of 25 programme type categories,
- the amount of total viewing time spend by television viewers per channel on any of these 25 programme type categories, and
- audience ratings per channel per programme type category.[11]

The quarterly estimates run from the first quarter of 1988 until and including the second quarter of 1999. From this dataset, one variable measuring the intensity of competition and several variables measuring different aspects of diversity were derived.

One major problem with our dataset is that RTL4, the first Dutch commercial broadcaster that entered the market as RTL-Veronique in October 1989, is only included from the 4th quarter of 1992 onwards. This implies that we may see changes in programme supply and viewer behaviour in between the 4th quarter of 1989 and the 4th quarter of 1992 that are related to increases in competition, whereas the effect of the entry of RTL4 on competition itself can not be observed. Table 2 presents the major broadcasters active in the Dutch market that are included in our analysis, as well as some of the smaller broadcasters that we could not include because of a lack of data.

---

10 Just at the time when we were finishing this paper, Veronica announced (on March 14, 2000) that it would sell all its shares in the Holland Media Group to CLT-UFA. CLT-UFA thus will become the only shareholder of HMG (Veronica stapt..., 2000).

11 All estimates are for people that are 6 years or older; and concern the time span between 18.30-24.00 hours for the period 1988-1992 and 18.00-24.00 for the period 1993-1999.

Table 2 Television channels in the Netherlands – not complete

channel	*market entry*	*data included since*
Nederland 1	October 1951	1st quarter 1988
Nederland 2	1964	1st quarter 1988
Nederland 3	February1988	2nd quarter 1988
RTL-Veronique/RTL4	October 1989	4th quarter 1992
RTL5	October 1993	4th quarter 1993
Veronica (VOO)	September 1995	4th quarter 1995
SBS6	August 1995	4th quarter 1995
Net5	March 1999	2nd quarter 1999
TMF	May 1995	not included
Sport 7	August 1996 (for 3 months)	
MTV	August 1987	not included
Kindernet	March 1988	
Eurosport	November 1989	
Discovery Channel	April 1990	
Euronews	January 1993	
NBC	June 1993	
Cartoon Network	November 1993	
The Box	June 1995	
BBC World	October 1995	
CNBC	January 1997	
CNN	January 1988	
National Geographic Channel	July 1998	

Sources: Commissie Ververs (1996: 8 and 18); Bakker & Scholten (1999: 99 ff.); Van Meurs (1999: Appendix 2); and personal communication various channel representatives.

To measure the *intensity of competition* we use the Hirschman-Herfindahl Index (HHI). The Hirschman-Herfindahl Index is a well-established indicator for the competitiveness of market structures. It runs between 0 (when an indefinite number of firms of equal size are active in a market) to 1 (monopoly). We will calculate the HHI for channels rather than firms, because we are first of all interested in competition between channels.

The $HHI_{channel}$ index is calculated by summing the squares of the audience shares of the major broadcasting channels (see Formula 1).

Formula 1

$$HHI_{channel} = \Sigma\, m_i^2$$

$$1/n \text{ (full competition)} \leq HHI \leq 1 \text{ (monopoly)}$$

where m_i market/audience share of channel i

Diversity refers to the relative amount of broadcasting time that is spent on various programme types. As argued above, diversity in programme types needs to be studied at the level at which viewers access television content. Here, three options are feasible. Firstly, consumers may choose between television and other media. Then the set of all individual units of information — programmes, articles, books, CDs — will be the appropriate level of analysis.[12] Secondly, viewers may watch television on a regular basis, actively selecting television programmes from all programmes offered at a particular point in time. Then the set of all programmes in a specific time slot is the appropriate level of analysis. Thirdly, viewers may be passive, selecting between channels rather than programmes. In that case the set of all channels becomes the appropriate level of analysis.

Bekkers (1998) argues that television viewers select by channel. "[W]atching television, for most people, is a type of leisure activity that one is not willing to put much effort in. Programme selection by the general public suggests that people actually appreciate that somebody else (the broadcaster) decides upon and makes the programming schedule." (1998: 15; in translation). Broadcasters capitalise on these viewing habits by developing programming schedules that keep viewers tuned to their channel. We can, however, not rule out that people are becoming more active television viewers. We will therefore analyse diversity both at the level of channels and the level of programmes.

Diversity increases when more different programme types are broadcasted. A first estimate of diversity can be calculated by using an indicator for entropy (Van Cuilenburg & McQuail, 1982: 38):

Formula 2

$$D \text{ (diversity)} = (-\Sigma\, p_i \log p_i) / \log n$$

$$0 \text{ (homogeneity)} \leq D \leq 1 \text{ (maximum heterogeneity)}$$

where n number of programme type categories

p_i proportion of programmes of programme type category *i*

---

12 The proper approach in this option would be to study diversity for all individual units of information across all substitutable media. However, for practical purposes and given the focus of our article, we will limit ourselves to broadcasting. Still, under option one we have to consider the usage of other media (i.e. not-viewing) as a positive alternative. We will do this by assuming that consumers choose from the set of all available programmes within a broad time frame (a week or month), rather than in specific time slots (e.g. Friday evening at 19.00 hours). Consumers thus can decide to read a book Monday evening, and watch television on Tuesday, because on Tuesdays their favourite show is broadcasted.

More specific indicators relate observed diversity to the standards of open and reflective diversity. There will be maximum *open diversity* when a relative equal amount of time is spent on each programme type. As we argued above, estimates of open diversity are very sensitive to the classification system used. A football channel can be said to be open diverse based on the criterion that all football clubs get even attention; and said to be completely not open diverse on the basis that it only broadcasts football.

Intomart traditionally uses 25 categories, developed by the Dutch broadcaster NOS, to classify programmes into distinctive programme types. We excluded children's programmes because we are interested in programme supply for and demand from adults. We regrouped the remaining 23 NOS categories into ten programme type categories that we believe should be given equal broadcasting time, given the fact that television is used for a broad range of functions by a broad range of people (see further the Annex: Classification of programme types). The formula for open diversity then becomes:

Formula 3

OD (open diversity) = $1 - \Sigma |y_i| / 2$

0 (minimum openness) $\leq$ OD $\leq$ 1 (maximum openness)

where y_i difference between the actual proportion of time devoted to programme type *i* and the norm for programme type *i* in a situation of maximum openness (i.e., 1 divided by the number of programme type categories)

There will be *reflective diversity* when supply of programme types matches viewer demand. To measure viewer demand, we can make use of two estimates that are included in our dataset: (audience) ratings, and estimates of average viewing time. Ratings (or *Kijkdichtheid* in Dutch) express the average proportion of potential viewers that actually watch a programme per unit of measurement time (usually a minute). Estimates of average viewing time express the average time that an average viewer watches a programme. Programme supply (PS), ratings (R) and viewing time (VT) are mathematically related: R/100% * PS = VT.

We opt to use viewing time as indicator for viewer demand. Ratings do express what proportion of the maximum audience watches a particular programme type, but does not take the length of programmes into account. Similar ratings may thus refer to situations in which viewers consume significantly different amounts of television programmes.[13] Viewing time does in that respect express viewer demand in a more straightforward manner.

Unfortunately, using viewing time to approximate viewer demand does not tell us anything about programme type demand of those that are not watching (but neither would ratings, for that matter). There is therefore the possibility that we overestimate reflective diversity. On the other hand, people that do not watch television do not necessarily have to do so because there is no supply to their taste.[14] To reduce the likelihood that our estimate of viewer demand is influenced by (changes in) programme supply as much as possible, we will use estimates of average viewing time per programme type for the whole period under investigation.

In conclusion, we will use an estimate of average viewing time over the period 1st quarter 1988-2nd quarter 1999 to approximate viewer demand. Our formula for reflective diversity will be:

Formula 4

RD (reflective diversity) = $1 - \Sigma |z_i| / 2$
0 (minimum reflection) $\leq$ RD $\leq$ 1 (maximum reflection)

where z_i difference between the actual proportion of time devoted to programme type *i* and the norm for programme type *i* given viewer demand (i.e., relative viewing time)

We assume that viewer preferences for different programme types are more or less (statistically) normally distributed. Perfect reflective diversity then implies less open diversity, because in a situation of reflective diversity popular programme types will be broadcasted significantly more than unpopular programme types. When programme supply shifts even more to popular programme types, so that popular programme types become over-represented and unpopular programme types become underrepresented given viewer preferences, we speak of *excessive sameness.*

Since there is no easy way to assess whether supply of popular programmes surpasses demand, we simply estimate excessive sameness by

13 Moreover, ratings may increase when programme supply is reduced. The more broadcasting time is spent on a particular programme type, the more viewers can spread themselves in time over these programmes and thus the fewer viewers will watch programmes on average for a particular unit of time. This interdependence between ratings and programme supply will of course bias our results.

14 The likelihood that people do not watch television because of a lack of attractive programming will decline with increases in open diversity. Therefore, when we observe a situation in which open diversity is low and a large proportion of potential viewers does not watch television, there is ample reason to investigate more closely whether non-watching is an indicator that supply does not reflect demand.

measuring the share of the two most popular programme types in programme supply.[15] Following the argument presented above with respect to reflective diversity, we will again use estimates of average viewing time to decide which programme types are most popular. That gives us the following formula for excessive sameness:

Formula 5

$$ES \text{ (excessive sameness)} = A_1 + A_2$$
$$0 \text{ (maximum diversity)} \leq ES \leq 1 \text{ (excessive sameness)}$$

where A_1 audience share of most popular programme type (i.e. the programme with the highest average relative viewing time)

A_2 audience share of second most popular programme type (i.e. the programme with the second highest average relative viewing time)

Given these variables and the general CoMInDi hypotheses presented in the previous section, we expect to find no linear relationships between competition (measured in $HHI_{channel}$) and diversity (measured in D, OD, RD and ES). Diversity will not increase nor decrease proportionally with competition intensity. On the contrary, we expect diversity to first increase and then decrease in response to a gradual increase in competition intensity since 1988.

Secondly, we expect that new entry will lead to a sudden increase in competition and hence to a decline of diversity in the period directly following new entry. Then, after a while, competition will de-escalate and diversity will increase again. Moreover, we expect that the magnitude and length of decreases in diversity following new entry will increase with the number of firms that are already active in the market.

In sum, we will test the following *hypotheses*:

- The Dutch broadcasting market shows an increase in competition intensity since 1988. Increasing competition is first accompanied by increasing open and/or reflective diversity and decreasing excessive sameness; and later by decreasing open and reflective diversity and increasing excessive sameness.

15 This estimate is similar to simple concentration indexes as C4 that are used to describe market structures.

- Each time a new major broadcaster enters the market, competition intensifies and diversity reduces. Then, after a while, competition de-escalates, and diversity increases again.
- The more broadcasters are already active in the market, the more intense competition will become in response to new entry, and the longer it will take before competition de-escalates again.

Empirical Results on Competition and Diversity

Figure 5 gives an overview of how competition intensity and diversity changed in the Dutch broadcasting market since 1988.

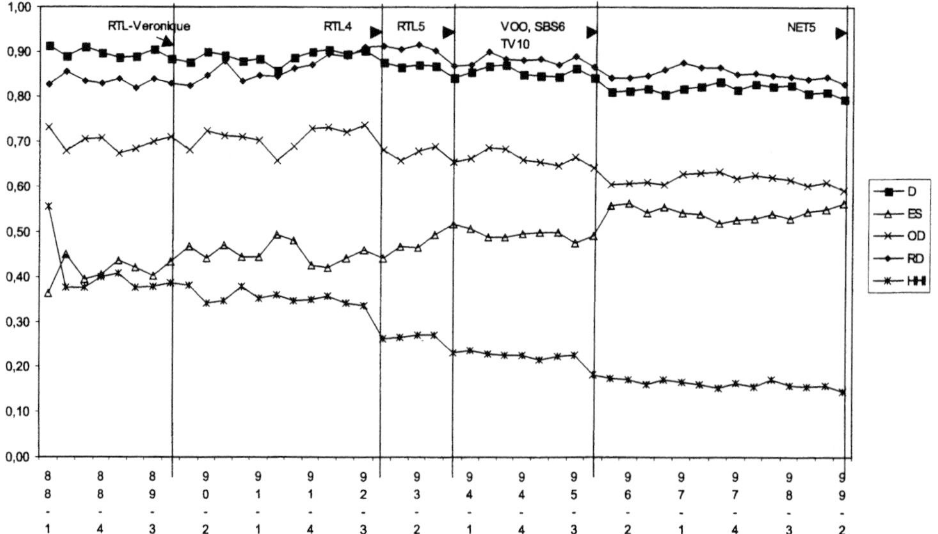

Figure 5 Overview of competition and diversity in the Dutch TV market

Figure 5 shows that the $\text{HHI}_{\text{channel}}$ index decreased and thus competition intensity increased gradually, with the rate of increase speeding up when new broadcasters enter the market. We also see that diversity (D) and open diversity (OD) declined over the period 1988-1999 and that excessive sameness (ES) increased in a similar pattern. This suggests that these three variables actually measure the same trend. When we look more closely, we can see an acceleration of the decline of diversity directly after (a) new broadcaster(s) entered the market, followed by a period in which diversity is more or less stabilised. Finally, we can see that reflective diversity (RD) first increased, and then in a meandering pattern started to decline.

Figure 6 presents the changes in competition intensity and reflective diversity in more detail. It shows that reflective diversity decreases until the 3rd quarter of 1989, when RTL-Veronique enters the market. After that, diversity offered by public broadcasters (remember, we have no data on RTL-Veronique/RTL4 until the 3rd quarter of 1992) starts to increase and reaches a maximum in 1993 (when data on RTL4 are included). Entry of RTL5 has a short-term strong negative effect on reflective diversity, after which stabilisation at a lower level than before occurs. Entry of VOO, SBS6 and TV10 in 1995 has a similar effect. Our first estimates suggest that entry of NET5 in 1999 might have the same effect for a third time. The end result of these changes is that supply matches demand in the 2nd quarter of 1999 equally well as in the 1st quarter of 1988.

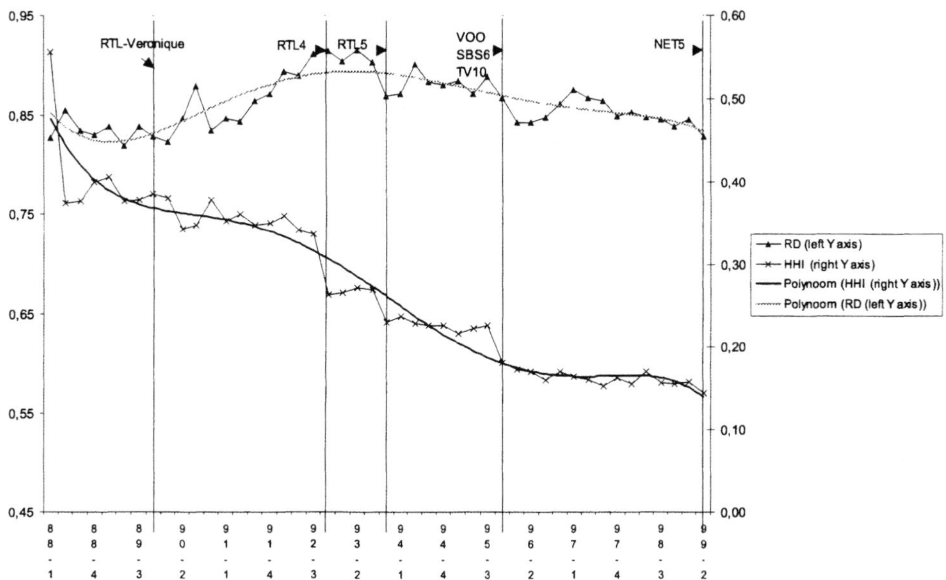

Figure 6 Competition and reflective diversity

Figure 7 presents additional information on changes in competition intensity and excessive sameness. Estimates of average viewer demand in the period under investigation indicate that 'light information' and 'TV-series' are the most popular programme types (with average viewing times of respectively 27% and 19% of total viewing time). Figure 7 shows that the relative amount of broadcasting time spent on these two programme types (i.e. ES) increased significantly, and even more so in periods of new entry.

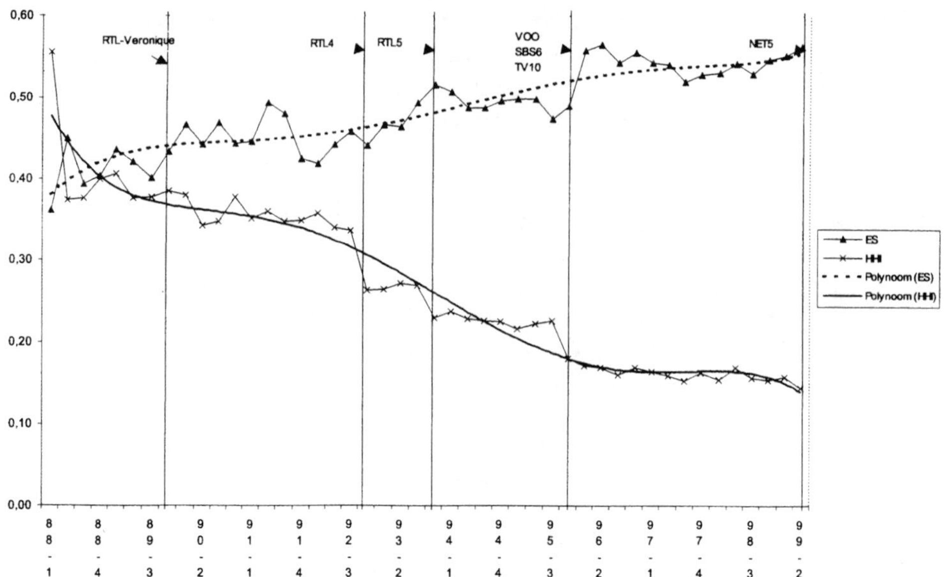

Figure 7 Competition and excessive sameness

A more thorough assessment of interrelations between our variables can be obtained by a correlation analysis. Table 3 presents the results of a simple bivariate correlation analysis. The table shows that diversity (D), open diversity (OD) and excessive sameness (ES) are closely related to each other, and also show a very strong relationship with competition intensity (HHI). Our estimate of reflective diversity, however, is much less strongly (linearly) related to competition intensity.

Our visual analysis also showed that new entry accelerates the general negative trend in diversity. This effect is especially strong with respect to reflective diversity (RD). To analyse the relationships between new entry and diversity more closely, we calculated a new variable 'Entry' (E). This variable reflects the relative strength of changes in HHI in a quarter due to new entry, and an assumed gradually withering away of this effect in the quarters following new entry. Table 4 shows that the explanatory power of this new variable Entry is not very high, other than with respect to reflective diversity (RD). This latter variable is much more strongly related to Entry than to competition intensity itself (see Table 5).

Finally, we look at the changes in *intra channel* diversity. The main question here is what diversity is offered to viewers who do not choose between programmes but between channels. Do separate channels offer on average more diverse or homogeneous programme types? And consequently, are people with a strong channel loyalty, thus people who tend to watch the same channel for an evening or longer period, offered more or less programme type diversity?

Table 3 Correlation analysis I

		D	*OD*	*RD*	*ES*	*HHI*
D	Pearson Correlation	1.000	.966**	.117	-.949**	.899**
	Sig. (2-tailed)	.	.000	.440	.000	.000
OD	Pearson Correlation	.966**	1.000	.193	-.894**	.855**
	Sig. (2-tailed)	.000	.	.199	.000	.000
RD	Pearson Correlation	.117	.193	1.000	.024	-.193
	Sig. (2-tailed)	.440	.199	.	.876	.200
ES	Pearson Correlation	-.949**	-.894**	.024	1.000	-.910**
	Sig. (2-tailed)	.000	.000	.876	.	.000
HHI	Pearson Correlation	.899**	.855**	-.193	-.910	1.000
	Sig. (2-tailed)	.000	.000	.200	.000	.

** Correlation is significant at the 0.01 level (2-tailed). N is 46 in all cases

Table 4 Correlation analysis II

		D	*OD*	*RD*	*ES*	*ENTRY*
D	Pearson Correlation	1.000	.966**	.117	-.949**	-.234
	Sig. (2-tailed)	.	.000	.440	.000	.117
OD	Pearson Correlation	.966**	1.000	.193	-.894**	-.236
	Sig. (2-tailed)	.000	.	.199	.000	.115
RD	Pearson Correlation	.117	.193	1.000	.024	.439**
	Sig. (2-tailed)	.440	.199	.	.876	.002
ES	Pearson Correlation	-.949**	-.894**	.024	1.000	.242
	Sig. (2-tailed)	.000	.000	.876	.	.106
ENTRY	Pearson Correlation	-.234	-.236	.439**	.242	1.000
	Sig. (2-tailed)	.117	.115	.002	.106	.

** Correlation is significant at the 0.01 level (2-tailed). N is 46 for all cases; except for correlations with Entry where N is 45.

Table 5 Correlation analysis III

Controlling for.. HHI			*Controlling for.. ENTRY*		
	RD	*ENTRY*		*RD*	*HHI*
RD	1.0000 (0) p= .	.4896 (42) P= .001	RD	1.0000 (0) P= .	-.1524 (42) P= .323
ENTRY	.4896 (42) P= .001	1.0000 (0) P= .	HHI	-.1524 (42) P= .323	1.0000 (0) P= .

(Coefficient / (D.F.) / 2-tailed Significance); ' . ' is printed if a coefficient cannot be computed

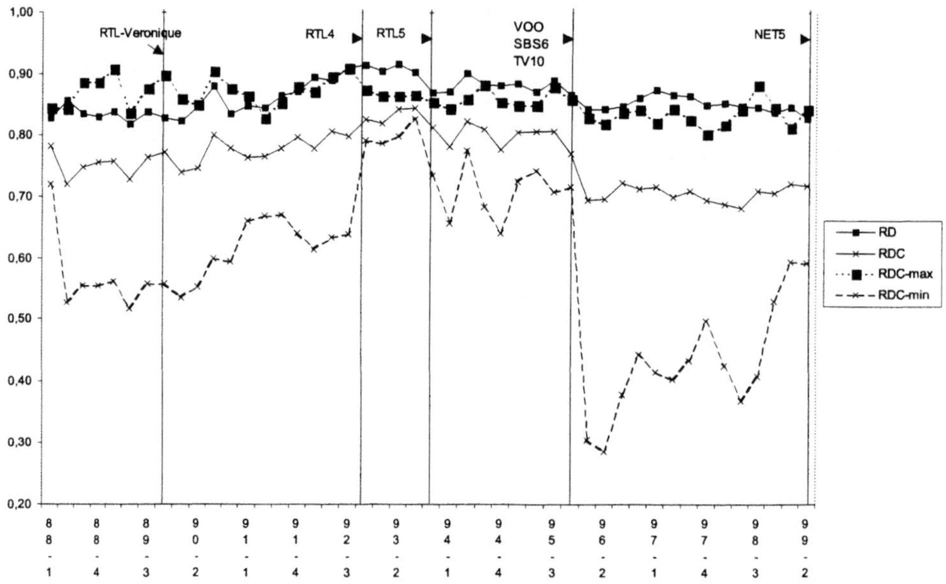

Figure 8 Intra and *intra* channel reflective diversity

Figure 8 shows us the development of maximum, average and minimum channel reflective diversity in comparison with the development of reflective diversity in the market as a whole. Firstly, we can observe that average channel reflective diversity (RDC-average) is throughout the whole period at the same level as market reflective diversity (RD). This suggests that most channels offer at least a moderately diverse supply of programme types and hence seem to aim for large, heterogeneous audiences. The same conclusion can be derived from the graphs describing the minimum level of reflective diversity that is offered by any channel (RDC-min). These graphs show a remarkably high level of minimum channel reflective diversity; that is the minimum level of diversity offered to viewers who continuously watch the same channel.

Secondly, we can observe that our estimate of channel reflective diversity shows the same non-linear relationship with competition intensity as market reflective diversity. Moreover, minimum channel reflective diversity (RDC-min) shows an even stronger non-linearity in its relationship with competition intensity then maximum and average channel reflective diversity. This confirms in our view that there is clear non-linear relationship between competition intensity and reflective diversity.

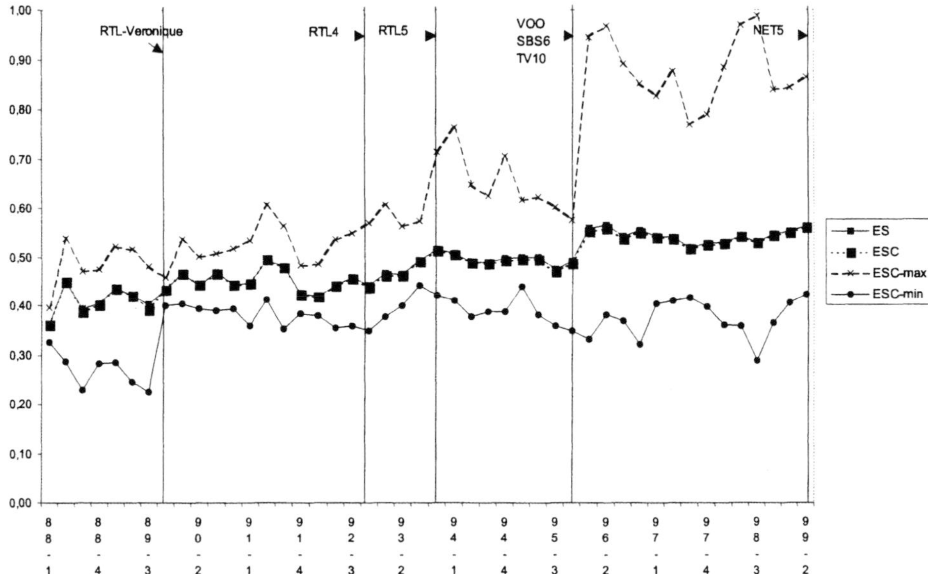

Figure 9 Inter and *intra* channel excessive sameness

Figure 9 and Figure 10 present similar data on intra channel open diversity and excessive sameness. What is most striking here is that new entry of RTL5 in 1993, and of SBS6, VOO and TV10 in 1995, but not of RTL4 in 1992, has a very strong effect on the minimum amount of open diversity (OD), and the maximum amount of excessive sameness (ES), that is offered by any channel. This suggests that new entrants enter the market with a substantially less openly diverse supply of programme types, or in other words, substantial more excessive sameness. A comparison of average channel profiles in Figure 11 confirms that new entrants of 1993 and 1995 indeed show less *intra* diversity than the 'older' broadcasting channels in the Netherlands.

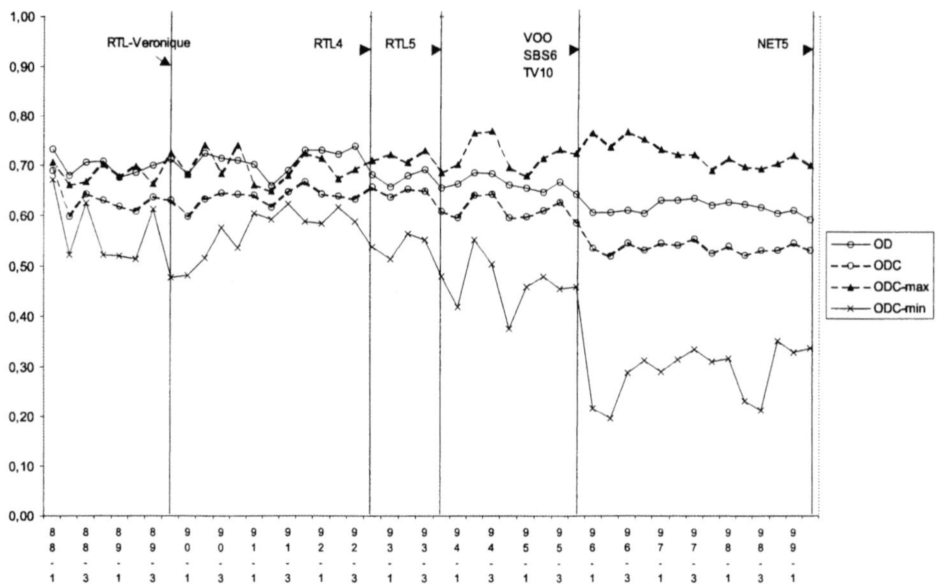

Figure 10 Inter and *intra* channel open diversity

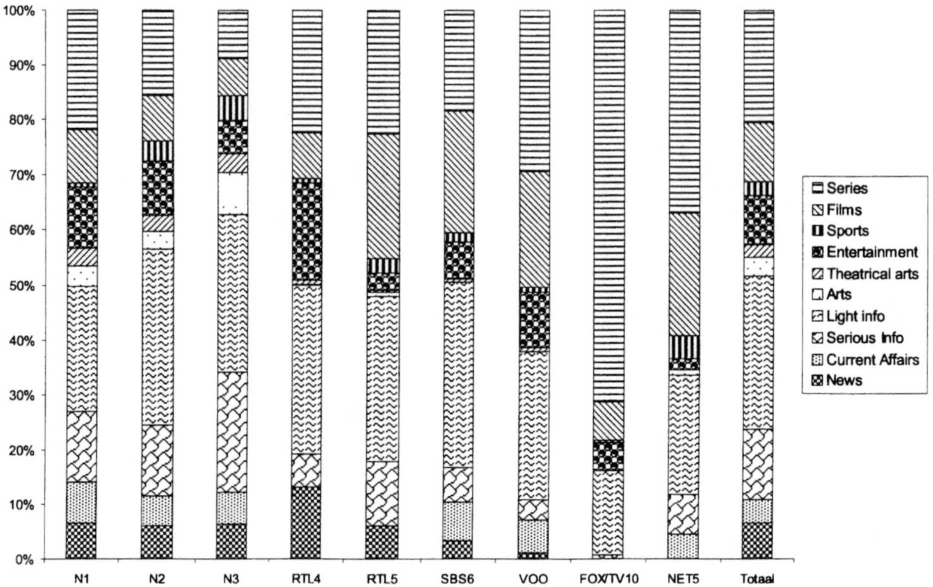

Figure 11 Average channel profiles

Based on our analysis presented thus far, we conclude that there is a clear and almost linear relationship between competition intensity (HHI), on the one hand, and diversity (D), open diversity (OD) and excessive sameness (ES) on the other hand. The more competition intensifies, the less (open) diverse programme types are offered, and *qualita qua*, the more excessive sameness is broadcasted. Only the relationship between competition intensity (HHI) and reflective diversity (RD) is clearly not linear. Our first hypothesis, that 'increasing competition is first accompanied by increasing open and/or reflective diversity and decreasing excessive sameness; and later by decreasing open and reflective diversity and increasing excessive sameness', therefore has to be rejected.

Our analysis also shows that new entry accelerates the general negative trend in diversity, and that especially reflective diversity (RD) is at least as strongly influenced by new entry as by competition intensity itself. In sum, we do not consider our second hypothesis, that 'each time a new major broadcaster enters the market, competition intensifies and diversity reduces, and that after a while, competition will de-escalate and diversity will increase again', falsified.

Thirdly, our estimate of competition intensity does not suggest that competition intensifies significantly stronger when there are already more broadcasters active in a market. On the contrary, the competition intensifying effect of entry (in our dataset) of RTL4 is larger than the competition intensifying effects of entry of RTL5 in 1993 and VOO, SBS6 and TV10 in 1995. With hindsight, this seems intuitively correct. A change from monopoly to a duopoly might have a larger impact on competition intensity than an increase of the number of oligopolists from 5 to 6. The first part of our third hypothesis, namely that 'the more broadcasters are already active in the market, the more intense competition will become in response to new entry', is therefore falsified. The second part of our third hypothesis, namely that 'the more intense competition will become in response to new entry, [...] the longer it will take before competition de-escalates again', can on the other hand not (yet) be falsified. After all, we observed that our variable Entry, which measures the relative strength of changes in competition intensity due to new entry, explains part of the variance in diversity.

A final verdict on our second and third hypotheses therefore has to be postponed. We will continue our investigation of the relationship between diversity and new entry in more detail in a follow-up paper that will be based on more detailed estimates of programme type supply and demand.[16]

Interpretation, Discussion and Conclusions

Let us summarise our findings so far. In general we observe a strong similarity between the development of diversity (D), open diversity (OD) and excessive sameness (ES). This suggests that these variables measure the same phenomenon, namely the extent to which channels offer only popular programme types or both popular and unpopular programme types. Secondly we observe that these three variables (D, OD and ES) strongly correlate with competition intensity ($HHI_{channel}$).

The last variable, reflective diversity (RD) shows a non-linear relationship with competition intensity ($HHI_{channel}$) and is in addition partially related to a simulated competition intensifying effect of new entry (E). The non-linear relationship with competition intensity suggests that increasing competition intensity indeed first increases and later decreases reflective diversity. The positive relationship between changes in competition intensity due to new entry (E) and reflective diversity (RD) confirms this conclusion.

Finally we observe that excessive sameness (ES) and reflective diversity (RD) increase both at the same time in the first phase of increasing competition intensity, whereas excessive sameness (ES) and reflective diversity (RD) tend to diverge in the second phase of increasing competition intensity, namely when intensifying competition tends to reduce rather that increase reflective diversity (RD).

These results suggest the following conclusions.

1 When there was a public monopoly, too few popular programme types were offered. Consequently, competition forced public and commercial broadcasters alike to offer more popular content. Since this resulted in increases not only in excessive sameness (ES) but also in increases in reflective diversity (RD), popular programme types were clearly underrepresented before the television broadcasting market became competitive.

---

16 For this follow-up study we will use monthly estimates of programme supply and demand, classified into more than 140 categories of programme types, for the period January 1993-June 1999.

2 New entrants tend to offer popular programme types when they enter the market. As a consequence, diversity reduces when new entrants enter the market. When they have acquired a position in the market, they then tend to expand their programme type offering, resulting in a stabilisation of diversity. The negative effect of new entry on diversity is however never completely compensated. This suggests that increasing new entry also in the future would continue to reduce diversity in both the short and long run.
3 All of the above confirm our supposition that moderate competition reinforces diversity, and that too much competition reduces diversity.

However, in our study we did not (yet) include the role of smaller, thematic channels that also entered the market in the wake of increasing competition. As we argued in the previous section, increasing competition may stimulate (or force) broadcasters to develop market niches, in an attempt to protect themselves against too strong competitive forces. The increasing number of thematic channels available suggests that diversity in the whole broadcasting market increased more, or decreased less, then our estimates of programme type supply of major channels suggest. This could imply that competition could intensify more before competition becomes ruinous, then we would conclude on the basis of our current data. We will take up this issue in future research.

References

Bakker, P. and Scholten, O.
1999 *Communicatiekaart van Nederland* [Communication Map of the Netherlands]. 2nd edition. Alphen aan den Rijn: Samsom.
Baumol, W.J. and Sidak, G.J.
1994 *Toward Competition in Local Telephony*. Cambridge, Mass.: MIT Press.
Bekkers, W.
1998 *Televisie en Publiek Nu en Straks* [Television and Audience, Present and Future]. Contribution to Conference on Broadcasting 2000, March 1998.
Brown, A.
1996 Economics, public service broadcasting, and social values. *The Journal of Media Economics* 9 (1): 3-15
Chae, S. and Flores, D.
1998 Broadcasting versus narrowcasting. *Information Economics and Policy* 10 (1): 41-57.

Chan-Olmsted, S.M.
1997 Theorizing multichannel media economics. *The Journal of Media Economics* 10 (1): 39-49.
Commissie Ververs
1996 *Terug naar het Publiek. Rapport van de Commissie Publieke Omroep* [Back to the Public. Report of Commission Public Broadcasting]. Den Haag: SDU.
De Jong, H.W.
1993 Market structures in the European Economic Community. In H.W. de Jong (ed.), *The Structure of the European Industry*, pp. 1-42. 3rd edition. Dordrecht: Kluwer Academic Publishers.
Ferguson, P.R.
1988 *Industrial Economics: Issues and Perspectives.* Houndsmill/London: MacMillan.
Gong, J. and Srinagesh, P.
1997 The economics of layered networks. In L.W. McKnight and J.P. Bailey (eds.), *Internet Economics*, pp. 63-75. Cambridge, Mass.: MIT Press.
Hendriks, P.
1995 Communicatie-economie: Tussen cultuur, markt en overheidsbeleid. [Communication Economics: between culture, market and state]. *Massacommunicatie* 23 (1): 19-40.
Hotelling, H.
1929 Stability in economic competition. *Economic Journal* 39: 41-57.
Intomart
1998 *Continuous TV Audience Survey in the Netherlands: A Methodological Description.* Hilversum: Intomart.
Keune, Genevion
1998 *Marktwerking en Pluriformiteit van Omroepprogramma's* [Market Mechanism and Broadcasting Programme Pluriformity]. Ministerie van Economische Zaken.
McQuail, D.
1992 *Media Performance. Mass Communication and the Public Interest.* London: Sage.
McQuail, D. and Van Cuilenburg, J.
1983 Diversity as a media policy goal: A strategy for evaluative research and a Netherlands case study. *Gazette* 31 (3): 145-162.
Noam, E.
1991 *Television in Europe.* New York: Oxford University Press.
Owen, B.M. and Wildman, S.S.
1992 *Video Economics.* Cambridge, MA: Harvard University Press.
Porter, M.
1985 *Competitive Advantage.* New York: The Free Press (reprinted 1998).

Porter, M.
1980/1998 *Concurrentiestrategie.* Groningen: Wolters-Noordhoff. [Dutch translation of *Competitive Strategy*, first published in 1980 by The Free Press, New York].

Rutten, P.W.M. and Buijs, T.S.F.
1999 *Concentratie in de Nederlandse Mediasector* [Concentration in the Dutch Media Sector]. Rapport STB-99-18. TNO.

Scherer, F.M.
1996 *Industry Structure, Strategy, and Public Policy.* New York: Harper Collins College Publishers.

Schoonhoven, R.
1995 Het wordt 'biggen' op markt voor commerciële omroepen [It will be hard work on the market for commercial broadcasters]. *Haagsche Courant*, 25 March 1995.

Soete, L. and Ter Weel, B.
1999 *Schumpeter and the Knowledge-Based Economy: On Technology and Competition Policy.* MERIT research memorandum 99-004. <http://meritbbs.unimaas.nl/rmpdf/1999/rm99_004.pdf>.

Van Cuilenburg, J.
1998 Diversity revisited: Towards a critical rational model of media diversity. In K. Brants, J. Hermes and L. van Zoonen (eds.), *The Media in Question. Popular Cultures and Public Interests*, pp. 38-49. London: Sage.

Van Cuilenburg, J.
1999 Between media monopoly and ruinous media competition. On media access and diversity in open societies. In Y.N. Zassoursky and E. Vartanova (eds.), *Media, Communications and the Open Society*, pp. 40-61. Moscow: Faculty of Journalism/Publisher IKAR.

Van Cuilenburg, J. and McQuail, D.
1982 *Media en Pluriformiteit* [Media and Pluriformity]. Den Haag: Staatsdrukkerij.

Van Cuilenburg, J. and Verhoest, P.
1998 Free and equal access. In search of policy models for converging communication systems. *Telecommunications Policy* 22 (3): 171-181.

Van Meurs, A.
1999 *Switching during commercial breaks.* Ph.D. thesis. University of Amsterdam.

Veronica stapt definitief uit HMG groep [Veronica definitely leaves HMG Groep]
2000 *Het Financieele Dagblad*, 14 March. <http://hfd.bvdep.com/ShowKrantArtikel.asp?KrantartikelId=6784>.

Waterman, D.
1989/90 Diversity and quality of information products in a monopolistically competitive industry. *Information Economics and Policy* (4): 291-301.

Wirth, M.O. and Bloch, H.
1995 Industrial organization theory and media industry analysis. *The Journal of Media Economics* 8 (2): 15-26.

Annex: Classification of Programme Types

Table 6 shows the ten categories of programme types that we use in our study (second column). It also shows how our categories relate to the 23 categories that have been used by Intomart to collect data on viewing and broadcasting time (i.e. our 'raw' data) (third column). Our choice for the ten categories mentioned is based on the normative assumption that these ten categories describe internally homogeneous and externally distinctive programme types, that each would deserve equal attention in a situation of open diversity, given the consideration that TV serves many purposes, interests and audiences.

Tabel 6 Classification of programme types

general heading	*our classification*	*NOS classification*
news and current affairs	news	news
	current affairs	current affairs
other information	serious information	- serious information
		- religion
		- small authorised broadcasting corporations
	light information	- nature/travel
		- light information
		- advertising
		- sports information
	information on arts	- arts magazine
		serious music
		- modern art
entertainment	stage/theatrical arts	- Dutch music
		- Dutch cabaret/satirical performance
	entertainment	- Dutch entertainment
		- foreign entertainment
	sports	- soccer coverage
		- other sports coverage
drama	film/cinema	- foreign film
		- Dutch film
	TV-series	- Dutch TV-series
		- foreign adventure series
		- other foreign TV-series

Media Competition: Greater Diversity or Greater Convergence?

Evidence from Two Empirical Studies

ELS DE BENS
Department of Communication Studies, University of Ghent, Belgium

Abstract

This paper argues that media competition can trigger innovation and stimulate diversity but that in a highly competitive media environment market imperatives will lead to more convergence. This hypothesis will be illustrated by a long term (ten years) programme analysis of the Flemish TV stations and an analysis of the marketing strategies of two leading Flemish newspapers.

Introduction

According to the free market model an abundance of many media suppliers and a 'sound' competition will stimulate diversity and innovation. The European Commission (EC) has always defended this hypothesis and has also argued that concentration will increase competition among media enterprises. The EC always was reluctant to media regulations (such as anti-trust and cross-ownership laws, subsidies, etc.) which could prevent the expansion of the media market. The EC only wishes to interfere when one media conglomerate tends to establish a dominant, oligopolistic market situation in which competition is threatened.

Media concentration has indeed often enlarged the market position of media enterprises and triggered product innovation. For smaller newspapers for example concentration often offered the only survival strategy and it improved and innovated the editorial output because 'the first copy costs' were diminished and more resources could be invested in content production.

In a highly commercialised media environment, concentration however often has the opposite effect: economics of editorial (content) production result in more convergence. Research has meanwhile demonstrated that media markets are not so fragmented as expected. Daily newspapers, weeklies of general interest (the so called *Publikumszeitschriften*), and 'generalist' TV stations aim at the same large audiences. The whole 'discourse' of the rapid growth of fragmented audiences, split up in 'niches' has largely been turned down. The big media enterprises are in competition for the same large segments of readers and viewers.

Advertisers also prefer media with a high potential range. Media consumers have been and constantly are screened by the media market research departments. The outcome results in the same strategies, the same trends, the same lifestyle and value-oriented directives, resulting in more of the same.

Innovation that happens to be successful is immediately imitated by competitors. This 'spiral' of initiatives often diminishes the financial resources so that on the long term less energy is invested in the production of content.

Two empirical studies (TV and daily newspapers) will illustrate that competition may indeed stimulate innovation and diversity but that in a highly competitive media environment market mechanisms boost convergence instead of diversity.

Case 1: 10 Years of TV Competition in Flanders: More Diversity?

In Flanders, like in most European countries, several new television stations were launched over the past decade. Do more channels mean 'more choice, more diversity'; or has competition between TV stations and the pursuit of high audience ratings provoked 'more of the same'?

The Flemish Broadcasting Market

Flanders offers an interesting case to study this question, because of its special television situation. Belgium has had the highest cable-penetration in the world for the past 20 years (93 per cent of television households). Apart from the 5 Flemish and 3 Walloon channels, some 15 to 20 general interest foreign channels are supplied (Germany, UK, Italy, Spain and the Netherlands) together with about 5 thematic channels (Eurosport, MTV, ARTE, CNN and Canal Plus).

The substantial foreign channel supply obviously increased structural diversity, but it also boosted competition between the home channels and the foreign ones, at a moment when in most European countries the public television stations still had an absolute monopoly. It was not until the end of the 1980s that Belgian commercial channels entered the scene. Until then, Luxembourg's RTL was the only commercial channel supplied through the Belgian cable network. Because of competition by the substantial foreign channel supply, home channels moved their more serious programmes to earlier and later hours, outside prime-time, and inserted more entertainment and especially fiction. However, these shifts were not very significant: the number of programmes on education and the arts remained practically unchanged in terms of total broadcasting hours, and Flemings and Walloons alike showed great loyalty to their home channels. Language and cultural barriers turned out to be decisive in the selection of foreign channels (De Bens, 1985, 1986, 1988; Geerts and Thoveron, 1979/1980).

In 1989 Flanders got its own commercial channel, VTM, which was immediately immensely popular; in 1995 the Scandinavian Broadcasting System followed with another initiative, VT4, which prompted VTM to set up a second channel of its own, Ka2. The result of all this is that Flanders now boasts three commercial channels. In spite of the many channels available on the Flemish cable network, Flemish channels are watched even more than in the past (De Bens & Van Landuyt, 1996). As the public broadcasting corporation is solely financed by public funds, it came under increasing pressure because of shrinking viewing figures. It was felt that these dwindling figures might be used against the public broadcasting system and might eventually lead to cuts in public funding. Consequently this situation meant that the public broadcasting corporation was more than tempted to imitate the commercial channels' 'success story'.

The Research

For our study we have chosen to use a quantitative content analysis method. We did not use the EBU-Escort system because this is a code system tailored to the programming of PBS stations. Our category system uses a rudimentary subdivision based on the 3 main traditional categories: entertainment, information and education (see Annex). We added 2 categories: children's programmes and arts. Children's programmes contain all programmes tailored to the needs of children and young people under the age of 12. With 'arts' we have deliberately avoided the term culture because it is too vague and can be confusing. With arts we refer to arts performance as well as programmes about these artistic performances (classical music, theatre, ballet, fine arts, literature, photography). The programme category arts together with education has often been neglected due to competition by the commercial stations.

We have analysed the programme output over a period of 10 years (1988-1998); for each year 3 months were examined (February, August and November); prime-time was set between 7 and 10 p.m.; the two public channels (BRTN-TV1 – BRTN-TV2) and the three commercial channels (VTM, VTM-Ka2 and VT4) were analysed.

Results: Broadcasting Time, Entertainment and Information

More TV channels, ever more broadcasting hours. The competition between the channels stimulated the extension of the total broadcast time (see Table and Figure 1). By expanding their broadcast hours, the commercial stations tried to attract and hold viewers earlier and later in the day. Obviously this extension was meant to allow for more commercial breaks and thus extra profits. PBS stations were forced to expand broadcasting hours as well but in the case of Flanders where there is no TV-advertising on PBS, this represented an additional financial burden. Core question is: has the extension of broadcasting time resulted in more programme diversity.

Table 1 Total broadcasting time (in hours)

	1988	*1989*	*1990*	*1991*	*1992*	*1993*	*1994*	*1995*	*1996*	*1997*	*1998*
BRTN	1132	12.28	11.11	11.59	14.46	13.25	13.13	15.06	15.38	17.55	17.53
VTM	-	7.11	7.55	8.29	9.35	10.34	10.28	16.34	18.14	21.04	20.48
VT4	-	-	-	-	-	-	-	8.02	10.23	11.53	11.38

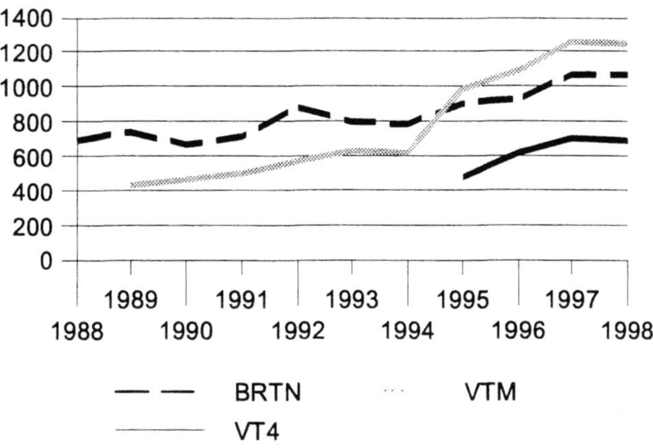

Figure 1 Total broadcasting time (in minutes)

Ever more entertainment. The entertainment share is particularly high for the commercial stations but the increase is most dramatic for the first channel of PBS. PBS and commercial stations are growing towards each other. On the second channel however, from 1993 on entertainment diminishes and takes on a more 'serious' profile (see Table and Figure 2).

Table 2 Percentage of entertainment programmes in total and prime-time broadcasting time

		1988	*1989*	*1990*	*1991*	*1992*	*1993*	*1994*	*1995*	*1996*	*1997*	*1998*
BRTN-	A	48.7	45.7	51.9	52.5	56.6	57.6	55	60.6	62.8	67.6	68.6
TV1	B	58.3	60.9	72.9	79.4	79.3	79.5	73.9	74.1%	77.8	78.7	74
BRTN-	A	73.7	60.9	52.9	44.2	62.9	56.5	50.2	42.5	33.4	33.6	33.7
TV2	B	77.2	58.3	43.8	32.3	53.6	36.9	37.6	43	27.7	42.5	42.6
VTM	A	--	66.8	72.2	76.7	78.9	81	82.1	81.5	78.1	73.6	65.9
	B		81.4	82.5	83.6	83.9	83.7	81	83.5	82.1	76.4	76.4
VTM-	A	--	--	--	--	--	--	--	71.2	79	75	82.4
Ka2	B								86.7	99.5	99.5	98.3
VT4	A	--	--	--	--	--	--	--	78.6	64.1	70.8	78.2
	B								97.2	97.7	97.7	100

A) in total broadcasting time
B) in prime-time

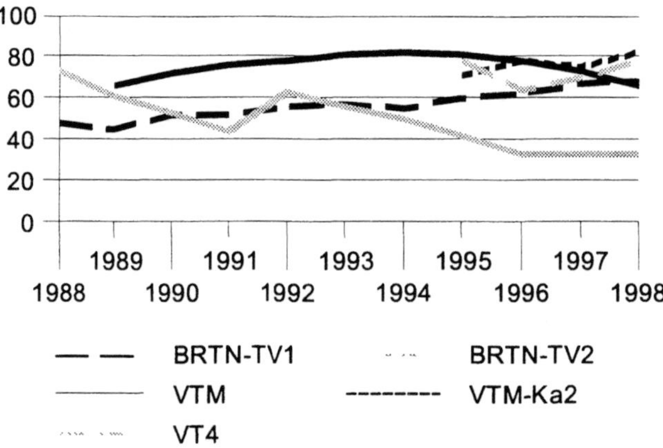

Figure 2 Percentage of entertainment programmes in total broadcasting time

Information: public and commercial channels are growing closer. For the public broadcasting station the information share of the first channel has remained almost unchanged until 1997; from 1998 on it is expanded to 21% (see Table and Figure 3). The second public channel has witnessed an increase especially during prime-time; from 1997 on it falls to 10%. The commercial channel VTM has kept its news share unchanged and it is almost equal to that of the first public BRTN-1 channel (especially during prime-time). TV4, the SBS commercial station, stopped its news programmes (too expensive).

Table 3 Percentage of information programmes in total and prime-time broadcasting time

		1988	*1989*	*1990*	*1991*	*1992*	*1993*	*1994*	*1995*	*1996*	*1997*	*1998*
BRTN-TV1	A	11.8	12.8	15.1	15.1	15.1	14.9	15	13.1	14.7	17.7	21.2
	B	17.9	19.5	18.2	19.2	19.4	19.2	19.4	16.1	14.9	16.5	22
BRTN-TV2	A	7.5	12.4	14.3	14.3	15.5	11.2	13.5	14.2	14.7	15.7	10.1
	B	11.5	16.3	16	19.3	13.9	14.9	18.6	23.3	27.8	15.6	13.7
VTM	A	--	15.1	15.1	15.8	15.8	12.9	12	12	13.3	16.7	14.7
	B		17.4	17.6	16.4	14.9	15	17.7	16	15.3	19.7	19.2
VTM-Ka2	A	--	--	--	--	--	--	--	9.4	8.7	3.2	3
	B								10.4	0.5	0	0
VT4	A	--	--	--	--	--	--	--	4.9	1.4	0	0
	B								0	0	0	0

A) in total broadcasting time
B) in prime-time

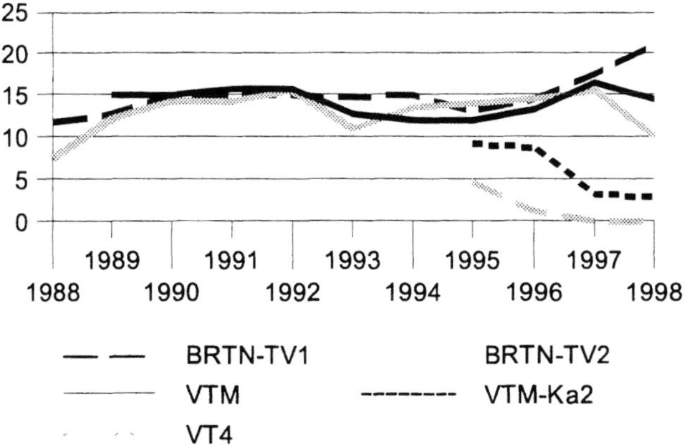

Figure 3 Percentage of information programmes in total broadcasting time

For the public broadcasting station, the news is still a major asset because most of the viewers remain faithful to its news broadcasts. Research abroad has confirmed that information is the public channel's stronger point but that the commercial channels have been seriously catching up lately (Krüger, 1996: 424).

Obviously, differences in news quality can only be demonstrated through more refined analysis. It is often claimed that commercial channels pay more attention to human interest topics, are more sensation-minded, present more 'parochial' news, but hardly any empirical quality research is available to support this hypothesis.

Results: Arts, Education and Children's Programmes

Increasingly less arts programmes. As far as the commercial channels are concerned, the figures in Table 4 confirm our expectations: no arts programming! (See also Figure 4) Ka2 which was started in 1995 has made a timid attempt but the third commercial network VT4 has virtually no arts programmes at all. This constitutes a major challenge for the public channel: but on the first public BRTN1-channel arts programmes have decreased over the years only to be reduced to zero during prime-time!

Table 4 Percentage of arts programmes in total and prime-time broadcasting time

		1988	*1989*	*1990*	*1991*	*1992*	*1993*	*1994*	*1995*	*1996*	*1997*	*1998*
BRTN-	A	4.9	5.2	3.8	3.8	2.7	2	2.6	2.1	1.7	0.3	0
TV1	B	3.2	2.8	0.9	0	0	0	0	0	0	0	0
BRTN-	A	5.7	5.2	8	11.9	8.3	12.6	10.3	7	7.9	4.3	2.9
TV2	B	2.8	4.1	8.9	9.9	8.8	15.1	12.3	6.2	11.3	3.9	3.3
VTM	A	--	0	0	0	0	0	0.3	0	0	0	0
	B		0	0	0	0	0	0	0	0	0	0
VTM-	A	--	--	--	--	--	--	--	1.7	0	0	0
Ka2	B								1.8	0	0	0
VT4	A	--	--	--	--	--	--	--	0.6	0	0	0
	B								0	0	0	0

A) in total broadcasting time
B) in prime-time

The second public BRTN2-channel could be used as a counterweight. Table 4 illustrates that this channel was reprofiled in 1991, 1993 and 1994 with more attention being given to the arts. However, in 1995 the arts share was reduced again and in the course of 1996 the management announced that on the second channel all arts programmes would be deleted! The arts programmes were said to be too difficult and too serious and would require a lighter approach. Most of the newspapers reacted using expressive headlines such as: 'culture slaughtered on the second public channel'. In 1998 only 2.1% arts programmes are offered. The public channel's complementary character is at stake here and diversity may in the future be even more threatened.

Yet, in *Media Performance* Denis McQuail stated that television has an important role to play when spreading arts programmes as it is a popular medium addressing a wide public: 'The popular media may be the only effective means of bringing some of the arts (e.g. opera, ballet, classical music and drama, art photography and film) to the wider public. They can also serve generally as a gate for awareness of all the arts' (McQuail,

1992: 284). This clearly represents a major mission for the public broadcasting system but in Flanders the policy required to take up this complementary assignment seems to be lacking.

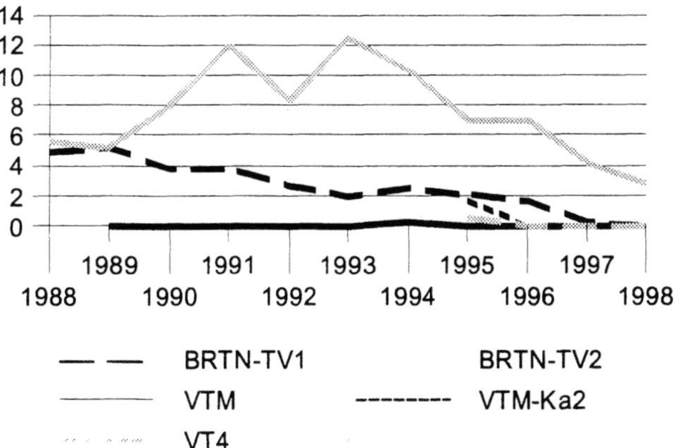

Figure 4 Percentage of arts programmes in total broadcasting time

Few and gradually even less education programmes. This programme category has been specified rather broad: not only educational and scientific programmes but also documentaries, service and consumer programmes were included because the information category was limited to recent news events.

On the public network BRTNI we have noticed a downward trend until 1994 followed by a slight rise in 1995 but halved in 1998. The second channel in particular brings more educational programmes which coincides with attempts in the past to give it a more serious complementary profile (see Table and Figure 5).

On VTM the supply of educational programmes is extremely limited although there was a growth of 2 % in 1995 so that in 1998 the public TV2 and the commercial VTM both program the same amount ± 7.5%; again we can conclude that both BRTNI and VTM are growing closer. The second channel of VTM, Ka2, and the SBS station VT4 program very few educational programmes; in prime-time 0%.

Children's programmes till 1995: a public broadcasting system's privilege. Children's programmes remained a kind of privilege for the public broadcasting corporation because the Flemish commercial station was not allowed to insert advertising directed at children before and after children's programmes; this meant that making and presenting children's programmes was loss-making.

Table 5 Percentage of education programmes in total and prime-time broadcasting time

		1988	*1989*	*1990*	*1991*	*1992*	*1993*	*1994*	*1995*	*1996*	*1997*	*1998*
BRTN-	A	17.7	16.6	12.5	12	8.8	8.5	10.5	14.5	8.3	6.6	7.5
TV1	B	12	9.7	4.1	0	1.4	0.9	4.4	7	6.2	2.7	3.4
BRTN-	A	10.1	12	18.6	21.8	12.2	17.2	11.4	13.7	13.1	12.6	13.6
TV2	B	4.6	12.6	22.4	30.9	18.6	29.6	19.5	21.2	20.8	19	20.2
VTM	A	--	0.9	1.5	0.7	1.3	1.2	1.2	3.5	3.9	3.7	7.3
	B		0	0	0	1	1.1	0	0.5	2.6	3.4	4.9
VTM-	A	--	--	--	--	--	--	--	2.7	0	3.2	4
Ka2	B								1.1	0	0	0
VT4	A	--	--	--	--	--	--	--	4.2	1.4	4.8	4.3
	B								1.2	0	1.8	0

A) in total broadcasting time
B) in prime-time

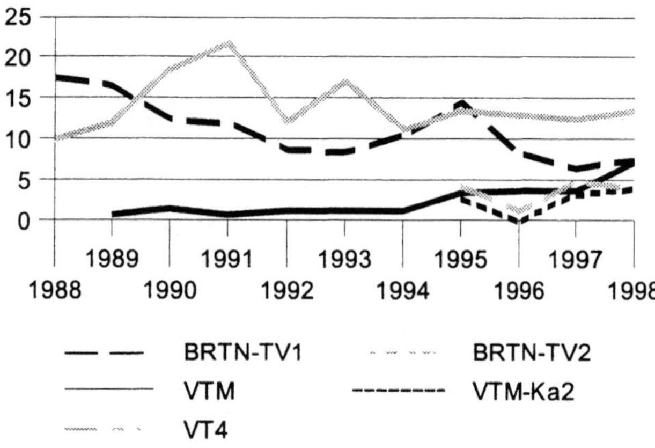

Figure 5 Percentage of education programmes in total broadcasting time

When in 1995 the new channel VT4, using the status of a foreign channel (unlimited from the UK) managed to get around the advertising-ban, it presented from the start 53 minutes of programmes for children (about 11% of the total programme supply); in 1998: 17.5% (see Table 6).

VTM was forced to counterprogram this and broadcasts about 1 hour a day of children's programmes without inserting advertisements. Due to the competition of VT4 the public and commercial stations are growing closer in terms of their share of children's programmes.

Table 6 Percentage of children's programmes in total broadcasting time

	1988	*1989*	*1990*	*1991*	*1992*	*1993*	*1994*	*1995*	*1996*	*1997*	*1998*
BRTN-TV1	11.2	16.5	14	14.8	14.1	14.4	11.7	5.8	9.2	4.6	0.3
BRTN-TV2	0	1.9	0	0	3.1	2.4	11.4	21.4	30.4	33.4	39.7
VTM	-	16.7	10.9	6.9	7.1	4.8	3.2	3	4.7	4.6	12.1
VTM-Ka2	-	-	-	-	-	-	-	15	12.2	18.7	10.6
VT4	-	-	-	-	-	-	-	10.9	29.3	24.4	17.5

Results: More American fiction, less cultural diversity?

Within the entertainment category, fiction is the most programmed and most often watched programme category: during prime-time almost half of the broadcasting time goes to fiction both on the public broadcasting system and on the commercial channels (see Table 7). Convergence between public BRTV1 and commercial VTM is manifest. During prime-time Ka2 (VTM) broadcasts 88.4% and VT4 80.7% fiction!

Many authors (Varis, 1985; Mattelart & Dorfmann, 1975; Pragnell, 1985: Silj, 1988; Sepstrup, 1990; De Bens, M. Kelly en M. Bakke, 1992; Biltereyst, 1995 etc.) have shown that the main share of the fiction programmes is of American origin and that the omnipresence of American fiction on European channels stimulates convergence and undermines the cultural diversity of the European programming-industry. All these studies also pointed out extensively that viewers invariably prefer home-made fiction which also yields the highest ratings. One of the consequences is that all European channels have made major financial efforts in recent years to produce more home-made fiction. Because of the extension of broadcasting time however they are forced to rely on foreign imports to fill the many programming hours. The scenario is the same everywhere: most of the import is of American origin because the American productions are cheaper than the European ones and on top of that they ensure high ratings. Yet the European Commission has set up a quota system in which 'a majority proportion of broadcasting needs to go to European works' (European Commission, 1996: Art. 4). The problem with this new guideline is that all programmes may be counted (except news, sports, games and advertising) which does not allow for the origin of the fiction to be assessed separately. The results are therefore misleading and according to the latest report of the Commission practically all channels comply with the norms set by Art. 4. If however one was to calculate the fiction category separately one might come to a totally different conclusion and indeed admit that the imports of American fiction are still immense.

Table 7 Percentage of fiction programmes in total and prime time broadcasting time

		1988	*1989*	*1990*	*1991*	*1992*	*1993*	*1994*	*1995*	*1996*	*1997*	*1998*
BRTN-	A	38.3	41	45.6	46.4	52.7	53.3	47.8	47.3	49.6	51.1	46
TV1	B	32.5	39.3	42.9	47.9	58.2	54.1	51.5	51	45.2	44.7	39
BRTN-	A	23	23.5	17.7	17.9	23.6	25.9	33.6	42.6	37.4	39.6	48.3
TV2	B	34.9	29.6	16.8	15.3	13.1	9.1	15.1	27.9	14.2	42.5	45.4
VTM	A	--	58.7	54.9	51.9	52	57.5	53.4	56	45.5	39	48.8
	B		56.2	46.1	40.8	44.1	45.3	38	46.5	36.7	39.3	42.3
VTM-	A	--	--	--	--	--	--	--	64.2	77	84.5	78.6
Ka2	B								67.3	93.2	92.9	88.4
VT4	A	--	--	--	--	--	--	--	74.9	79.9	88.1	85
	B								79.8	61	78.4	80.7

A) in total broadcasting time
B) in prime-time

Table 8 and Figures 6 and 7 illustrate that Flemish fiction series and serials have increased both on the public broadcasting system and on the commercial channels. In the top 10 of the most popular programmes we always find the Flemish series. So to comply with their viewers wishes both the public and the commercial channels have made substantial financial efforts to produce more Flemish fiction.

On the public broadcasting system we notice a gradual rise until 1994 followed by a decrease in 1995. The same year turns out to be a breaking point for the commercial channels as the home productions are suddenly reduced by half. The main reason for this is the new commercial channel VT4 which mainly presents fiction of American origin but also the fact that Ka2, the second commercial VTM network channel does not have the financial means to produce its own fiction and is therefore an avid buyer on the American market: in 1998 the American imports are very high: 42.3% for VTM; 91% for Ka2 and 88% for VT4.

On the public broadcasting system American series remain important although there is no further increase. However, the available time is not taken up by more European productions but by Australian ones!

As for films (see Table 9 and Figures 8 and 9) the USA remain the most important supplier, also in 1998: 60% for the public broadcasting service and 81% for the commercial channels. The share of European film remains too low and the overwhelming presence of American movies obviously stimulates cultural globalisation in the long term.

Table 8 Origin of series and serials on the public and commercial TV channels (in %)

	series and serials (public broadcasting)									
	1989	*1990*	*1991*	*1992*	*1993*	*1994*	*1995*	*1996*	*1997*	*1998*
Flanders	4.6	5.7	8.7	7.5	11.9	12.2	10.4	18	20.7	17.2
Europe	17	25.7	21.6	26.3	19.6	25.8	18.7	23.4	28.7	20.2
U.S.A.	17	27.5	48.4	48.4	47.3	39.8	36.1	43.9	29.1	31.5
Australia	45.4	24.3	19.4	17.8	16.2	19.2	25.9	14.3	20.7	28.6
rest of world	16	16.8	1.9	0	4.9	3	8.9	0.4	0.8	2.5
	series and serials (commercial broadcasting)									
	1989	*1990*	*1991*	*1992*	*1993*	*1994*	*1995*	*1996*	*1997*	*1998*
Flanders	2.7	2.6	3	10.8	17.8	18.6	9.3	11.6	13.6	15.5
Europe	3.7	1.1	8.3	5.8	6.7	6.3	15.4	11.8	6.5	4.9
U.S.A.	74.6	74.7	64.5	54.6	55.5	65.3	67.2	67.4	74.9	75.3
Australia	12.8	21.2	23.4	28.1	15.5	8.2	7.9	8.1	4.8	3.7
rest of world	6.2	0.5	0.7	0.7	3.7	1.5	0.2	1	0.2	0.6

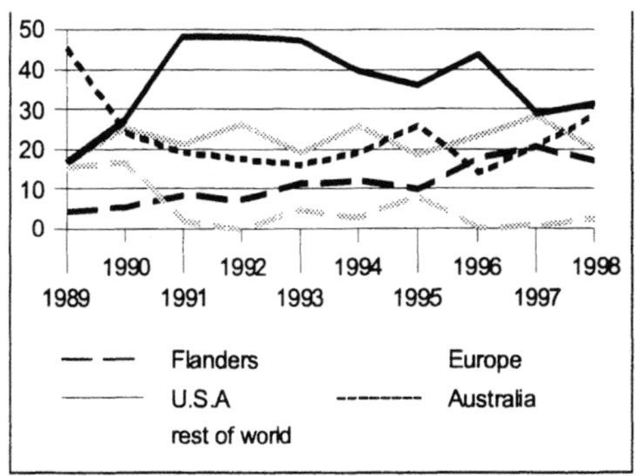

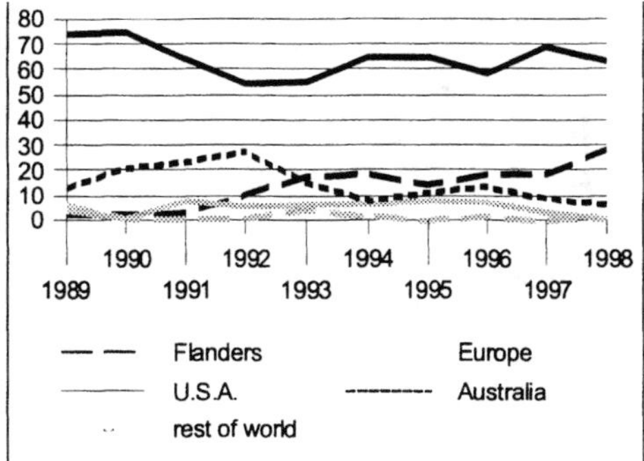

Figures 6 & 7 Origin of series and serials on the public and commercial TV channels (in %)

We also have looked into the origin of children's programmes and we found an extremely high share of American programmes on the commercial stationd Ka2 (± 90%) and VT4 (97%) in 1998. The American import on VTM and BRTN1 is almost the same: 41.4% and 40.5%. It is obvious that as a result of competition among public and commercial stations the import of American TV drama has increased and has stimulated convergence.

Table 9 Origin of movies on the public and commercial TV channels (in %)

movies (public broadcasting)										
	1989	*1990*	*1991*	*1992*	*1993*	*1994*	*1995*	*1996*	*1997*	*1998*
Flanders	10.2	10.3	14.5	7.6	1.9	2.5	5.5	6.3	6.7	5.7
Europe	23.8	30.8	31.5	21.1	23.4	28.2	25.9	16.6	15	23.7
U.S.A.	50.8	48.5	42.1	66.1	66	64.5	59.3	71.9	73	60.1
Australia	3.4	2.9	1.3	0.8	1.9	2.4	1.9	0	0.8	1.6
rest of world	11.8	7.5	10.6	4.4	6.8	2.4	7.4	5.2	4.2	8.9
movies (commercial broadcasting)										
	1989	*1990*	*1991*	*1992*	*1993*	*1994*	*1995*	*1996*	*1997*	*1998*
Flanders	2	0	5.2	11.4	6.6	0	2.2	0.9	0.4	0.9
Europe	7.9	3.4	6.4	8.3	7.4	12.3	13.6	5.1	10.4	7.8
U.S.A.	86.3	92.8	83.7	79.6	81.1	83	81	92.2	87.3	87.4
Australia	0	0	0	0	0	1.3	0	1.3	1.1	0.4
rest of world	3.8	3.8	3.8	0.7	4.8	3.4	3.2	0.5	0.8	3.5

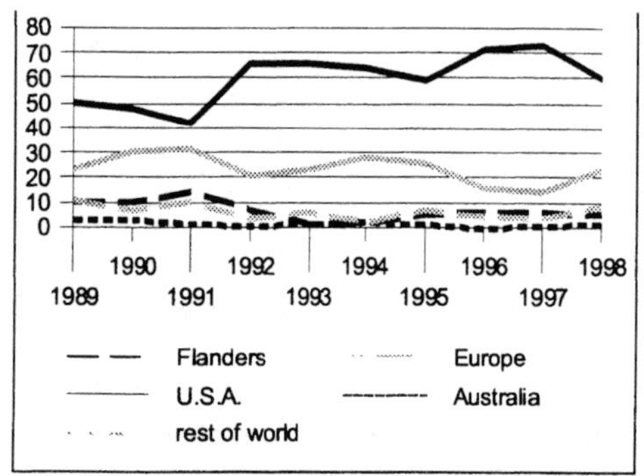

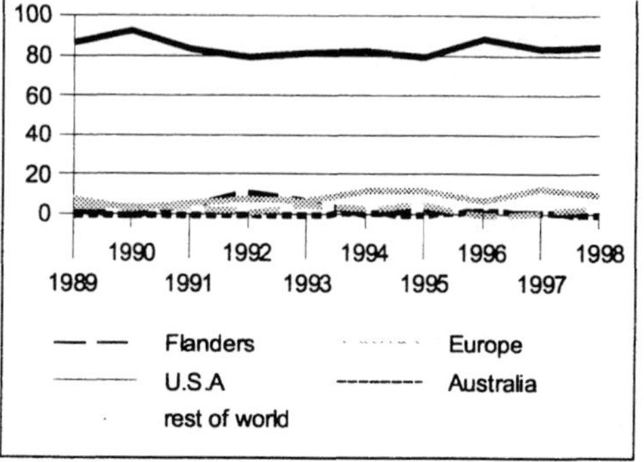

Figures 8 & 9 Origin of movies on the public and commercial TV channels (in %)

Conclusion

It seems that the commercialisation of TV broadcasting has become a spiral movement and that it has not stimulated diversity but has lead to more convergence (see also Figures 10-15).

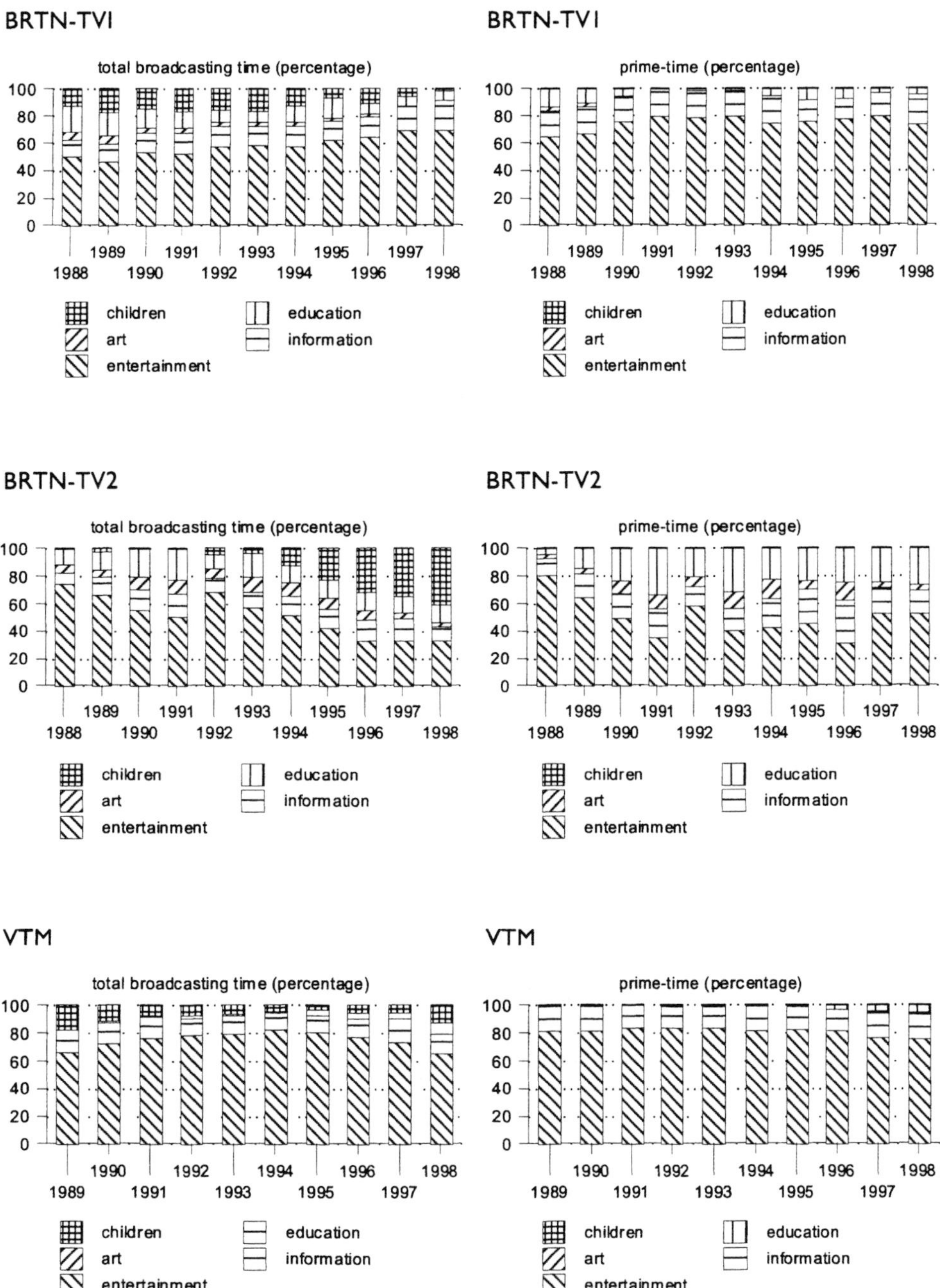

Figures 10-5 Percentages of programme type in total and prime-time broadcasting time on Flemish channels

The public stations still offer a more diverse programme supply but over the last 10 years public and commercial stations have grown closer, especially the first channel of the public service BRTV1 and the first commercial channel of VTM; on the other hand both commercial stations Ka2 and VT4 are engaged in a head-to-head race and their programme output is very similar. The growing import of American programmes on both public and particularly on the commercial stations stimulates convergence.

We have limited our research to quantitative programme analysis; we are almost sure that a more qualitative research would reveal even more convergence: the TV stations often use the same formats (mostly 'clones' of American formats): formats of games, quizzes, reality shows, TV confessions, blind dates, etc.

The obsession for high audience ratings is one of the main reasons for this convergence. For the commercial stations it is an inevitable evolution: high ratings guarantee high revenues. The main budget of the public stations however still comes from public money (licence fees). In many countries a debate is going on whether public stations need to have income from advertising so that competition with the commercial stations becomes less relevant (the BBC-model). Maybe a topic for discussion as an advertising ban for public TV is on the political agenda of Germany, France, Holland and Belgium.

Case II: Media Competition among Daily Newspapers in Flanders: More Innovation, More Diversity?

Competition among daily newspaper enterprises in the Belgium newspaper market had become severe. The concentration process has created an almost oligopolistic market situation (see Table 10).

Of the 50 dailies that were published in 1950, only 24 have survived and they are published by only 6 newsgroups. Some of the mergers took place quite recently: in 1994 the VUM, market leader in Flanders, took over *Het Volk*; in 1996 two newsgroups (NV De Vlijt: *Gazet van Antwerpen* en NV Concentra: *Het Belang van Limburg*) merged into RUG (Regionale Uitgeversgroep).

In French speaking Belgium Mediabel (*Vers L'Avenir*) took in 1997 a share of 51% in IPM (*La Libre Belgique/La Dernière Heure*) creating a duopoly together with the other pressgroup Rossel, market leader in the French speaking part (*Le Soir, La Lanterne, La Meuse, La Nouvelle Gazette*). Another *coup de théatre* occurred in 1999 when the VUM, the market leader of the Flemish press, took a share in Mediabel (through SBE), that obtained 58.9% of Mediabel (see Figure 16).

Table 10 Decline of the number of dailies and of news enterprises

	Flanders		*Wallonia*		*Belgium*	
	Titles	*Enterprises*	*Titles*	*Enterprises*	*Titles*	*Enterprises*
1950	19	14	31	19	50	33
1980	12	7	23	9	33	16
1999	9	3	15	3	24	6

Note: Without the two financial dailies *De Financieel-Economische Tijd* (Flanders) and *L'Echo* (Wallonia)

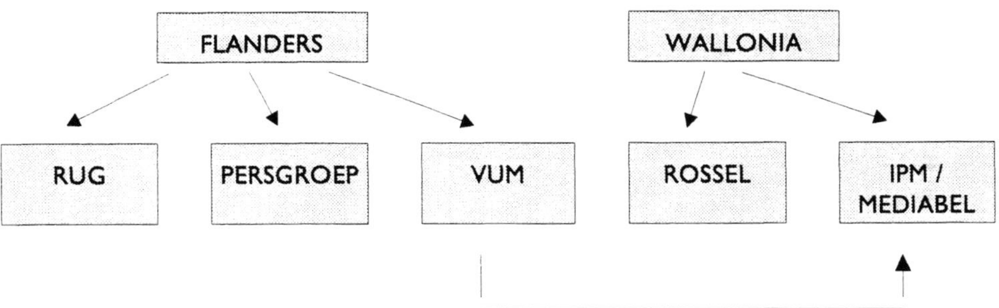

Figure 16 Five remaining press groups

Press Groups in Belgium and Their Market Share in 1996

These '6' (almost 5) groups control the newspaper market; small newspapers have disappeared or have been merged; every initiative to launch a new newspaper failed because the daily newspaper market has become saturated.

Circulation is slightly declining over the past 5 years. The total circulation of the Belgian press in 1998 is 1.543.624, the Flemish press taking 64% and the French speaking 36%. Belgians do rarely subscribe to their newspaper (about 35%) so that most dailies are sold in single copies so that publishers are having a varying high number of unsold copies.

Revenue from advertising is also declining because of competition of commercial television. Classified advertising has increased slightly as a result of economical revival but in Belgium revenue from classified advertising is still limited in comparison with most other European countries.

Effect of Concentration and Competition

Concentration has been for some newspapers quite positive. The 'first copy cost' declined, production as well as distribution costs diminished so that merged newspapers benefited from a stronger market position. If the financial resources are used to improve the editorial output, mergers can trigger more editorial quality and diversity.

As competition is severe among the dominant pressgroups, the publishers have invested in a lot of marketing strategies: all dailies recently developed a new look, have added columns, new inserts, new and better distribution, and also have developed strategies to make their newspapers more attractive to advertisers.

Competition among newspapers enterprises seems to have stimulated more innovation and diversity than competition among national TV-stations.

On the other hand, competition of the daily newspaper sector has often boasted tabloidisation: more human interest, more trivialisation and more sensationalism. Crime, sex, disaster, celebrities, sports have become core topics. As a result of strong competition and pressure from the commercial department, hunting for the ultimate 'scoop' becomes compulsive.

Many authors claim that all dailies, quality as well as popular, once have given in to down market model. The Guardian launched the term 'broadbloids', an amalgamation of the words 'tabloids' and 'broadsheets' (synonym for quality paper).

We must admit that in spite of the fact that many communication researchers have referred to 'tabloidisation' of the daily newspapers, it is not so evident to work out a methodology that reveals the tabloidisation trend.

We are engaged in a comparative study of two Flemish quality papers *De Standaard* and *De Morgen* in which we try to point to the positive effects of competition and at the same time to the increasing tabloidisation. The study is not yet finished but we can already indicate some tentative conclusions.

Competition between De Standaard en De Morgen

De Standaard belongs to the VUM (Vlaamse Uitgeversmaatschappij); this pressgroup publishes 4 dailies: *De Standaard*, a quality paper, *Het Nieuwsblad*, a popular version of *De Standaard*, *De Gentenaar*, a regional edition of *Het Nieuwsblad*, and *Het Volk*, a tabloid that VUM received in 1994.

VUM is the market leader of the Flemish daily newspaper press and *De Standaard* has for many years have been the leading quality newspaper. Since two years however *De Morgen*, a former small socialist newspaper, identifies itself as a quality paper.

De Morgen made his come back some years ago after having faced several bankrupts. The newspaper went bankrupt in 1986 after the socialist party had decided to cut its financial support. The reasons for the socialist party's decision were twofold: the party had lost its grip on the editorial staff and at the same time the newspaper had accumulated huge debts. The newspaper was 'saved' by its readers, who raised money. The paper managed to persist until the end of 1988, when the financial losses were discovered to have become even larger.

In 1989 the newspaper was taken over by the Persgroep, that publishes the leading Flemish tabloid *Het Laatste Nieuws*. *De Morgen* was promised editorial autonomy and the newspaper designed itself as 'progressive and independent'.

Until 1995 *De Morgen* did not succeed to increase its sale figures nor its advertising revenues. Already in 1993 De Persgroep considered to sell or to liquidate the newspaper. From 1996 on *De Morgen* succeeded however in increasing its circulation and attracted more advertising revenue. This success was the result of an aggressive marketing strategy: the format, and lay-out were changed, an increasing amount of supplements, inserts with all kinds of gadgets had to attract readers. The number of journalists was substantially increased and De Morgen advocated itself as a quality paper, offering its readers investigative and critical journalism. Advertising campaigns supported this new quality label. *De Morgen* turned out to be a competitor of *De Standaard* and from 1997 on they were engaged in a head-to-head race.

From 1996 till today *De Morgen* sold much more copies compared to *De Standaard*'s circulation that stabilised the past five years (sold copies) (see Table 11).

Table 11 Circulation numbers

	De Morgen	*De Standaard*
1994	24.516	75.534
1995	30.251	76.691
1996	35.474	77.499
1997	42.545	75.955
1998	44.172	76.095
1999*	47.242	75.596

* april-june 1999

Tabloidisation Strategies

Meanwhile *De Morgen* had introduced more human interest, more popular news, so that many authors argue that *De Morgen* has enlarged his market segment as a result of this tabloidisation strategy. Especially on the front page human interest articles have increased as well as the size of the photographs. The boundaries between investigative journalism and sensation became vague. In response to the Dutroux-scandal *De Morgen* published the famous x-files, in which a young woman gave evidence of ritual murders; in spite of the fact that *De Morgen* was aware of the erratic emotional state of the witness, the newspaper continued to publish her horrible testimonies. The sale of *De Morgen* increased with 4.000 copies a day...

The chief editor of *De Standaard* blamed his colleague of *De Morgen* for his lack of journalistic ethics and for giving in to commercial pressure. A few months later, *De Standaard,* on the front page, revealed the homosexual affair of a Walloon socialist Minister with an underage boy. Afterwards, this disclosure too turned out to be mainly based on a doubtful source.

This was only the beginning of a non ending war and rivalry. In several 'open letters' in their newspaper both chief editors blamed one another. In those days, the journalistic ethics of the competitor became a news item.

It is obvious that competition has triggered tabloidisation. *De Standaard* introduced larger photographs on the front-page; both newspapers changed their lay-out so that with bigger titles and less text they hoped to attract more readers. Some weeks ago the chief editor of *De Morgen* sued the general director of the public service broadcast corporation after he had declared in an interview in *De Standaard* that *De Morgen* always takes side for the commercial station VTM (De Persgroep, publisher of *De Morgen,* is main shareholder of the commercial television station VTM).

Both editors of *De Morgen* and *De Standaard* have become mediastars, taking part in several television-shows and recording radio publicity spots for their paper, talking about quality. Since September 1999, the chief editor of *De Morgen* started his own political program on the commercial television station VTM. Its seems that the quality newspapers in Flanders tend to be personified in their chief editors; this personification of newspaper editors is a new phenomenon in Flanders.

In spite of the manifest tabloidisation, both editors recently announced to become the leading quality newspaper. *De Standaard* (1 October 1999) described its new quality strategy referring to the definition of quality by Le Monde journalist D. Schneidermann: '*court, rapide, distrayant et percutant*' (short, quick, to give release and accurate). Two weeks later, *De Morgen* designed itself as the quality paper of 2000 that '*will lead readers in a concise way through all important events*'.

We are confronted with an ambiguous situation: competition has stimulated innovation and diversity (more supplements, more columns, more inserts) but at the same time has triggered tabloidisation.

References

Biltereyst, D.
1995 *Hollywood in het Avondland: Over de Afhankelijkheid en de Impact van Amerikaanse Televisie in Europa* [Hollywood in the Evening Country. On the Dependence on and Impact of American Television in Europe]. Brussel: VUB-Press.

De Bens, E.
1985 L'Influence de la cablodiffusion sur le comportement télévisuel des Belges et sur les stratégies de programmation [The impact of the diffusion of cable on television behaviour of Belgians and programming strategies]. In IDATE (ed.), *Actes des 7es Journées Internationales de l'IDATE*, pp. 318-329.

De Bens, E.
1986 Cable penetration and competition among Belgian and foreign stations. *European Journal of Communication* 1 (4): pp. 478-492.

De Bens, E.
1988 Der Einfluz eines grossen ausländischen Programmangebotes auf die Sehgewohnkeiten. Belgische Erfahrungen mit einen dichten Verkabelung [The impact of a large supply of foreign programmes on viewing habits. Belgian experiences with a dense cable system]. *Publizistik* 33 (2/3): 352-365.

De Bens, E., Kelly, M. and Bakke, M.
1992 Television content: Dallasfiction of culture? In K. Siune and W. Truetzschler (eds.), *Dynamics of Media Politics*, pp. 75-100. London: SAGE/Euromedia Research Group.

De Bens, E., and Van Landuyt, D.
1996 *Video on Demand.* Research report. Department of Communication, University of Ghent.

European Commission
1996 *Communication from the European Commission to the Council and the European Parliament on the Application of Articles 4 and 5 of Directive 89/552/EEC, Television without Frontiers.* Brussels, July 15.

Geerts, C. and Thoveron, G.
1979/1980 *Télévision Offerte au Public, Télévision Regardée par le Public. Une Enquête Internationale* [Television Offered to the Public, Television Watched by the Public. An International Survey]. Brussel: RTBF.

Hellman, H. and Sauri, T.
1994 Public service television and the tendency towards convergence. Trends in prime time programme structure in Finland 1970-1992. *Media, Culture & Society* 16 (1): 47-71.

Hellman, H.
1999 *From Companions to Competitors. The Changing Broadcasting Markets and Television Programming in Finland.* Tampere: University of Tampere.

Krüger, U.M.
1996 Programm-analyse: Tendenzen in den Programmen der grossen Fernsehsender 1985-1995 [Programme analysis: Trends in Programming of the major broadcasters, 1985-1995]. *Media Perspektiven* (8): 417-440.

Mattelart, A. and Dorfmann, A.
1975 *How to Read Donald Duck: Imperialist Ideology in the Disney Comic.* New York: International General.

McQuail, D.
1992 *Media Performance. Mass Communication and the Public Interest.* London: Sage.

Pragnell, O.
1985 *Television in Europe.* Media Monograph No. 5. Manchester: European Institute for the Media.

Sepstrup, P.
1990 *Transnationalised Television in Western Europe.* London: Libbey.

Silj, A.
1988 *East of Dallas. The European Challenge to American TV.* London: BFI Publishing.

Varis, T.
1985 *Flow of Television Programmes in Western Europe.* Tampere, Department of Journalism and Mass Communication.

Annex: Category System

Entertainment
quiz and games
sport
leisure time (hobby, house, garden, etc.)
infotainment:
– talkshows
– human interest
popular music and shows
cabaret, humor en satire
series:
– 'series'
– 'mini-series en -serials' (maximum 4 episodes)
– 'serials'
TV- and feature films

Information
newsbulletins
newsmagazines

Arts
classical music
theater and ballet
fine arts
literature
mixture of fine arts
other arts programmes (architecture, photography, etc.)

Education
schooltelevision
scientific programmes
documentaries
consumer programmes
other education programmes

Children- and teenage-programmes
information programmes
entertainment programmes:
– non-fictional entertainment (quiz, games, etc.)
– fictional entertainment (films, series and cartoons)

Miscellaneous
religious programmes, lotto, tiercé, etc.

Audience Fragmentation and Structural Limits on Media Innovation and Diversity

ROBERT G. PICARD
Media Group, Turku School of Economics and Business Administration, Finland

Abstract

This paper explores the requirements for innovation and diversity. It contrasts these necessities with how fragmentation has diminished resources available to content producers, the nature and effects of labour pool limitations, the role of competition in programming choices, and the strategies employed by content packagers and producers to respond to the new economic environment. The author argues that the economics of content production and distribution interfere with the goals of innovation and diversity. These desirable outcomes can be produced by commercial entities only when the number of commercial competitors and audience fragmentation is limited and/or public policies encourage or demand such outcomes. The author suggests some policy strategies to promote innovation and diversity within the commercialised media environment that exists throughout much of the world today.

Introduction

The maturation of media markets, the development of new technologies, and changes in media policies have resulted in an increasing number of published titles and broadcast channels, a rise in the number of broadcast hours, and the appearance of a variety of new electronic sources of information, ideas, and entertainment.

Proponents of liberalisation and privatisation have greeted the increasing number of sources of content as evidence that their projected outcomes of economic development, content innovation, and diversity are being achieved. Even critics of traditional media during the past decade have argued that increased communications channels are creating the means to increase innovation and diversity and thus empower democratic participation.

The desire to have multiple outlets for communications has been widely embraced by capitalists intent on profiting from media development. But support for the policy is much broader and has been well grounded in Western political theory. Under liberal democratic theories of communication, multiple sources of information and ideas and different perspectives of human development are desirable to help individuals and societies make informed responses to events and issues they confront. This idea of plurality of sources is widely accepted by a wide range of political theorists as a necessity for free expression and the carriage of multiple views. Basic to this philosophy is the idea that multiple media outlets create conditions in which it is possible for diverse views to be disseminated. Without that plurality, the number of voices that can potentially be heard is restricted.

It is difficult to disagree with this proposition. Those who look deeper at plurality, however, soon come to the conclusion that plurality itself is not a necessary and sufficient condition to create diverse content. 'Although the existence of multiple media outlets makes it theoretically possible for a larger number of views and opinions to be communicated, the mere existence of media plurality does not ensure message pluralism, that is, diversity of viewpoints' (Hilliard & Picard, 1989: 56). This gap between the provision of media plurality and the goal of diversity occurs because communications are clearly influenced by cultural, philosophical, political, and economic factors. Whenever communications is produced by or distributed through organised channels, the forces that affect their operations – such as time constraints and organisational structure, norms, and behaviour – play significant roles as well.

The problem of the limited effectiveness of channel pluralism has become increasingly evident in the 1980s and 1990s. The inability of media plurality to produce diverse content has been increasingly documented as producing homogenised, central viewpoints that promote dominant or acceptable frameworks of society and politics (Graber, McQuail & Norris, 1998; Brants, Hermes & Van Zoonen, 1998; Bennett, 1996; McQuail, 1992; Nimmo & Combs, 1990; Entman, 1989; Jamison & Campbell, 1988).

Although media pluralism alone cannot achieve the goal of diversity, it remains a condition that is necessary to ensure that the possibility can exist. Even the most well-meaning public service media monopolies produce limitations on diversity. Pluralism is needed to overcome such constraints, much less the hindrances to diversity inherent in commercial media. A variety of other factors are needed to overcome its limitations, including limited social and organisational constraints, autonomy on the part of those who create and select content, and avenues for effective public access (Picard, 1985). Even those factors are not sufficient conditions for innovative content and diverse viewpoints rising to the level of widespread awareness. Diversity and, indeed, the ability to truly innovate content are themselves limited by audience developments and structural limits inherent in contemporary communications systems.

Although it is clear that the number of communication products and services has clearly increased, any serious consideration of the content immediately leads one to the conclusions that innovation is limited and that significant diversity is not appearing in the generally available sources of information and entertainment.

Audiences and Audience Fragmentation

Discussions of communication rarely seriously dissect the concept of audiences, but rather make sweeping assumptions about their nature and behaviour by merely assuming their existence and structure. This is especially evident in the most widely read books about audiences of the 1990s (Webster & Phalen, 1997; Neuman, 1991; Webster & Lichty, 1991). In order to discuss audience developments and their effects on diversity and innovation, it is important to turn our attention first to the basic elements of audiences.

We need to understand the idea of the audience as an abstract concept denoting those persons who attend to a communications channel. It is not the population. It is not those who have access to a medium or channel. It is those who actually select a channel for use. The audience is the whole of those persons that is measured as a collective. Nevertheless, it is made up of individuals and the behaviour of these individuals dictates the behaviour of the audience. These individuals are different persons who use communications to satisfy their different wants and needs for information, ideas, and diversion in different ways. They spend different amounts of time serving their different wants with different media and in doing so create multiple audiences, that is, multiple collections of individuals seeking to serve those needs simultaneously.

The audience for a particularly media channel is never stable. It is a constantly changing collective. There is rarely a single audience for any media channel but rather there are many audiences in most channels. A central reality of audiences in a multiple channel world is that they cannot be controlled but can merely be courted.

The basic problems of audiences are compounded as the number of channels of communications increases. As the number of choices rise and individuals' behaviours diverge, the former audience fragments. Audience fragmentation, then, is then the process and result of de-massification of the audience, that is, the breakdown of a mass audience into smaller audiences. Audience fragmentation is the inevitable and unstoppable consequence of increasing the channels available to audiences. It is true whether one is discussing publishing, broadcasting, Internet, or other forms of communications involving multiple individuals.

The result of fragmentation can be clearly seen in the decline of average television audience share when the number of available channels increases (Figure 1). The share of the total television audience drops dramatically with the addition of each new channel. Whereas the share of the total audience is 100 percent with one channel, it plummets to an average share of 20 percent of the total audience with only 5 channels and then to 5 percent at 20 channels.

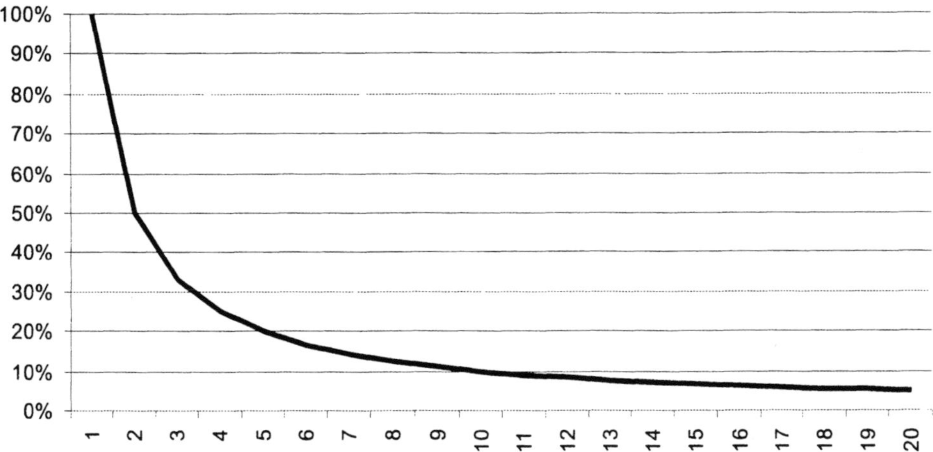

Figure 1 Effect of increasing channels on average share of television audience

When one looks beyond averages at actual television and cable markets, one finds that some channels must struggle to survive with only 1 or 2 percent shares after about a dozen channels are available because they fall below the average share of the total television audience. This occurs because it is rare that audiences watch each of the channels equally. This, of course, raises the question of whether individuals view channels or programmes. When the number of channels is low it appears that viewers tend to watch channels but as the number increases it is particular programmes that become attractive. Nevertheless there is a tendency for individuals to focus most viewing on a relatively few number of channels even in a multi-channel environment.

There appear to be some national and industry structural factors that reduce the rapid decline of audiences in some markets, however. National language can be a significant protection and higher than average ratings for domestic channels appear if other channels operate in other languages. Similarly, when domestic news, culture, and entertainment are available only from a few channels, these tend to get higher than average ratings.

All of these factors combine to create an environment in which managers' choices are significantly constrained and most pursue similar types of strategies that limit innovation and diversity.

Managerial Responses to Fragmentation

In order to survive in the highly competitive environment of fragmented audiences, media managers in broadcasting, cable, and publishing – especially magazine publishers – tend to engage in audience segmentation. This means that they work to serve an audience with characteristics that differ from the general audience for their medium.

The forces promoting these segmentation efforts are made possible by advances in audience measurement that stem from the audience fragmentation created by multiple channels, from audience polarisation to specific content of their choice, and from advertiser interests in reaching specialised audiences. Although some critics are willing to assign the causes of segmentation easily, no research has yet clearly answered the question of whether different communication channels create segmented audiences by content choices or whether segmented audiences create conditions in which managers seek to provide what the audiences wish. It is the basic question of whether the chicken or the egg came first, but it may be answerable by research.

New television and cable channels have typically tried to differentiate their audiences from the inception of the channels. They have adopted earlier strategies seen in magazines and radio of producing content with narrow appeal. From the business standpoint, these approaches are linked to strategies of product differentiation and the creation of brand identities. Audiences are increasingly being asked to think of different communications channels as distinct brands with distinct qualities.

It comes as no surprise to anyone who has studied the market economy that commercial communications firms have adopted these strategies. Differentiation and specialisation are means of business survival in a competitive environment if one wishes to avoid the inherent difficulties of price and cost competition. In terms of media, firms pursuing the segmentation strategy must seek narrowness of interests and topics. This occurs even in information content. One firm may chose to focus its content on business and financial news. A competitor may arise who carries business and financial news only of Europe. Another competitor may appear who focuses upon such news in Denmark and yet another firm may differentiate its product by including only business and financial news of Copenhagen.

These product differentiation choices are made to reduce the substitutability of content and audiences. The choices result in variety in content and appearance, differences in tone of presentation, and differences in the locations in which the products are primarily available. Such differences either serve or produce different audiences and thus different access to audience.

The growth of communications products and services has been primarily the result of managers finding content niches that serve increasingly fragmented audiences. The result of this proliferation of media has been *variety* rather than diversity. Television viewers at any time of the day can choose among a variety of genres (news, comedy, drama, action, talk shows) and – in markets with a large number of channels – between multiple shows of the same genre. Magazine readers can chose among scores of women's magazines or computer magazines. Listeners can chose among dozens of radio stations and formats. This is arguably a benefit to the public but it is not the same as receiving material with diverse viewpoints.

Limits to Diversity and Innovation

We would do well to consider whether the lack of diversity is real or whether diverse content is just not perceived or rejected.

I would like to suggest that the primary limitation to diversity is not the result of conspiracy, media structure, or economics but stems from the fact that most human beings do not wish to be confronted with diverse views and opinions. Although political theorists argue strongly that the public needs such diversity, behavioural scientists have clearly established that the public – for the most part – is uninterested in diversity and will typically reject it through selective perception and recall even if they are exposed to it. I also believe that audiences may not have a very high regard for diversity because the persons who most argue for diversity are persons like us with particular agendas with which they may disagree. If content providers – no matter how benevolent or malevolent – believe the public does not wish to hear certain viewpoints, it becomes difficult to convince them to seek and carry large amounts of diverse materials and ideas.

Second, I would like to argue that there is a large availability of diversity in voices of organisations and their communications, opinion journals, and new media. The problem is not the lack of diverse voices but rather that the mere availability of diverse voices is insufficient because potential readers, listeners, and viewers do not know that other voices exist. The result is that those who are directly interested in these diverse views share them only among themselves. Others are left ignorant of the availability of these views. This problem exists even in the relatively unrestricted Internet because there are significant limitations on the ability to gain notice in order for diverse voices to be heard. Even if persons wish to find diverse information their search on the net is constrained because the best search engines today cover only about one-fifth of the total sites.

It is as if one is speaking in one's seat in a premier league football match and hoping other spectators can hear what you have to say. Even if a spectator across the stadium might wish to hear if they knew something interesting is being spoken, there is no way for them to gain that knowledge or to effectively hear.

The babel of the Internet can only be partly overcome through significant search engine improvements and dramatic improvements in indexing of sites and contents. Even if those steps are achieved, the attention of significant groups of persons can only be achieved if one gains prominent display on a well-used portal.

Structural Limits to Diversity

But even that will not solve the problem. For all our complaints about the lack of diversity in media, we have scores of examples of diverse content that has not had a significant impact on the perceptions of the general public. This ranges from well-organised public access television and community radio to all manner of print materials and online sites carrying information and propaganda for many diverse organisations and groups.

One must also recognise that there are some structural limits that hamper the ability of managers of more widely utilised media to carry diverse materials. We all recognise how the need to increase audience consumption through better ratings or circulation affects managerial choices in commercial media but we need to remember that similar forces are at work in non-commercial media as well. Personnel in both types of institutions receive career rewards – if not significant monetary rewards – for serving broad audiences that are most responsive to comfortable content.

At the same time, significant financial limitations caused by audience fragmentation tend to create situations in which whatever diversity existed is diminished or when it is presented or conveyed in a way designed to enhance social norms.

Spiral Effect of Increasing Media Outlets and Declining Content Investment

The increase in media cannot be expected to increase diverse views reaching audiences because it constantly reduces the size of audiences and resources available to managers to pursue quality and diversity. As shown in Figure 2, there is a direct link between the increasing number of media outlets and resources available for content. The fragmentation of the audience ultimately requires that the cost of content be reduced.

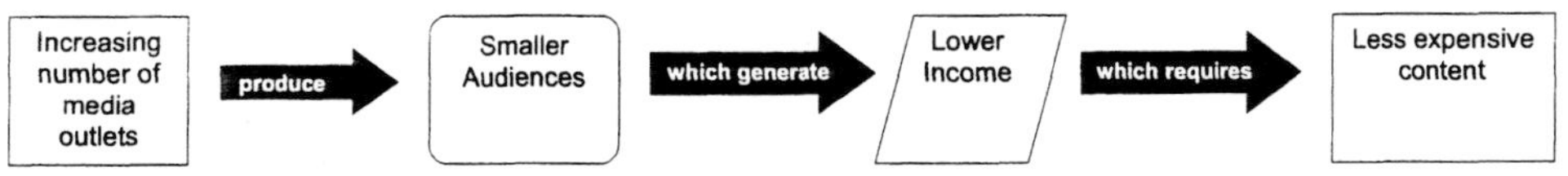

Figure 2 Effect of increasing media outlets on audiences, income, and content

The process compounds itself and transforms into a spiral, however, because cheap content becomes less desirable to audiences as illustrated in Figure 3.

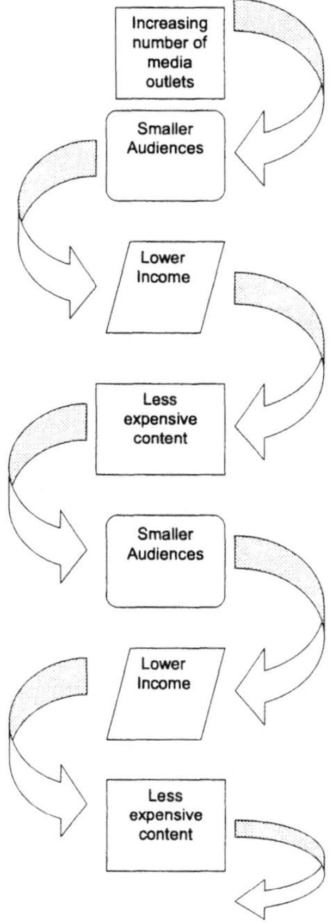

Figure 3 Spiral effect of increasing media outlets and declining content investment

In television, for example, this link between the effect of the average audience, programme investment, and type of programming is manifest in the production of game shows, café programmes, inexpensive children's shows such as cartoons, and phone-in shows, as well as longer programmes, more reruns, and the acquisition of syndicated programmes. Today, when productions are created there tends to be the use of fewer cameras, less expensive actors and personalities, less taping on location, and less time for editing and other post-production. In addition, television programmers are increasingly outsourcing production because it is less expensive, often requires a commitment to fewer episodes, and can be cancelled more easily if the shows are unsuccessful.

Structural Limits to Creativity and Risk Taking

The willingness and ability of managers of media to truly innovate content are also affected by the resource problem. Innovation is also limited by a variety of other factors, not the least of which is creativity in developing new formats, genres, modes of presentation, and type of media products and services. The limitation of creativity is present in both commercial and non-commercial media.

In considering and proposing programming, both programmers and producers seek to duplicate successful formulas to attract a different part of the fragmented audience. This again limits creativity and innovation. It must be recognised that the persons who make such decisions are few and that they operate in an environment in which employment is increasingly tenuous. Because success is critical to their continued employment, the measurement of successful performance is immediate and short-term. In commercial television, for example, performance in terms of achieving ratings is measured daily, weekly, and monthly and a programmer's employment is measured in months, not years. Even magazines tend to measure the success of publishers and editors monthly.

Another limit on diversity is the economies of scale and scope in producing programmes and publications of similar formats in the television and magazine industries. If a television studio is set up for a talk show, one can more cheaply produce other talk shows within the same facility. If a magazine company produces multiple magazines for different audiences, it can use common formats, the same infrastructure, and common production and distribution mechanisms to achieve significant savings.

An added problem is that that professional media education and the norms of professionalism in content, design, and methods of operation also hinder the ability to innovate or limit the willingness of managers to take risks.

Another hindrance to innovation is that managers cannot project how audiences will respond to innovation and, in the case of commercial operations, how advertisers will respond. These factors create significant risks that investments in innovation will be lost and that innovation may then produce negative results on careers of the those who innovate.

Conclusions

Diminished resources for content producers and the development of product differentiation and audience segmentation strategies have accompanied audience fragmentation resulting from the proliferation of media units.

It is clear that the economics and management of media plurality, content production, marketing, and distribution conflict with the goals of innovation and diversity. It is arguable that the desirable outcomes of significant innovation and real diversity can be produced only when the number of competitors and audience fragmentation within mainstream communications is limited and/or public policies encourage or demand such outcomes.

If we accept these views, we are led to the conclusion that the trends toward fragmentation and narrowness run counter to the social needs of European integration and global understanding. This, of course, leads to the very real questions of how one can force the public to attend to diverse messages that exist outside the mainstream, and even if such force is desirable, or whether mechanisms can be sought to ensure that the main media enhance diversity within themselves.

The Need for Stimulation Policies

I would like to suggest that the most effective way to overcome the constraints on innovation and diversity in commercialised and other primary media is not merely to argue over whether and the extent to which concentration exists and how to respond to it, but to provide incentives for publishers, programmers, and producers that overcome the financial and internal constraints on innovation and diversity.

One of the reasons for failure of European Union and other organisations to effectively respond to the problem is that legal and philosophical bases of competition and industrial policies are based on arguments and precedents that cannot effectively address issues of diversity and content innovation. All is not lost, however. I would like to suggest that national and regional cultural policies – which have significantly different bases – can be utilised to provide incentives for including diverse content within existing programmes and publications and for encouraging risk taking through innovation.

By being provided with access to new financial resources, both commercial and non-commercial media can be induced to broaden or enhance their offerings. This might take the form of subsidies for audio, video, or multimedia productions, publications, or articles that improve the quality of content and serve the interests of diversity and innovation. Such aid might take the form of grants for travel to gather information or other materials. It might also take the form of support for marketing and distributing less commercial and less widely available materials.

Similarly, support can be provided to enhance access of diverse groups to existing channels and publications in a way that it is also desirable to programmers and publishers. This is important to ensure that the material is of high quality and not placed within ghettos of unpopular time slots or distribution channels less widely available or utilised. One can also use policies designed to lessen some of the economic and structural problems for individuals and groups who wish to communicate by encouraging the creation of facilities with competent personnel and facilities that can be commonly used. Similarly, joint production and distribution schemes should be encouraged. These processes would extend the economies of scale and scope that commercial content producers seek to those who create diverse content.

There are no easy solutions to the difficulties caused by audience fragmentation and the structural limits inherent in the contemporary media and communication system. Some may argue that there is a need to completely alter the current structure and operations of the system to achieve the goals of diversity and innovation. The environment in which the system is operating, the forces promoting its current operations, and the forces directing in into the next century clearly make that impossible without significantly altering the capitalist and liberal democratic system that has spawned the current milieu.

In short, providing inducements to better performance to overcome existing constraints is the only effective method of respond in the near future.

References

Bennett, W. L.

1996 *News: The Politics of Illusion.* 2nd edition. New York: Longman.

Brants, K., Hermes, J. and Van Zoonen, L., (eds.)

1998 *The Media in Question: Popular Culture and Public Interests.* London: Sage.

Entman, R.M.
1989 *Democracy without Citizens: Media and the Decay of American Politics.* New York: Oxford University Press.

Graber, D., McQuail, D. and Norris, P.
1998 *The Politics of News: The News of Politics.* Washington, DC: Congressional Quarterly Press.

Hilliard, R.L. and Picard, R.G.
1989 Plurality, Diversity, and Prohibitions on Television-Newspaper Crossownership. *The Journal of Media Economics* 2 (1): 55-65.

Jamison, K.H. and Campbell, K.K.
1988 *The Interplay of Influence.* 2nd edition. Belmont, Calif.: Wadsworth.

McQuail, D.
1992 *Media Performance. Mass Communication and the Public Interest.* London: Sage.

Nimmo, D. and Combs, J.E.
1990 *Mediated Political Realities.* 2nd edition. New York: Longman.

Neuman, W.
1991 *The Future of Mass Audience.* Cambridge, Mass.: Cambridge University Press.

Picard, R.G.
1985 *The Press and the Decline of Democracy: The Social Democratic Approach in Public Policy.* Westport, Conn.: Greenwood Press.

Webster, J. G. and Lichty, L.
1991 *Ratings Analysis: Theory and Practice.* Hillsdale, NJ: Lawrence Erlbaum Associates.

Webster, J. and Phalen, P.
1997 *The Mass Audience: Rediscovering the Dominant Model.* Mahwah, NJ: Lawrence Erlbaum Associations.

Competition, Innovation and Diversity in Media

National Newspaper Markets

IORDAN IOSSIFOV
The Amsterdam School of Communications Research *ASCoR*,
University of Amsterdam, The Netherlands

Abstract

This paper presents a research project that studies the interrelations between competition, innovation and diversity in national newspaper markets. The objective of the study is to test a general hypothesis on competition, media innovation and diversity (called the CoMInDi hypothesis) by comparing newspaper markets in the Netherlands, the United Kingdom, Spain and Germany. This paper presents the theoretical model and the research outline.

Introduction

In recent years the world has been through some notable changes. Among the most significant of these changes is that fast moving industries like IT, telecommunication and media intersect their development in a point which could be regarded as one of the fundaments of the information society. Competition and new technologies are seen as central forces leading to these changes. Competition is a primarily economic phenomenon but also has social impacts.

Some aspects of the social importance of competition are discussed in this paper. It presents a research project into the dependence of innovation and diversity of general news services on competition. The objective of the study is to test a general hypothesis on competition, media innovation and diversity that was developed at The Amsterdam School of Communications Research *ASCoR* and initially presented by Van Cuilenburg in several papers (Van Cuilenburg, 1999a; Van Cuilenburg, 1999b; Van Cuilenburg, 1999c; Van Cuilenburg & McQuail, 1998). Since it concerns the relationship between competition, media innovation and diversity, this hypothesis is called the CoMInDi hypothesis. This paper proposes that the CoMInDi hypothesis should be tested by studying competition among media organisations, innovation and diversity concerning a particular media product and public policy applied to media. The study will compare newspaper markets in the Netherlands, the UK, Spain and Germany over a period of 15 years.

The results of the study could be useful for several categories of professionals in their work:

- for policy makers in formulating the objectives and means of policy towards media;
- for audiences – ultimately this research studies factors that influence one of the most important elements of media performance for audiences, namely diversity;
- for media analysts and managers in formulating their competitive strategies; and
- for consultants, especially media consultants and people from trade and professional organisations (publishers, advertisers, journalists) in their efforts to help media organisations improve performance.

The Theoretical Model of the Research

The model of the research is based mainly on the CoMInDi hypothesis. However, it incorporates other theoretical developments in the field of (media) economics and communication science, including industrial organisation theory and especially the Structure-Conduct-Performance (SCP) paradigm (as presented by Wirth & Bloch, 1995); the media organisational model (McQuail, 1992: 87); and Porter's model of competitive forces that drive competition (Porter, 1980: 4).

Competition as Structure and Behaviour

The research addresses competition as dual category which could be expressed in terms of competitive structure and competitive behaviour. Competitive structure provides the framework in which media organisations operate. It describes the economic environment in which media function. It is a relatively static category.[1] Its dynamic correspondence is

1 The phrase 'relatively static category' should not be interpreted as if competitive structure is unchangeable. Competitive structure is stable only in short to middle term period of time. In long term periods competitive structure also changes. The term 'static' is used only to underline the opposition with the dynamism of competitive conduct.

the competitive behaviour of the same media organisations that form the market structure. Through their behaviour they interact with the market and social actors.

The theoretical model presented here follows the classical SCP paradigm. Structure has a fundamental role in the model. However, competition is a dynamic concept. Structure and conduct are regarded as two sides of the same coin. They are different expressions of the same phenomenon: competition. Structure gives the snap-shot of it and conduct is its dynamic dimension.

Competition as structure in the model refers to industry concentration, revenue distribution, industry dynamics, consumer loyalty and audience concentration. The selection of these variables follows from the fact that the research studies oligopolistic newspaper markets.

There are different types of oligopolies and it is necessary to distinguish between them in order to define what kind of oligopolistic structure dominates each market. Defining the type of oligopoly will be done by measuring industry concentration. On the basis of the level of industry concentration, a market could be defined as a tight or a loose / symmetric oligopoly. The former represents a moderate competitive structure; the latter presupposes fierce competition.

The other variables mentioned will help to refine the picture of the competitive structure for each market studied. These variables measure the relevant competitive forces that drive competition according to Porter's model (Porter, 1980: 4).

Competitive conduct encompasses the different strategies that media organisations apply. It refers to pricing, product strategy, advertising and innovation (McQuail, 1992: 87). When companies define their strategies, they take into account different factors. Among the most important ones is the environment in which they operate: the structural characteristics of the market. Under different structural circumstances companies choose different strategies. This is the way competitive structure influences competitive conduct.

Degrees of Competition, Innovation and Diversity

Different competitive structures and related competitive strategies can be expressed in terms of different degrees of competition. 'Fierce' competition is competition on prices to acquire a market share in rivalry with another media organisation, whereas 'moderate' competition is competition on content (Van Cuilenburg, 1999c: 4).

As explained above, the newspaper markets are oligopolistic and the terms 'moderate' and 'fierce' should be positioned in this oligopolistic context. Table 1 presents what correspondences are expected between 'moderate' and 'fierce' competitive structures and competitive strategies on the researched markets.

Table I Competitive structure and competitive conduct

Competition	*Structural Aspects*	*Behavioural Aspects*
Moderate	- Tight/asymmetric oligopoly - Industry growth/stagnation - Equal/optimal revenue distribution - High consumer loyalty - Level of audience concentration less than thisl of industry concentration	- *Product* Innovation - Strategy based on product differentiation - Publishers target more than one consumer group
Fierce	- Loose/symmetric oligopoly - Industry decline - Unequal revenue distribution - Low consumer loyalty - Level of audience concentration corresponding to this of industry concentration	- Process innovation - Strategy based on price - More than one publishers target one consumer group

Innovation is regarded part of the competitive conduct of companies (McQuail, 1992: 87; Wirth & Bloch, 1995: 17). Under different circumstances companies focus on different types of innovation. This choice depends on companies' basic competitive strategy. If publishers compete on prices they need to produce cheaper, therefore they need to implement innovations that lead to a lowering of costs and prices, i.e. process innovation. On the other hand, strategies that are built on the basis of introducing new products should rely on product innovation.

Diversity is one of the criteria for media performance. As such its importance has been well recognised (McQuail & Van Cuilenburg, 1983; McQuail, 1992; Wirth & Bloch, 1995; Van Cuilenburg 1999a; Van Cuilenburg 1999b; Van Cuilenburg 1999c; Van der Wurff, Van Cuilenburg & Keune, 2000).

Diversity on media markets could be defined as 'the variety of media products that are available to media users' (Van der Wurff, Van Cuilenburg & Keune, 2000: 120).

There are different types of diversity. On the one hand, there is reflective diversity where 'media content proportionally reflects differences in politics, religion, culture and social conditions in society' (Van Cuilenburg, 1999a: 190). This is somehow 'quantitative' diversity: it is a kind of diversity where the 'bigger' (the larger consumer group) gets the more (i.e. content supplied). On the other hand, there is open diversity, where 'perfectly equal attention is given to all identifiable preferences streams or groups or positions in society' (Van Cuilenburg, 1999a: 190).

This 'perfectly equal access' (Van Cuilenburg, 1999a: 190) provides opportunities for qualitatively different preferences to be expressed or satisfied.

The main CoMInDi hypothesis suggests that fierce competition and presumably process innovation lead to reflective diversity, whereas moderate competition and product innovation convey open diversity. Fierce competition is associated with competition on price and process innovation. This ultimately leads to reflective diversity i.e. following and reproducing existing preferences. Moderate competition allows media organisations to invest in product innovation and consequently to provide open diversity to the public. Innovation is thus considered to offer the connection between competition and diversity.

Public Policy

The research takes into account the fact that the media business is not 'business as any other business' and that it has a specific political and cultural role. Thus it is normal that social pressure on media is stronger than on most other businesses. As a rule this social pressure is institutionalised in public policy.

Van Cuilenburg and McQuail define public policy as follows: '[p]olicies in general refer to conscious (public) projects for achieving some goal, together with the proposed means and time schedule of achieving them' (Van Cuilenburg & McQuail, 1998: 57). In some countries public policy has an objective to secure specified characteristics of media performance. Means to achieve the goals of such a policy could be economic (e.g. subsidies, tax exemptions etc.) or legal (e.g. special regulations) intervention. In contrast in other countries the main objective of public policy is to guarantee freedom from any intervention. The means to accomplish such an objective could be to create rules for a market oriented environment where authorities act as an arbiter (i.e. they act only when there is a claim that the rules have been broken). The former type of policy is called 'specific' (referring to its objective of providing' specified output) whereas the latter is called 'general'. The term 'general' points out that newspapers are not treated differently from any other media and that even the rules for the media are general free-market-economy rules of non-intervention.

Given the definitions above it could be suggested that specific media policy has a mitigating effect on competition, possibly encouraging product innovation which is beneficial for open diversity. On the other hand, the more general approach towards the media as an industry underlines the existing competitive structure and forces the media to take competition into greater consideration when formulating their competitive strategies. This is due to the fact that media organisations cannot rely on assistance from outside the market. Thus, presumably the output of 'general' public policy inclines towards reflective diversity.

The Model

Presented graphically the theoretical model of the research is as follows:

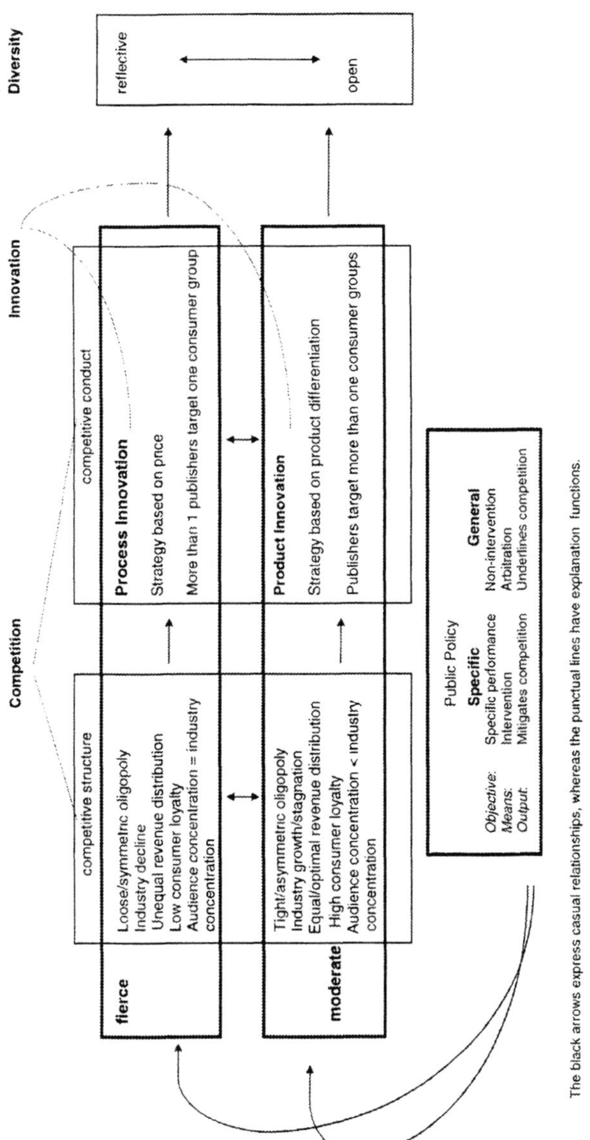

Figure 1 Theoretical model

This theoretical model is the starting point for the research. The research question will runs as follows: What is the impact of competition among media organisations on innovation and consequently on diversity of daily news services for the general public and how does public policy influence this impact?

The Research Design

The answer to the research question follows from the sum of the answers to the following sub-questions:

1. What is the degree of competition between media organisations in the relevant markets? What type of competitive strategies do media organisations apply?
2. What type of innovation do media organisations apply in the researched markets?
3. What type of diversity is typical for each of the researched markets?

Answering these sub-questions provides the data for the major categories of the research. Once this information is available it should be possible to check if developments in the real markets confirm the hypothesised relations among the different categories. Thus the next set of questions to be answered is:

4. What is the impact of (different degrees of) competition among media organisations on innovation? Do different degrees of competition lead to different types of innovation?
5. What is the impact of (different degrees of) competition among media organisations on diversity? Do different degrees of competition lead to different types of diversity? What is the mechanism of influence?
6. How does innovation on national newspaper markets influence diversity? Is there a relation between different types of innovation and different types of diversity?

The research question addresses also public policy towards the media. This is necessary because public policy could have its own impact on the whole relationship between competition, innovation and diversity. So yet other questions to be answered are:

7. What are the different policy approaches implemented in the different countries? To what extend does public policy towards media have an impact on the relationship between competition, innovation and diversity and what is the mechanism of this impact?

Definitions and Methods

The research studies national newspaper markets of four member states of the European Union. The countries were selected after a preliminary research. The objective of the selection was to identify markets with different degrees of competition and different public policies. The four selected countries are the Netherlands, the UK, Spain and Germany.

It is worth noting that only when competition is concerned the term 'national newspaper market' is proper. In order to make the research feasible, innovation and diversity will be addressed only for a part of the newspaper content: namely, the news supply, for which the term 'daily news services for the general public' is being used.

As mentioned, national newspaper markets are oligopolistic. This feature is taken into account in the theoretical part when defining 'moderate' and 'fierce' competition. On the methodological level the oligopolistic nature of the national newspaper markets influences the way all theoretical concepts (except for diversity) are transformed into variables. Competition is studied in its two dimensions: competitive structure and competitive policy. The main variables defining competitive structure are: degree of oligopoly, industry dynamics, revenue distribution, consumer loyalty, and ratio between audience concentration and industry concentration. The degree of oligopoly is identified by the level of concentration (by using the Hirschman-Herfindahl Index). Industry dynamics shows if there are conditions for competition on market share. Revenue distribution reflects the fact that media operate on a dual product market (Picard, 1989: 18). Consumer loyalty and the ratio between audience concentration and industry concentration address the 'bargaining power' of readers.

Studying competitive conduct emphasises the type of competitive strategies: if the publishers on the respective market compete on price or on product, if they compete with other publishers for one and the same consumer group and what type of innovation they focus on.

Public policy is to be studied in terms of its objectives, means, and effects.

Diversity is the most difficult concept to be transformed into operational variables. In the theoretical framework a definition of diversity is given and a distinction between reflective and open diversity is made. According to the theoretical framework, reflective diversity mirrors public preferences in a proportional way. Thus the starting point for studying types of diversity should be public preferences. Then an assessment should be made as to what extent these and the actual newspaper supply overlap. Such assessment can be made only after studying the type and content of the news supplied. In order to make the research feasible, only part of the content is to be studied. This part is the leading news. Measuring diversity of 'top news stories' is to be done by assessing the space and the place devoted to different news items. The news that is placed on the front page and that is given larger space is to be regarded as 'top news'.

The research applies a multiple-method design. In order to compare the four markets, analysis of primary and secondary sources, interviews and front-page analyses are to be used. Studying competitive structure and public policy will be mainly done by analysis of primary and secondary sources. Interviews will be used to provide information on competitive conduct of publishers. By analysing to what topics newspapers devote their front pages the diversity will be studied.

Conclusion

Competition has always had its social impact but the recent developments have made it an increasingly important topic for social science and particularly for communication science. The proposed research is part of this trend. The suggested study takes into account the economic nature of competition but is also concerned with its social impact. The model introduced in this paper is a starting point for the study. The model is based on the CoMInDi hypothesis that suggests an approach to explain how different degrees of competition could lead to a different output in terms of media performance.

References

McQuail, D.
1992 *Media Performance. Mass Communication and the Public Interest.* London: Sage.
McQuail, D. and Van Cuilenburg, J.
1983 Diversity as a media policy goal: A strategy for evaluative research and a Netherlands case study. *Gazette* 31 (3): 145-162.
Picard, R.
1989 *Media Economics. Concepts and Issues.* London: Sage.
Porter, M.
1980 *Competitive Strategy.* New York: The Free Press.
Van Cuilenburg, J.
1999a On competition, access and diversity in media, old and new. Some remarks for communications policy in the information age. *New Media & Society*, 1 (2): 183-207.

Van Cuilenburg, J.
1999b Between media monopoly and ruinous media competition. On media access and diversity in open societies. In Y.N. Zassoursky and E. Vartanova (eds.), *Media, Communication and the Open Society*, pp. 40-61. Moscow: Faculty of Journalism/IKAR Publisher.

Van Cuilenburg, J.
1999c *Design, Notes and Hypothesis CoMInDi-Research Project.* Mimeo. *ASCoR.*

Van Cuilenburg, J. and McQuail, D.
1998 Media policy paradigm shifts. In search of a new communications policy paradigm. In R.G. Picard (ed.), *Evolving Media Markets: Effects of Economic and Policy Changes*, pp. 57-80. Turku: The Economic Research Foundation for Mass Communication.

Van der Wurff, R., Van Cuilenburg, J. and Keune, G.
2000 Competition, media innovation and diversity in broadcasting. In J. van Cuilenburg and R. van der Wurff (eds.), *Media and Open Societies*, pp. 119-157. Amsterdam: Het Spinhuis.

Wirth, M.O and Bloch, H.
1995 Industrial organization theory and media industry analysis. *The Journal of Media Economics*, 8 (2): 15-26.

Part IV

NEW MEDIA AND EMPOWERMENT

Reinventing Roots

New Media and National Identity

PIET BAKKER
The Amsterdam School of Communications Research *ASCoR*,
University of Amsterdam, The Netherlands

Abstract

The Internet can be a very important vehicle for the transmission of ideas concerning a national identity, particular for people who have lost or left their homeland. This identity is presented as very complete and historic enduring, and going back for several thousand years. Completeness of the identity means presenting it with as many aspects as possible: art, culture, music, cuisine, flags, anthems, tourism, politics etc. These finding are derived from a pilot study on 30 websites of Kurd, Armenian and Macedonian origin.[1]

Introduction: Internet Users

In the second half of the nineties the amount of Internet users has grown beyond imagination. Never before we saw such a rapid introduction of a new medium. Although research on Internet use and Internet users is often badly documented, confusing and contradictory, it is clear that the vast majority of Internet users are found in the Western world and in some parts of Asia. In the US 60 to 90 million people (20 to 30% of the population) can use the Internet. In the Netherlands the estimated amount is 2.7 million (14% of the population above 16). In Scandinavian and other North European countries these figures are even higher, in Denmark 22% of the population uses the Internet; in Finland 28%, in Sweden and Iceland almost half of the population is accessing the Internet. In Southern and Eastern Europe these figures are lower (France: 5%; Czech Republic 3%, Greece: 1%) and in most African, Asian, and South American countries figures stay well below 1% (Headcount, 1999;

---

1 A web-version with all relevant hyperlinks of this article is available on <http:// home.pscw.uva.nl/bakker/roots.html>.

Digital Living Room Consumer Index, 1999; National Telecommunications and Information Administration, 1999). (All figures are estimations made for 1998 and 1999.)

The unequal distribution of Internet users is somewhat superficial. When we look more closely at some of the users, it is clear there are many users from so-called 'underdeveloped Internet countries' online. Immigrants, students and professionals, who left their countries of birth, devote much of their time (and webspace) to their region of origin. In this research we will concentrate on this group of users: strangers in a strange land, but keeping a close tie with their roots.

Internet Use

The amount of pages people could access has reached an astonishing figure. It was estimated at 800 million in the middle of 1999 (Lawrence & Giles, 1999). The possibilities of the Internet are growing likewise; we are far beyond just sending and receiving e-mail and watching www-pages with text and pictures. We can listen to live radio, concerts, CD-tracks, watch television or movies, download software, participate in a chat session, a video conference or an online game and buy things online. This last possibility is one of the most recent Internet 'hypes'; it is responsible both for the high prices that are paid for Internet companies and for the bulk of publicity about the Internet.

This publicity distracts our attention from questions like who are these users, how do they use the Internet, and how does this affect their lives? In this article we will focus on these questions. More specifically, we will study the relation between the content of Internet pages and their users.

Virtual Communities

When we look more closely at the way people use the Internet, we see that a fair amount of usage is not exactly 'new'. Like before, people book holidays, collect pictures of their favourite movie star or take a quick look at today's headlines. The means of finding information is new, the information sought is not. But not all usage can be written off as 'a new means for old habits'. Sometimes people participate in activities that cannot be compared to any other media use, most of all because of the interactivity of the Internet. The classic example is *online gaming*; people participate in a *virtual community* and play a chosen role, they communicate with others, form clans, become friends with other users, send each other messages etc. This sort of usage is tied to the medium; these communities are impossible without the Internet.

These virtual communities are responsible for only a small part of Internet usage. Much more common are existing 'communities' with a virtual 'branch'. Soccer fans are not a virtual community but participate also in virtual communities, they have mailing lists, websites and chat channels. This also applies to Rolling Stones fans, Macintosh users, white supremacists, believers in the flatness of the earth, Muslim fanatics and breeders of Dalmatian dogs. These 'communities' existed before the Internet and can exist without it. They had other ways of communicating; newsletters and magazines and personal communication: local or regional gatherings, phone conversations and letters. The Internet gave these communities extra possibilities: communication is faster, can be more frequent and is possible for more people.

We use the term 'communities' without a definition but as the above examples indicate, there are many different sorts of communities. The main difference seems to lie in the scope of the communities: there are 'one issue' communities (music lovers, dog breeders, Mac users, believers in the flatness of the earth) while white supremacists and Muslim fanatics share some sort of common ideology. We are mainly interested in this last sort of communities, people who share common ideas or believes which are not limited to one topic and participate in one way or another in sharing, promoting and defending these ideas or believes.

National 'Homeless' Communities

We will concentrate here on one special category of communities with a very strong common feeling: national communities without a nation. People like the Kurds or Armenians who have been scattered all over the earth, still have succeeded in maintaining a national identity without a nation state. This used to take place within local or regional communities but the Internet offers different possibilities for these communities. For the first time they can organise world-wide, reach new members and communicate with these 'members' more often.

Our research question is how these communities use the Internet; how do they organise their information, how do they present their tradition and how do they define their national identity.

Case Studies

Three different 'virtual nations' are selected for this research:

- KURDS. A true virtual nation. Kurds are living in the traditional Kurdish regions in Turkey, Iraq, Iran, Syria and Russia and of course all over the world.
- MACEDONIANS. Only a nation state since a few years and having a conflict with their neighbour Greece over territories.
- ARMENIANS. Spread all over world after the genocide in 1915. Since 1991 they are an Armenian nation but according some Armenians, a great part of western Armenia is still occupied by Turkey.

For every nation 10 websites were chosen. This was done with the search engine DirectHit <www.directhit.com> which ranks sites by popularity. Only sites with a lot of visitors were chosen. In some cases there were more than 1.6 million visits. A first finding is that there is no problem finding these sites. There are hundreds of sites devoted to 'virtual nations'. They do exist.

Research questions concentrated on the 'how'. How do people see their identity, what do they show to visitors, how do they define their national identity? A more general question is how important is the Internet in constructing this national identity? We cannot really answer this question because users should be interviewed to shed some light on this question. But the fact that there are so many websites devoted to virtual nations is an indication it could be very important. Analysis of guestbooks, forums or webboards gives us additional information: the virtual nation lives.

Results

Analysing 30 websites is not an easy task but after seeing only a few the pattern becomes clear. Almost every site devoted to a virtual nation has the same elements: completeness, symbols, maps, history, news, politics and actuality.

COMPLETENESS. In most cases the webmasters (who for the most part do not live in their regions of birth but in the USA, Sweden, Denmark, the Netherlands, Germany, Canada) want to cover every aspect of life on their websites: history, culture (art, music, architecture, poetry, literature), economics, women's issues, geography, geology, anthropology. But things like traditional recipes, folktales and tourism are not forgotten.

SYMBOLS. Flags, coats of arms and anthems are very prominent displayed. The same goes for historic relics and places of interest.

MAPS. Making clear what belongs to their country and what does not is an important aspect. Kurdish maps show how their region is in five different countries, Armenians show that Turkey occupies the western part of their country while Macedonians show that half of their country lies in Greece.

HISTORY. Important facts are repeated over and over again. In particular massacres by Turkey, Iraq, Iran, Bulgaria, Greece. History is ancient. Macedonian history goes back to a time before Alexander the Great, Kurds go back to Mesopotamia while Noah's ark (and the roots of the whole western and Christian civilisation) is located in Armenia.

NEWS, POLITICS AND ACTUALITY. Links to al kinds of media, reprints of articles in elite news media (New York Times), reprints of documents of international organisations (UN, Human Rights Watch, and Amnesty International). Conflicts with other parties are covered: with the Kurdish community, between Armenians and Turks, between Macedonians and Greeks.

Conclusion

These websites are more than a virtual nation. Their aim is to construct a true nation. And it is done by presenting it as complete and historic as possible. It is very possible that the Internet plays an important role in the creation of this kind of identity. It is almost impossible to create it with other (traditional) means. Further research should be more systematic and explore more complex dimensions of national identity while it could be extended to other virtual nations. Users and visitors (and the people behind the websites) could be studied in more detail.

References

Digital Living Room Consumer Index
1999 <http://www.greenfieldcentral.com/dlrci/index.html>.
Headcount
1999 <http://www.headcount.com/>.
Lawrence, S. and Giles, C.L.
1999 *Accessibility of Information on the Web*, 8 July. <http://www.nature.com/server-java/Propub/nature/400107A0.frameset?context-toc>.
National Telecommunications and Information Administration
1999 *Falling Through the Net: Defining the Digital Divide.* <http://www.ntia.doc.gov/ntiahome/fttn99/execsummary.html>.

Annex: Websites studied

Kurdistan

Homepage of KAMARAN KAKEL with map, brief history (who are the Kurds) and the story (with pictures) of the attack on the village of Halabja in March 1988 by the Iraqi government. (Hosted in Canada).

Homepage of AZAD with history, map, flag, culture, language, literature, music, mailinglist etc. (Hosted in Sweden).

ROJBAS: Magazine in Kurdish and Turkish. (Hosted in Sweden).

KDP: Kurdistan Democratic Party-Iraq. Founded in 1946 by Mustafa Barzani (14.03.1903 - 01.03.1979) who features still very prominent on almost any KDP-site. The site has links to Australian, French, Danish, Spanish, Canadian and German branches of the party. It further contains documents about KDP, links to Kurdistan television, press releases and information about culture, media, history, tourism, industry etc. (Hosted in Sweden).

The WASHINGTON KURDISH INSTITUTE (WKI): History, links, geography, culture. (Hosted in the USA).

The PATRIOTIC UNION OF KURDISTAN (PUK). Founded in 1975 in Iraq (split from Barzani's KDP party). Links to UK, Australian, Canadian, American, Kurdistan, Russian and French branches. (Hosted in Germany).

The KURDISH INFORMATION NETWORK. Culture, music, language, history. (Hosted in The Netherlands).

KURDISH WORLDWIDE RESOURCES. Origins, demographics, language, geography, geology, maps, literature, art etc. (Hosted in the USA).

KURDISTAN WEB. Hosted on the German human rights server. Art, people, geography, anthropology, maps, literature, architecture, history, language, news, music, flag, links to personal pages etc. (100,000 visits since 1995). (Hosted in Germany).

AKAKURDISTAN. Images and stories on history and culture of the Kurds: 'a place for collective memory and cultural exchange'. (Hosted in the USA).

Macedonia

VIRTUAL MACEDONIA. Culture, religion, people, cuisine, sport etc. (Hosted in the USA).

FYROM. Former Yugoslav Republic of Macedonia. Economy, defence, geography, government, people. (Hosted in Macedonia).

MACEDONIA FOR THE MACEDONIANS. Pleading for an undivided Macedonia: surrender of the Greek part to Macedonia; history, human rights, language, Greek propaganda, culture, music, books, current events, latest news. Discussion forum. (55,000 visits since July 1997). (Hosted in the USA).

REPUBLIC OF MACEDONIA. Art, history, politics, flag, anthem, constitution, movie, facts and figures, tourism. (Location of host unknown).

MACEDONIA FAQ. Information, cuisine, politics, economy, religion, art, history. (Hosted in the USA).
WHAT ABOUT MACEDONIA. Personal page with pictures and some information. (Hosted in the USA).
SLAVIC RESEARCH CENTRE. Links and information: history, culture, people, news on conflict with Greece, geography. (Hosted in Japan).
PAN-MACEDONIAN NETWORK. In English and Greek, '4000 years of Greek civilization'. Emphasis on history. And information on culture, sports, news, organisations and tourism. From a Greek perspective. (Hosted in Greece).
MACEDONIA BY NIKOLAOS MARTIS. Former foreign minister. History and politics. Author of: *The Falsification of the history of Macedonia.* (Hosted in Greece).

Armenia

ARMENIA ONLINE COM. books, music, news, weather, famous Armenians, culture and art. 'Armenians have been scattered all over the world as refugees. Living in unfamiliar lands, we as Armenians, have made our mark in many different places and fields' (1.6 million visitors). (Hosted in the USA).
CILICIA.COM. Famous Armenians, genocide, cookbook, church (375 pages.) (Hosted in the USA).
ARMENIA. History, economy, defence, geography, government, people. (Hosted in the USA).
SOROS.ARMENIA. General information on current situation. (Hosted in the USA).
ARMENIA. Extensive links-collection. (Hosted in the USA).
WESTERN ARMENIA INSTITUTE. Site 'dedicated to the history and future of western Armenia which is, for now, occupied by the Republic of Turkey.' (Location of host unknown).
EMBASSY OF THE REPUBLIC OF ARMENIA. Facts, history, foreign relations, news. (Hosted in the USA).
FRANCE/ARMENIA WEBSITE. Pictures and some information. (Hosted in the USA).
ARMENIAN HIGHLAND. Culture and History. 4000 views in 1999. (Hosted in the USA).
ARMENIA, KARABAGH, AND THE ARMENIAN GENOCIDE. 'The Armenian Genocide was carried out by the "Young Turk" government of the Ottoman Empire in 1915-1916 (with subsidiaries to 1922-23). One and a half million Armenians were killed, out of a total of two and a half million Armenians in the Ottoman Empire.' (Hosted in the USA).

The Web Paradigms of the Russian Media

MARIA LOUKINA
Faculty of Journalism, Moscow State University, Russia

Abstract

This paper assesses media behaviour and media resources in the Russian sector of the Internet (RuNet), and discusses the political significance of trends that can be identified. The author shows that RuNet is growing in terms of users and available information. A shift can be observed from online publishing of traditional publications to the development of new online products. Information agencies are major players in this respect. Yet, Russian Internet content is also heavily politicised. This reduces opportunities to realise social goals.

Introduction

Over the past two years the Russian sector of Internet has become the fourth player in media broadcasting, leaving behind by growth rate the traditional channels like press, radio and TV. In the sense of current trends, especially political mediation, Internet in Russia is treated today not only as an elite network for intellectuals but also as a new channel available to all participants in the media sector. The Internet audience forms a special kind of media consumers, not typical for the Russian media environment.

Another thing is that the content of new media broadcasting is changing rapidly and crossing over from the field of professional interests and entertainment to the field of political matter and conflicts of interests. Today these three factors: a new channel of media broadcasting, its special audiences and its challenging content are demonstrating new paradigms in Russian media and show a good example of the power of new information technologies.

General Overview of Online Communications in Russia

The first Internet hosts in Russia have been set up at the end of 1980s by academic institutions. Most of them have been located in industrial and university centres. It was a starting point for Internet developments in Russia. The first three providers became monopolists in national networking and until the middle of 1990s over 70% of individual users received Internet connections via 'The Big Three'. The second period could be characterised as 'networking' in a technical and geographical sense: in the last three years of 1990s there appeared more than 300 commercial providers which gave access to a large number of local users.

To the end of 1998 in the Russian Internet zone (RuNet) there were about 200,000 individual active hosts with unique IP-addresses (ROCIT, 1998). Until now their distribution through Russian territory is rather irregular: 40% is concentrated in Moscow, 35% in Saint-Petersburg, 26% in the European part of Russia and 23% in the Urals, Siberia and the Far East (ROCIT, 1998). The Internet networks remain to be dominant in big industrial cities and university centres, giving access to a large amount of users. In addition and due to the Internet projects of The Open Society Institute (The Soros Foundation), potentially every Russian academician, researcher or student could be an online user.

Russian Internet Audiences and Their Media Behaviour

In the middle of 1999 the number of Internet users in Russia was 1.5 million which is only 2.5% of the grown-up population or 1% of the whole nation. But poor traffic, high prices of services, which are extremely expensive by world standards, and lacks of state support are delaying Internet developments in the country.

The growth in the number of Internet users was rapid before the financial crisis of August 1998. Within a month (January-February 1998) it increased from 840,000 to 1 million (Gallup, 1999). Since then, the number of Internet users has stabilised, and in the spring-summer period of 1999 even has gone down. Yet this could be a seasonal fluctuation. The last quarter of 1999 and the beginning of 2000 have demonstrated again a rapid animation of Russian Internet life: different sources announced that the number of users increased from 1.5 to 3.5 million. But still this is only 1% of the total Internet world population, though Russia forms 2.5% of the planet's inhabitants.

Portrait of the Internet Audience

According to the results of a number of Internet media studies, run by Gallup Media, Comcon-2 and ROCIT, the social-demographic portrait of the Internet audience could be described like this. A young male (80% of Internet users in Russia are males) between 16 and 34 (the largest group of the users is of the age from 20 to 24), with a university degree, with middle or high income and a high level of consumption (Gallup, 1999). Over 50% of them drives a car and uses a mobile telephone or pager. An average Internet user is employed mostly in a commercial structure connected with finances, sciences, high technologies, mass media, advertising or management, though part of them has their own private business. Often he is a decision-making person.

As far as professions are concerned, computer specialists, academicians, students, managers of different levels, and specialists in different spheres make up a disproportionate share of Internet users (see Table 1).

Table 1 Spectrum of Internet users

Specialists, employees	50%
Students	18%
Top-managers	15%

Source: ROCIT (1998)

Compared with North American trends, which demonstrate a process of democratisation and show that Internet becomes a part of everyday life of a wide range of 'ordinary' Americans, the Russian Net population is a more educated and elite group. The social groups of unemployed and housekeepers, as well as workers are practically excluded.

Sociological interviews of lecturers and students from several universities conducted in three biggest urban Russian centres (Moscow, St. Petersburg, Ekaterinburg) demonstrated that 40% of academicians and 80% of students have an opportunity for Internet access. At the same time only one half of them use Web resources in reality (ROCIT, 1998).

Only 80% of the Russian-speaking users live in Russia, 10% are residents of the CIS countries, 10% live abroad (ROCIT, 1998). Most of the Internet users live in Moscow, but only 3.5% of the Moscow population has Internet access. Because of high prices, places of Internet usage tend to be non-private. Online connection is usually activated during working hours in offices or in places of study, and on a whole access during working days is three times more than during weekends. That is why educational and corporate networks still remain dominant. In contrast, in the USA 70% of users has online connection at home; in Great Britain 40% of the Net population use their own computers.

Approximately 20% of private users are women (ROCIT, 1998), but you should take in account that the great number of private hosts is registered by the name of the head of the family.

The main interests of the Internet Russian-speaking audiences are concentrated in areas like political and business news, weather, popular sciences, travel, and arts (see Table 2). In another study you may find information that Russian audience is showing its interest to evidently erotic and porno sites.

Table 2 Sphere of interests

Political News	20.55%
Business News	16.73%
Weather	16.33%
Sciences	16.00%
Travel	15.24%
Arts	13.98%
Job Opportunities	12.40%
Sports	12.02%
Electronic Commerce	11.16%
Health	10.67%

Source: Infoart Agency, in ROCIT (1998)

For searching purposes Russian Internet users prefer visiting both national (Rambler, Yandex, Aport, etc.) and international (Altavista, Yahoo) search engines. Table 3 below demonstrates the amount of different Web-sites visitors presented as a percentage of the adult population of Moscow.

Table 3 Percentage of adult population visiting search engines

Rambler (Russian)	4.4%
Altavista	4.4%
Yahoo	4.2%
Yandex (Russian)	3.3%
Aport (Russian)	3.4%

Source: Gallup (1999)

Preferences of the Internet audience are still not studied and clear. But we know that online versions of popular offline publications are not necessarily as popular as the offline versions. On the contrary, little known portals can become popular producers of news or analytical reviews. For example, the offline magazine *Za Rulem* for car drivers has its specific and regular offline readers, but their profile characteristics are not the same as for the online version of this magazine <www.zr.ru>. At the same time the Web-site *Auto in Russia* <www.auto.ru> is much more popular, though the content is practically the same as the content of the previous one.

Russian Media Resources in www

Different Russian Internet catalogues are containing different numbers of mass media published on the Net. Figures vary from 1,500 to approximately 2,000 links. In comparison, the most popular section 'Business and Finances' counts from 7,000 to 7,500 links, and 'Leisure and Health' from 3,000 to 3,500 links. The classification system for mass media includes headings for different sorts of mass media, including online editions, electronic versions of print and broadcasting media.

Because of a fundamentally democratic nature the Web network is practically uncontrolled and non-hierarchical. Therefore there are no exact data on the figures and typological structure of the Web's content. According to some experts, the main content producers are traditional media institutions, publishers, broadcasting companies and information agencies, who are publishing web-versions of their offline media product. But the media sector is participating in the Russian Internet with new online forms as well. Since the middle of 1999 the net media market is enlarging its territories by several numbers of pure online professional editions. These new media projects started up by net communicators are shaping special, dedicated types of media products and become really popular.

Information Agencies

Currently practically every Russian information agency has published its Web-version. Among them ITAR-TASS <www.itar-tass.com>, RIA-Vesti (Novosti) <www.rian.ru>, Interfax <www.interfax.ru> and other agencies that are working in the traditional information space. Publishing their Web pages, these media institutions declare their willingness to develop new communication territories. Today most information agencies do not limit themselves to 'displaying' their information commodity. They offer access to the main content, although in some cases they ask money for full disclosure of information.

The concept of online news services reflected the 'open access' ideology from the very beginning. The National News Service <www.nns.ru> broadcasts on the Web since 1994 under conditions of openness and mass access. Besides the selection of hard news, this agency is publishing its archives, reviews of press, catalogues of the main political and public figures. It had its own radio channel, which stopped its offline and online broadcasting after the economic crisis in August 1998. The citation index of 'Nns.ru' is one of the highest.

Lenta.ru <www.lenta.ru> is a new information online agency that works mostly in the field of political news with timely coverage of national and international events. This agency also produces an important database on different kinds of issues.

Today offline and online news agencies compete on the market. News pages come from different sites and portals that in some cases produce quality online news. The site of RosBusinessConsulting <www.rbc.ru> in the days of financial crises has demonstrated a good example of market strategy, by publishing openly exclusive financial data. The number of visits at this period approached the circulation of a daily newspaper.

Table 4 Percentage of Moscow adult population visiting most popular Web sites

RosBusinessConsulting <www.rbc.ru>	3.8%
Interfax <www.interfax.ru>	4.2%
ITAR TASS <www.itar-tass.ru>	3.4%
National News Service <www.nns.ru>	2.6%
Lenta.Ru <www.lenta.ru>	1.2%

Source: Gallup (1999)

In the days of a new wave of political activities, RosBusiness Consulting started up a new daily format project called 'Utro.ru' <www.utro.ru>, that produces information on the whole spectrum of political, economic, social and cultural events.

Newspapers and Magazines

During the last two to three years, most of the national periodicals have published their web versions, attracting advertisers and attracting new audiences. A year ago 'leaders' in the Moscow region were sites of the most popular offline newspaper *Moskovskij Komsomolets'* <www.mk.ru> and daily periodicals for businessman and top-managers called *Kommersant-daily* <www.kommersant.com>.

In the starting period of the web, some papers had several online variants with different forms of subscribing (i.e. *Nezavisimaya Gazeta* had 5 different sites). These days they are concentrating on regular web formats with professional design and dedicated content. *Nezavisimaya Gazeta* opened a new site that includes not only the web-version of the offline edition but also extra online timely news bulletins with rather frequent updates.

Local and regional newspapers are also rather active in assessing Internet possibilities. The European part of Russia and its Asian part have different numbers of net issues and different dynamics of web media developments.

Experts consider that in the eastern part of the country, especially the Urals and Siberia, web media developments are more advanced. The most popular issues in Siberia are economic issues called *Delovaya Sibir* <hope.nsk.su/BS/> and *Kommersant-Sibir* <www.nsk.su/~daily/>.

'Gazeta.ru' (the second place in the Citation Index) was started up as the first Internet media institution with a professional staff and clear goals in covering political and economic news and conveying information to audiences. During the first period of its development, a number of competitive issues was published that attracted audiences of similar size as audiences of regular, solid daily papers (22,000 host connections per day). Nevertheless, the number of staff is only 8 persons plus several regional free-lancers. The project was launched in the beginning of 1999 by The Foundation for Effective Politics, known as a consulting institution in media and political technologies. This was not the first Internet project run by this institution. It linked this project to a number of other Internet projects like *Russkij Zurnal* <www.russ.ru>, the *Pushkin* magazine <www.russ.ru/pushkin>, the site of the Millennium Committee <www.millennium.ru>, sites of several young Russian politicians, including Sergey Kirienko <www.kirienko.ru> and Boris Nemtsov <www.nemtsov.ru>, and to *Modern Arts on the Net* <www.guelman.ru>.

During the last two months of 1999 several other Internet media projects have been launched: a new information agency Lenta.ru <www.lenta.ru>, a new daily 'Vesti.ru' <www.vesti.ru>, a new site for professional communicators concentrated on media issues 'Smi.ru' <www.smi.ru>, and 'The Moscow Alternative' <www.msk.ru>. These new media initiatives (today there are 19 links in total) can be expected to be used as new resources during two political campaigns for the parliamentary and presidential elections. The ideological initiator of all these projects is Gleb Pavlovsky, famous as consultant for Yeltsins' election campaign in 1996 and involved in several political scandals. The political goals of all these media projects were focused on supporting non-communist forces, and they achieved some good results, using a wide spectrum of journalism, PR and propaganda methods.

Web Radio and TV Broadcasting

Russian Internet catalogues mention from 130 to 170 links to different radio broadcasting or production companies. But only few of them have live transmissions in the format of RealAudio. Foreign radio stations broadcasting in Russian were the pioneers here (i.e. radio 'Liberty' <www.rferl.org/bd/ru/russian>, 'Deutsche Welle' <www.dwelle.de/russian>). The majority of the native online radio belong to radio stations who have formed a solid reputation in the offline broadcasting market ('The Echo of Moscow' <www.echo.msk.ru>, 'Europa Plus' <www.europaplus.sb.ru>). Some local radio stations as well have been broadcasting on the Web (radio 'August', Tolyatti <www.august.ru>, radio 'Randevu', Nizhniy Novgorod <www.randeu.ru>).

New technologies have expanded broadcasting possibilities: besides the audio information, the user can receive a selection of hot news in a text format, as well as the program announcements. At the same time net broadcasting changes the nature of information consumption: on the one hand, it transforms consumption of other types of media, while on the other hand it creates an opportunity to postpone consumption by recording the sound.

Television Web-technologies are developing in Russia with a delay. The reasons for this are not only economical and technological; also the uncertainty of the technological perspectives of Web-TV in the world play a role here. Until now there are several dozens of Web-sites of TV companies. But in contrast with radio, Web TVs have only few *live* video broadcasting. Most are transmitting recorded programs. The channels with live online transmission are, for example, RTR or TV-6. The remainder of TV sites are designed in a 'presentational' manner, including news in text formats, timetables of transmissions, some extra information about presenters and projects, advertising and announcements.

TV news is published in a hypertext format, covering the content in a vertical line, page by page, from brief headings to a detailed description. Internet technologies also allow to extend content horizontally, including much more information than has been transmitted offline. For example, the 'Vesti' news program (RTR) includes some extra news and background stories, which could not be transmitted online, due to the different characteristics of the medium. Besides that, push-technology gives users the opportunity to choose packages with useful information.

There are approximately 150 links to TV companies or other companies close to the TV sphere in Russian catalogues, including local and regional broadcasting TV companies (such as the 'Volga' TV company or the 'Kuzbass' state TV channel), and different production companies ('VID', 'ATV') and projects. Ratings show that the most popular are servers of the private NTV+, the 'Vprok' program of the NTV channel and the server of the ORT channel.

To summarise all this we can draw the following conclusions:

- It is obvious that the Russian Internet now plays an important role as mediator for a wide public. For some 'traditional media' the Internet is an effective means to reach a wider audience.

- The Russian part of the Internet offers a wide number of media products. The largest amount of them are web versions of traditional media. But there is also a new type of media institutions that use the possibilities of electronic technologies and produce a new product with hypertext characteristics that are more similar to databases.
- The most effective new media model can be compared with an information agency that is distributing non-exclusive news; the main news sources are concentrated in the Web as well.
- Web radio and TV are still on the margins of the Russian Internet.
- The content of new media is focused mostly on political issues and evidently serves interests of definite reformed-minded population but does not represent the whole nation. This political emphasis reduces opportunities to realise social aims and pay more attention to human-interest issues.

Perspectives of Internet Media Developments in Russia

The Net media system that includes online publishing and Web versions of offline issues is a dynamically developing sector of media market in Russia.

Factors contributing to the democratic developments of Russian net media include:
- the democratic nature and openness of new media (equal equality);
- the possibility to connect different parts of a large country (a new national medium);
- the possibility to overcome the national borders;
- the interactive, dialogic nature of Internet communication;
- the efficiency and searchability in covering news;
- the availability of multimedia formats.

And here are the factors, which hinder developments:
- the low quality of communication traffic;
- the undeveloped state of the financial infrastructure, including a lack of credit payment and plastic card systems;
- the poor state of computer equipment, which is mostly produced by local industries;
- the fact that the Ministry of Communications has a monopoly on domain registration;
- the high prices that are charged for online connections and services.

The last factor is especially important in the days of economic difficulties.

The development of online media is terribly hindered by gaps in the legislation system: copyright is not protected, resulting in piracy, and lack of protection for personal databases, resulting into breaches of human rights to keep information confidential.

However, in spite of these social and economic difficulties the dynamics of the net population in Russia are going up. Some experts affirm that Internet developments here are running even faster than in the West, though the number of servers is less compared with the average abroad. In any case the density of information saturation, that is the density of Web-sites as compared to the whole amount of hosts, overdraws the European and is approaching North American standards. Besides that, the Internet will go out from the narrow corporate sphere and start to attract a wide social interest.

Internet and Politics

The Russian sector of the Internet most probably will become more active in the year 2000 in connection with the presidential elections. I should mention here, that to the end of 1999 most of the political parties, that were claiming to participate in the parliamentary structures and working out the strategies of influence, have formed their presentation in the Web. This is especially the case for political parties, whose electorate groups potentially could coincide with the Internet media audiences.

The last two years also demonstrated that a political factor is probably one of the most important in new media developments all over the world. Media experts in the United States consider that the global, non-national character of the Clinton-Lewinsky scandal was produced on the Web. All details of this story were available to everyone in all parts of the world via the CNN Web-site. Since that time the Internet has occupied the dominant position among other news resources, and became a concrete media phenomenon independent from print and electronic broadcasting. In the opinion of communicators, just that very case had the same meaning for Internet media as President Kennedy's murder for TV.

The Kosovo crisis coverage strengthened the position of the Internet as a new media channel, which has been conquering a specific territory in the world information structure. In Russia these days every online user can search for information on the Chechnya crisis and obtain a balanced picture via different news services, national and foreign as well.

All these factors form a new media consumer, described above as a well-educated young man under 35 with high income, an active participant in economic and social spheres of life, who demonstrates his interests also in politics. He is not satisfied with traditional print and especially TV coverage of political issues and finds new information sources in Internet media. On the other hand, the new Web media projects are searching for new electorate groups that have been traditionally at the margins of the active part of the voting citizens, but that offer an attractive target group from a social-demographical point of view. The profile of audiences and the palette of new media together are contributing to new paradigms of Russian media, which are tending to openness and diversity, as the very nature of the Internet.

References

Gallup

1999 Several studies on 'Internet Audiences in Moscow', held between 1998-1999 (in Russian). <http://www.gallup.ru/publications.html#net>.

ROCIT

1998 *Ezhegodnyj Otchet ROCIT 'Rossiya v Internete'* [Annual Report 'Russia in the Internet']. <http://www.rocit.ru/page.plx?d=inform&t=shablon&m=menu&p=russia>.

The Open Society and the New Urban Culture as Presented in the Public Communication Process

IVAN ZASSOURSKY
Faculty of Journalism, Moscow State University, Russia

Abstract

This paper argues that the notion of 'open society' forms an attractive positive idea that can form the basis of a reformulated liberal ideology in Russia, especially if it is related to ideas of a 'new city generation' or to other, similar instrumental concepts that exist in the urban regions which have the most developed media systems.

Introduction

The 'open society' as a concept is not well-known in Russia. It is somewhat popular in academic circles and among fund-raisers, at least those trained to work with the vast Soros network. But this does not mean that the 'open society' concept lacks potential needed to enter the public communications process. On the contrary, a bit transformed and simplified, it looks like one of the most promising ones. Especially if the political context is appropriate.

Ideas enter public communication in peculiar ways. New trends emerge and develop outside political discourse, gaining more and more support on the grass-roots level. They inspire intellectuals, provide ground for academic debate; inch by inch they gain more virtual ground in the Internet and slowly penetrate mainstream media until they are ready to be used by politicians to mobilise and politicise voters. If voters 'buy' them, they simultaneously support political actors. And this is exactly what is happening with the open society concept and the new urban culture.

Mapping Russian Politics

The divide in Russian politics used to be between communists (or self-proclaimed social democrats) on the one side and liberals on the other. Voters were mobilised by anti-Communist campaigns. It is all different now.

Liberals are discredited by the wealth of compromises on the one side and cruel social policy and inefficient management of the economy on the other. They also have more strong opponents now. While communists remain strong, etatists (among them extremely popular politicians such as former prime minister Evgeny Primakov and Moscow mayor Yuri Luzhkov) created a very strong block. Even Yavlinsky and his 'Yabloko' party try to keep distance from the liberals, also known as the 'young reformers'.

To get 5% of votes necessary to enter parliament as a party would be quite an achievement for these young reformers. At this point the search for new ideas has started. At this point one of the liberals, former prime minister Sergey Kirienko, decided to run in the Moscow mayor elections against one of the leading paternalists-etatists politicians, Yuri Luzhkov (who in the last elections received almost 90% of the votes).

As earlier noticed, liberals share an extremely narrow social base and worn-out image. Kirienko has almost no chance to win. But even to loose with dignity he and other liberals in parliamentary elections (that take place simultaneously) had to re-emerge with a distinct political profile.

They had to build their new political identity in the opposition to other political actors, especially paternalists-etatists, extremely strong both in Moscow and parliamentary elections. But the economic discourse is too limited and complicated to make a difference. In post-communist Russia it is extremely difficult to turn such differences into a dramatic divide. Liberals had to look someplace else. Anti-Communist campaign is not going to work – at least not as much for the benefit of the liberals as before.

To put it in another way, liberals could not count on a mass audience anymore. Their only hope is to create a niche on the political market. This dictates a change of style from banal all-embracing political rhetoric and to abandon their much cherished middle-class construct. They needed something more fresh, much more appealing and energetic, more distinct.

No matter how many political experts work for a political party, it is always a matter of coincidence when and how a group of politicians meet their new political face. Lucky for the liberals, Kirienko met Marat Guelman, an energetic producer, who organised the First Moscow Art Festival *Unofficial Moscow* that took place at City Day, September 3-5,

1999. The festival managed to consolidate leading art makers on the wave of irritation towards cultural politics that are promoted by the city administration of Moscow – the 'turbo patriotism' of mayor Luzhkov.[1]

The 'New City Generation'

The concept of the 'new city generation' emerged in no time. This construct was definitively a step further from weakened formulas of 'independent people'.

The 'new city generation' has its roots in the new urban culture with all its lively contradictions mixed with post-modern elan, their high self-esteem, creativity and vital energy. All those in their 20-ties, 30-ties and early 40-ties, almost everybody, whose identity was forged in the stormy nineties, can qualify.

Yet to make this identity more appealing, it had to be filled not only with irritation at those, who stand for a paternalist state (no difference is made at this point between indeed appealing Primakov, populist Luzhkov, frightening regional governors-hardliners and communists), but with positive ideas as well.

'Open society' values and ideals were indispensable here. Together with the somewhat dated (that is, after cyberpunk) but still striving utopia of metropolitan paradise, and a fresh Castells-inspired vision of ever growing urbanisation it is exposed as a 'future'. Well, *the* future, to be more exact.

Although realistic assumptions of the future still vary according to attitudes, utopias are sometimes ignited in the maturing generation. Capable political leaders engaged in search for the new electorate in the highly concurrent political market, try to position themselves with them.

According to Sergey Kirienko, one of the prominent political leaders of the Right Forces Union, a remake of a broad democratic coalition constructed upon the liberals old guard, his political block is representing the interests of a grand new group of people that emerged in Russia during the nineties. Those, who are by now used to make important decisions

---

1 For example, you can not stay in the city without a registration that is hard to arrange if you do not stay at a hotel, but with friends. The metropolitan police from time to time provides convincing samples of xenophobia and racism towards people from southern provinces, etc. Ironically, after the Chechen war and the presidential elections in the year 2000, in which most of the 'young reformers' and Kirienko personally supported Putin, Luzhkov's policies seem mild, but during the parliamentary campaign he was marked as a political scapegoat by the liberal community.

about their life solely by themselves, and would not tolerate state interference in their life-planning and lifestyles. As a new class these people are concerned primarily with the future, not with the past.

And indeed there turns out to be quite a generation gap.

A Generation Gap between Paternalists and Liberals

Paternalists naturally gravitate towards tradition almost everywhere. Count Uvarov, a visionary and a minister of education in the Emperor Alexander government had lucidly stated their credo back in 1834 as '*Orthodox church, absolute monarchy and national roots*'.[2]

Luzhkov is a good example of that. He controls everything in the city, starting from the city administration to the city parliament and the city press. He also helped to build and provides vital support for one of the biggest private corporations, AFK-Sistema.

As for national roots, Luzhkov is famous for his position on Sevastopol, a city in Crimea that became part of Ukraine in the late fifties, when Nikita Khruschev changed its status. Luzhkov believes Sevastopol should be Russian and never looses the chance to boldly state his claim.

Last but not least, under his auspices a couple of large monuments did appear: one for Peter the Great; another is the remake of Christ the Saviour church, the biggest in the city by far. Situated one across the other, together they dominate on the Moscow river embankment near Kremlin. And there is good reason for their king size: if they were small, they simply would not be noticed, they would not proclaim, they would not look solid and, at last, they could not be able to represent (and thus *create*) tradition, this fake construct, one of the leading commodities these days in the rootless mother Russia and everywhere else, where globalization shock has coincided with a major crisis.

Instead of isolationism, 'historical destiny', the unbearable weight of 'common fate' and a 'final solution' (it is no surprise that the 'openness' recipe fits well into the liberal pattern), the open society concept offers plurality, freedom of personal choice and the natural optimism. All of these are innate qualities of the 'new city generation'. They offer a different solution for the globalization shock. The traditional oppositions of closed society versus open society, or rigid society versus network society, or rural society versus post-industrial (information, knowledge etc.)

---

2 This formula was articulated when Uvarov was *sous-ministre* of education, in the Moscow State University report in the winter of 1832-1833. It was published for the first time when he was appointed minister as his official directive in the *Journal of the Public Education Ministry, 1834, vol.1* C.XLIX-L. (See also Barsukov, 1891: 83).

society provide a profound distinction and a fool-proof value-laden discourse, and a nice basis for the campaign.

Adapted to the needs of the liberals, the open society concept may penetrate the public communication process. However, it will not be as popular itself as much as the adaptation of it to the 'new city generation' concept or to other pragmatic schemes. People may learn no more of it than fits into the fundamental principles of the new right – individualism, freedom and private property – with the 'new city generation' somewhat widening this political platform and stretching it into the future.

By the way, the definition for the 'new city generation' concept has emerged already as well. It consists of those, who share 'an *openness to the future*, an interest in the *other*, and a quest for the *new*', as written in the press-release of the *Unofficial Moscow* art festival (quoted in Zassoursky, 1999). It is easy to notice how this formulae mimics the classical one, and it was certainly created with Uvarov's dictum in mind and in opposition to it as well.

Counting on the Domino Effect

However, the fact is that if the 'open society'-based new city generation concept will not prove itself reality-based, it might be counterproductive. At least that is what the researchers should have thought about while attaching moral values to a vague social group. Indeed, the rules impose the limits of risk – you have to collect at least 5% to enter parliament as a party. This is why the title of 'Right Forces Union' appeared where simple 'New Right' would be bright. This is why the 'new city generation' concept was not embraced officially as the main origin of political support.

However, the concept is still applied and is being used. Just how? And here is the trick. The 'new city generation' concept was originally created as a self-extracting social construct, that is based upon Western research in sociology and identity theory. It works the same way as the concept of the 'proletariat' did. A strong social group is identified, symbolised in the most attractive ways by advertisement or propaganda, then broadcasted on to the general public – because the ideology it conveys is supposedly demanded by larger social groups as well. Presented as the most fashionable identity of modern times, it offers those that are addressed a new affiliation, a new description of a generation that they might (or still might not) embrace.

Progress goes in the direction of more individualisation, more effectiveness and boldness, more towards a count-on-your-own kind of approach. Proponents of these developments survived the crash of the nineties, that is the Soviet system crash. Most of them had to create new lifestyles without role-models, in cultural exteriors of the post-modern age, yet disconnected from the knowledge about it. They are used to discovering the unknown, they are inventive and flexible.

The existing power structure of the new Russian state seems no longer able to integrate them. Once again, 'young reformers' are on their own in politics. Together with the new city generation, they were able to move against the tide, ride the new conservative wave towards their small electorate victory.

It is quite unfortunate that in the presidential elections of 2000, the 'young reformers' were swayed to support nationalist politics of Mr. Putin. There are still no institutions in Russian politics – everything can change in five minutes. In this mediated political system, the communication channels create 'parties' as modes of reality perception. That makes media the strongest generator of identities. At least their liaison with their audiences is more stable.

There is at least one new publication inspired by the 'new city generation' concept and articulating it – while there remain a dozen more that had initially provided the fundament for the concept. This comes as no surprise, considering 20 to 30-year-olds are the most important section for advertisers, where brands can be positioned for life – and that is still an extremely long period of time.

Identity politics of the Internet age are certainly emerging as the new show of the political spectacle, attaining the place once occupied by traditional politics. Yet their 'liberated' space is still so narrow, that it accounts only for a single niche among many still unoccupied islands in the country-wide ocean of a paranoid TV-galaxy. This galaxy is inhabited by totalising myths and other archaic conscience structures, like the good and evil, heroes and monsters, in a comfortable asylum for the Soviet era identity, yet an immensely poisonous environment for any mind that attempts to think.

References

Barsukov, N.

1891 *Zhizn' i trudy M.P.Pogodina* [Life and Works of M.P. Podogin]. Vol. IV. St-Petersburg.

Zassoursky, I.

1999 About 'Unofficial Moscow': The old and the new. *Nezavisimaya Gazeta*, August 31.

The Distribution of Online Resources and the Democratic Potential of the Internet

COLIN SPARKS
Centre for Communication and Information Studies,
University of Westminster, United Kingdom

Abstract

Some of the content of the media is migrating on to the Internet, and more and more people have access to the Internet. This paper considers the implications of these shifts from the point of view both of the range of views, news and opinions that can be placed in the public domain and the degree to which the ability to access these is widely distributed amongst the population. The paper reviews the unequal distribution of Internet resources globally (with particular reference to newspapers), shows that within the USA social differences map closely on to the distribution of Internet access, and argues that complete accessibility will depend upon either a social initiative to overcome the inadequacies of the market, or the re-invention of the technology in to a form that is capable of finding the same kind of mass acceptance as has television. The consequences of these two conclusions are then explored.

Introduction

This paper is concerned with data about the diffusion of the Internet and the patterns of use that can be observed developing. The reason for looking at these questions is that the development of the Internet clearly has important implications for a wide range of human activities. What these might be are hotly debated, and none more so than the issue of the relationship of this new technology to the established patterns of governance. Very crudely, there are many who hail the development of the Internet as the mechanism that will destroy dictators and tyrants, and greatly extend the scope of democratic government both within the boundaries of states and at a global level. I have examined the theoretical basis of these arguments elsewhere (Sparks, forthcoming a). In this paper, I want to concentrate my attention on more empirical questions.

I therefore take it as given that the dialogic and searchable nature of the Internet, particularly as embodied in its current, PC-based, format has enormous potential. It presents the possibility of a great extension of the citizen's power to enter the public arena and to participate in debates and decision-making. It also allows the citizen far easier and greater access to a huge range of information and opinion about their situation, and thus empowers them to reach informed decisions about their political choices. The technology, at least as presently realised, represents a vast democratic gain compared with the traditional mass media. These were, and are, essentially point-to-multipoint in structure, and the role of most users is necessarily confined to that of an audience. The best that most citizens can hope for with such a technology is that their opinion will be polled and may form some sort of feedback. The mass media are technologies incapable of anything more than the most limited and crippled forms of democratic function. The Internet, which permits point-to-point as well as point-to-multipoint communication, has the potential to overcome these limitations. It provides the possibility of reconstructing the dialogic features of the classical *agora* in the conditions of contemporary, large-scale and dispersed societies.

The problem, however, is not the potential of the technology, but the ways in which it comes to be embedded in societies. A potential can be realised, or it can be stultified and atrophy. Which occurs depends upon the ways in which the technology is developed and implemented, the social uses to which it is put, and the degree to which it is diffused throughout society. It is what is known about the social uses of the Internet and its social diffusion that is under consideration here.

Diffusion and Use of the Internet

From the point of view of the realisation of the democratic potential of the Internet, two issues are of central importance. The first concerns diffusion. It is, today, a generally-accepted feature of theories of democracy that all adult citizens have equal political rights; the epoch in which theories and practices could pass as democratic that were premised on the exclusion from the franchise of the poor, or women, or people with brown skins, are long past. The measure of the realisation of the democratic potential of any technology is the extent to which it is available to all citizens. Thus, while the freedom of the printed press is a central democratic right, it is an extremely limited one in societies that are predominately illiterate. Overcoming illiteracy has thus been one of the key objectives for those who wish to make democracy a social reality rather than just a desirable ideal. I am therefore concerned to consider what is known about the distribution of the Internet, both internationally and within societies.

Finding out who has access to this technology is the first step to deciding whether its democratic potential is being realised or not.

Most technologies have multiple potential uses, and many have several real social uses. Again, the newspaper press provides a good example. The technology of the newspaper can be used to provide information and opinion about the business of the world. It can also be used to provide information that is about scandal and gossip, as well as commentary on television, music and sport. As a matter of fact, both of these usages are present in most newspapers to varying degrees. To the extent that a newspaper is concerned with the former material, it clearly plays some role in the democratic process. To the extent that it is concerned with the latter, it clearly plays some role in the entertainment industry. In order to understand whether the democratic potential of the Internet is being realised, we need to know what kinds of social uses it is being put to, and what these tell us about its likely development.

The Availability of Public Information

These two issues concern the extent to which all citizens are, or will be able to, participate in public life through the Internet. In addition, however, it is important to consider the nature of the public information that is likely to be available. While the Internet makes it much easier to gain access to a wealth of information, it does not alter the length of the day. The realities of the time budgets of the mass of population mean that, even in the most wired of societies, there is still an important role for the intermediary organisations that gather, process, validate and interpret news for the citizen. Against the limitations of the mass media discussed above, one has to set the positive point that they are the only currently available mechanisms that carry out those tasks. To a large extent, the availability of information and opinion on the Internet is dependent upon the development of online versions of these offline media that are the sole organisations that are in a position to provide it. As studies of international news and news flows have long demonstrated, the domination of the offline news world by a few large players can have negative effects for the provision of material about the less materially-advantaged regions of the world. This, in turn, limits the ability of citizens of those countries to play an active role in political life. It also, as it happens, limits the access of citizens of materially advantaged regions to alternative views of the world, and thus restricts their abilities to arrive at informed opinions about international issues.

The potential of the Internet here is enormous. Sitting at a desk in London, or anywhere else for that matter, one can communicate with people in Amsterdam or Moscow or Los Angeles as easily as with people in the same city. It is possible to access the *New York Times* or the *Times of India* as easily as the London *Times*. To the extent that the Internet provides a social space in which information and opinion from all sources is given equal prominence, it transcends the limits imposed by political geography. The extent to which the Internet is providing a home for information and opinion from around the world is thus one of the measures of the degree to which it is realising its democratic potential.

The final issue that this paper confronts is that of the paucity of data. It is, of course, entirely true that mass diffusion of the Internet is a phenomenon of the 1990s, and the data runs available are thus so short as to render any projections hazardous. The conclusions that I draw in this paper are thus open to objections based on the claim that the mature shape of the Internet will be entirely different from its current state. In order to take account of potential criticism of this kind, I thus consider what is known about the diffusion of innovations in society, and try to apply this knowledge to the data about the Internet. In particular, I am concerned with the issue of whether the short-term trends under discussion here provide the basis for any kind of generalisation about the future.

The International Distribution of Access

The growth of the Internet is a well-documented phenomenon, and recently knowledge about its unequal distribution has become more widespread (UNDP, 1999). It is, however, worth spelling out some of the data in detail, since the evidence is so striking. Between August 1981, which is the earliest record available, and January 1999, the number of Internet hosts rose from 213 to 43,229,694.[1] Methodological difficulties with the ways in which the data was collected make it difficult to construct meaningful series over that whole period, but Figure 1 illustrates the growth between January 1993 and January 1999, on a more or less consistent basis.

---

1 The material in this section of the paper is based on data from the Internet Software Consortium <http://www.isc.org>. Since I use 'host' as one of the most important terms in this paper, it is as well to be clear about exactly what is meant by this term. It is not a measure of users, but of the number of computers connected to the Internet. The formal definition is: 'A host used to be a single machine on the net. However, the definition of a host has changed in recent years due to virtual hosting, where a single machine acts like multiple systems (and has multiple domain names and IP address). Ideally, a virtual host will act and look exactly like a regular host, so we count them equally' (ISC, 1999). I follow other writers in taking this to be a measure of the extent to which the physical infrastructure of the Internet is internationally distributed.

As can clearly be seen, not only is the total number of hosts growing, but also the rate of increase itself appears to be growing. There is no sign whatsoever that the explosion in connectivity might be coming to an end.

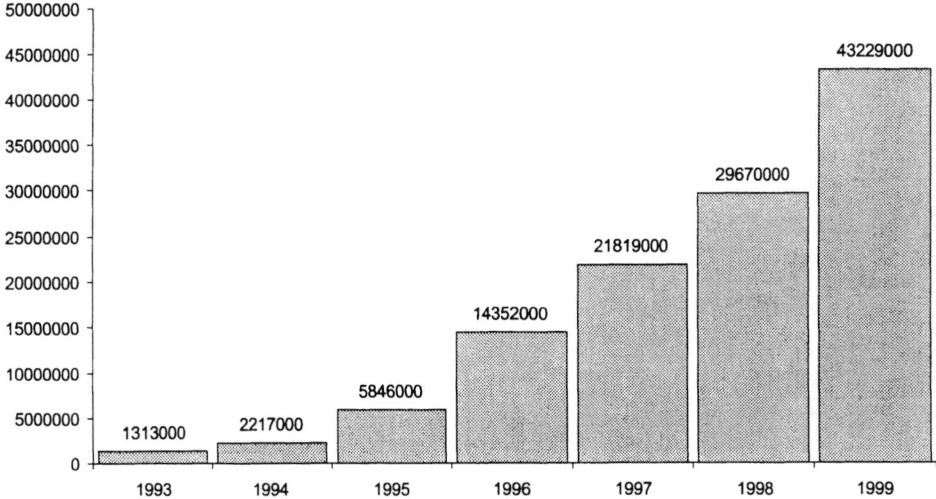

Source: Based on data from the Internet Software Corporation <http://www.isc.org>

Figure 1 Number of internet hosts 1993-1999

It is much more difficult to say what the geographical spread of these hosts is. The physical location of a host is hard to determine, since the geographical identifiers at the end of domain names (e.g. '.uk' for the United Kingdom, '.nl' for the Netherlands, '.ru' for the Russian Federation and, still in January 1999, '.su' for the Soviet Union) do not necessarily correspond to an offline location. A host can have a '.uk' domain name and be physically located in Australia. What is more, the fastest-growing class of domain names end with '.com', and it is difficult to say exactly where they are located. Although the USA is probably the home of most of them, a host can have a '.com' domain name and be in Zaire. The best we can do is to use the figures as publicly available, and to try to take account of their limitations. At the very least, they give us an indication as to what the distribution of online resources is. As Figure 2 demonstrates, Internet hosts are disproportionately concentrated in the developed countries. Even taking the minority of US sites that have a '.us' domain name, the number of hosts per head of the population in the USA is far higher than in the world's most populous countries, India and China. What is more, there is little evidence that they are catching up, at least over the time span of one year. While this is a very short period, it should be recalled that, during the same time, the total number of hosts rose from 29,670,000 to 43,229,694, an increase of

46 per cent. This is the same rate of growth as for India, and higher than that for China, so it is reasonable to argue that they are not closing the gap noticeably at the present moment.

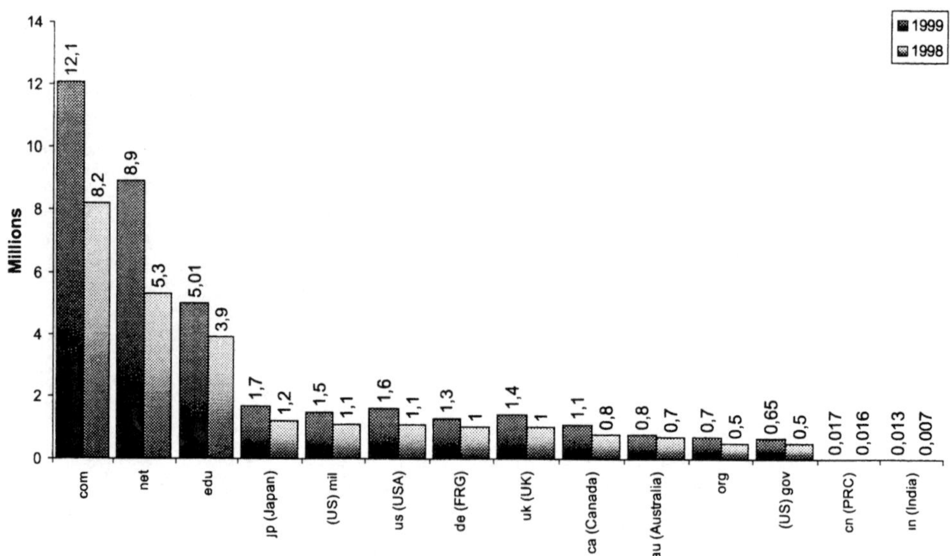

Source: Based on data from the Internet Software Corporation <http://www.isc.org>

Figure 2 The distribution of Internet Resources, January 1998 and January 1999

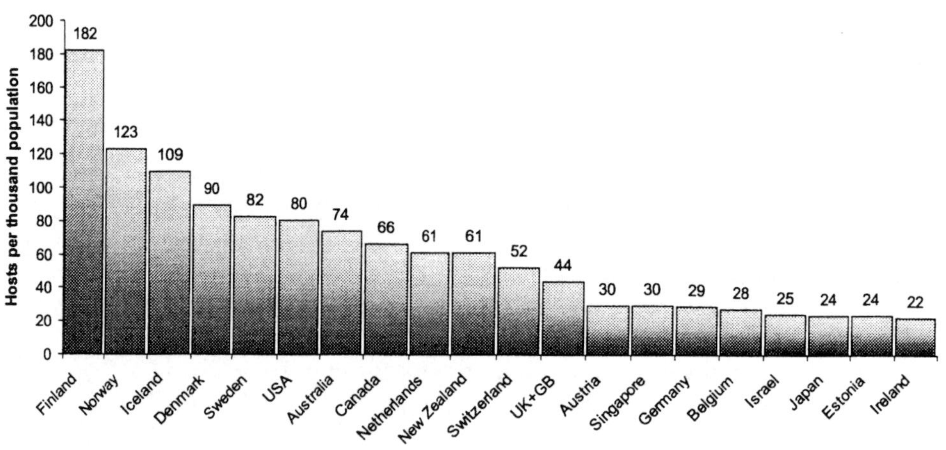

Source: Based on data from the Internet Software Corporation <http://www.isc.org> and UNDP (1999)

Figure 3 Top twenty states by density of hosts per thousand of population

Global Income Distribution and Internet Access

Giving a more detailed picture of the distribution of hosts poses some difficulties. Common sense suggests that high-income countries would tend to have a higher number of hosts per head of the population. In order to test this hypothesis, I studied the relationship between the density of hosts and the per capita wealth of as many countries as possible. It seems to hold good, at least within certain assumptions.[2] The country with the highest density of hosts emerges as Finland, with 182 per 1,000 of the population. The USA has 80; the Netherlands 61; the UK 43; and the Russian Federation 1.9. The top twenty countries with regard to host density are

2 The assumptions upon which this graph is based require spelling out in full. Apart from the difficulty of the possible non-correspondence between domain name and geographical location, some 21,742,617 of the hosts recorded in January 1999 (approximately 50 per cent of the total) were in the categories '.com' (12,140,747), '.net' (8,856,687), '.org' (744,285) and '.int' (898), and thus not directly classifiable. In order to try to take account of these realities, my procedure was as follows: I started with the geographically-tagged sites, and added to them those that were variations (so the US total was made up of '.us' plus '.edu' plus '.mil' plus '.gov'; the Russian Federation was the total of '.ru' and '.su' and so on). Obviously, not all US military sites are in the USA, but it seemed sensible to include them in that country's total. I discarded all domain names that had no sites and some that were unclassifiable (notably '.arpa' and '.unknown'.) Having done that, I then faced the problem of allocating the unaccountable 21 million. I made the assumption that around 60 per cent of these sites were likely to be located in the USA. I thus multiplied the raw US total by 2.5. I then carried this principle forward by multiplying domains according to the following formulae: those with more than one million were multiplied by 1.8; those with less than one million but more than 100,000 by 1.7; those with less than 100,000 but more than 10,000 by 1.5; those with less than 10,000 but more than 1,000 by 1.25; those with less that 1,000 but more than 100 by 1.2; those with less than 100 by 1.1. In adopting this procedure I was trying to reflect the fact that states with larger Internet populations are likely to have a higher proportion of commerce etc. located online. The adjusted total was 43,024,542. This is about 200,000 less than the overall total recorded by a survey, but since I had ignored some classes of domain, this seemed a close enough approximation. These figures were all based on data from the Internet Software Consortium <http://www.isc.org>. I then gathered data about population, $GNP per capita and $GDP at PPPs from the UNDP's 1999 Human Development Report. After discarding those cases for which data was incomplete, I was left with 150 domains. I then calculated the ratio of hosts to the population and regressed this against the two wealth measures. As a test of the distribution of the indirect classifications, I also regressed the raw counts against GNP. The result was a slightly higher degree of correlation, which suggests that my distribution was reasonable.

presented in Figure 3. As will be obvious, these are all wealthy countries, apart from Estonia, which has a per capita GNP of $3,360, which is about one fifth that of the next richest country in the list (New Zealand).

Previous studies have shown that there is a relationship between GNP per capita and host density within the OECD (Hargittai, 1999). It is possible to extend this to a much larger number of countries, and the results are presented in Figure 4. While there clearly is not a complete relationship between the two variables, there is obviously some correlation and these findings would provide a good starting point for a more detailed analysis that would regress multiple variables in an attempt to gain greater accuracy of prediction.[3] For our purposes here, two things stand out. The first is that, while are there are some notable outliers, the general proposition that rich countries have large numbers of Internet hosts in proportion to their population, and poor countries have few, is clearly generally true. Secondly, the fit between host density and dollar GNP is rather better than the fit between host density and GDP adjusted for purchasing power parities. This suggests that the key variable is the absolute wealth of the country on a world scale, rather than the local level of prices.

Although the world of the Internet is notoriously fluid, there is little apparent change at the top end of the scale of host distribution. As Table 1 demonstrates, the top ten domain names have remained relatively constant in composition, if not in exact order, over the last five years.[4] To the extent that the domain names are those of countries, the dominant ones throughout are those of developed nations. In January 1999, the first non-developed country in the unadjusted list of domain names was Taiwan, at number nineteen. All of the first ten named countries had a per capita GNP of more than $US19,000 per annum in 1997, as compared with a world average of $US5,257 (UNDP, 1999: 180-83).

---

3 The first one that suggests itself is the result of observation of the data. A number of small, rich undemocratic states are outliers in their low density of hosts. A 'democracy index' which took account of these factors but was not ideological in construction might improve the fit. My concern with finding a non-ideological measure is provoked by the fact that Hargittai negates a lot of her valuable work by introducing a variable of competition in telecoms policy. The problem with using this is that while the USA now has a policy of competition in the local loop, this was not present in law until the passage of 1996 Federal Communications Act, and is not really present in reality up to the present. There was, and is, competition in the long distance market, but of course local calls are what the vast majority of Internet users employ. It is likely that she has here ignored an intervening variable that would have greater validity.

4 If the netties are to be believed, and one Net year last three months, then this represents effectively a 20 year period.

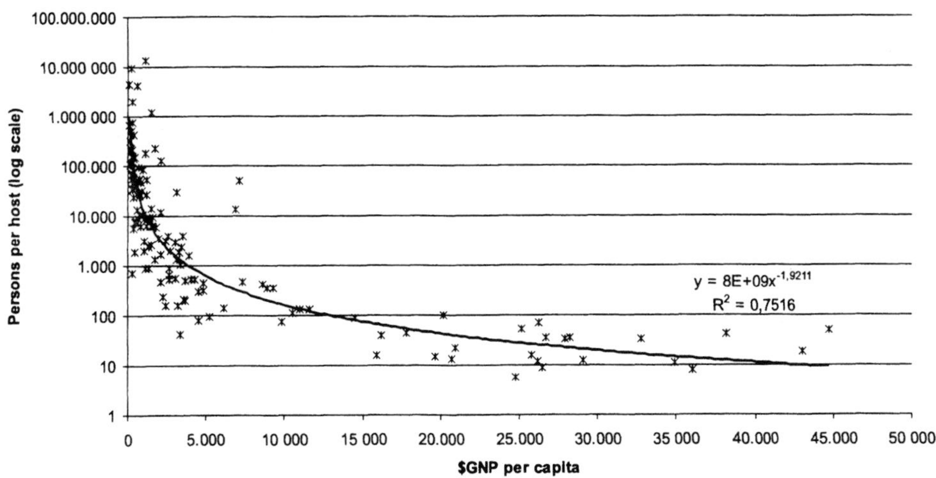

Source: Based on data from the Internet Software Corporation <http://www.isc.org> and UNDP (1999)

Figure 4 Density of hosts plotted against $GNP per capita

Table 1 Ten most frequent top-level domain names 1995-1999

1995	1996	1997	1998	1999
.com	.com	.com	.com	com
.edu	.edu	.edu	.net	.net
.uk	net	net	.edu	.edu
.gov	.gov	.jp	.jp	.jp
.de	.org	.de	.mil	.us
.ca	.mil	.mil	.us	.mil
mil	de	.ca.	.de	uk
.au	.uk	.uk	.uk	.de
.org	.ca	.us	.ca	.ca
.net	.au	au	.au	.au

Source: Based on data from the Internet Software Corporation <http://www.isc.org>

Internet Usage

Measuring Internet usage is another matter, and here there are no authoritative international figures. The well-known Irish Internet consultancy Nua gave, at the time of writing, the estimates reproduced in

Table 2, which they describe as an 'educated guess'. These are not broken down by country, but it is notable that around 75 per cent of the total estimated numbers of users are to be found in North America and Europe. No doubt a breakdown of the figure for Asia/Pacific would reveal that the richer countries, notably Japan but also Australia and New Zealand, Hong Kong (not, of course, a separate state but with its own economy and domain name) and Singapore, accounted for a disproportionately high number of the connections.

Table 2 One estimate of world Internet usage

World Total	201,000,000
Africa	1,720,000
Asia/Pacific	33,610,000
Europe	47,150,000
Middle East	880,000
Canada and USA	112,000,000
Latin America	5,290,000

Source: Nua (September 1999)

All of the evidence that we have about the distribution of the Internet thus suggests that it is, in world terms, a club for rich countries. There is a very strong, although not exact, relationship between the per capita GNP of a particular country and the number of Internet hosts per thousand of the population. Finland has one Internet host for every 5.5 members of the population, and the USA has one for every twelve. The population of the ten countries with the highest density of hosts, all with one host for less than twenty people, amounts to 363.8 million people. This is around six per cent of the world's six billion people. More than 2.2 billion people, or around 37 per cent of the world's population, live in China and India. China has one host per 48,071 people. India has one host per 48,668 people. It is clear from these figures that the infrastructure of the Internet has not, so far at least, developed in a way that would equitably distribute the opportunities for people to participate in any form of online activity, let alone in the governance of their countries. The online world is very unequal indeed.

Access in One Country

Differences in the provision of online resources between countries tell us relatively little about what the distribution of resources is within countries. After all, not all people in rich countries are themselves rich, and not all people in poor countries are actually poor. While much attention has been devoted to inequalities of wealth and other resources between countries, it is also legitimate to enquire what the distributions are within those countries. This is, of course, a rather more contentious area since it immediately raises political questions about the way that societies are run. It is also the case that in many countries, for example the UK, reliable data on the social distribution of the Internet does not exist, at least in the public domain. There does exist, however, reasonable data that allows us to draw conclusions for the USA. It is legitimate to concentrate on this country as a prime example since not only is it very large and very rich, but it is also generally recognised as the 'home' of the Internet. Trends that are only just visible in other countries have been running for some years in the USA and, to the extent that it is possible to avoid speculation in this field, it is there that we have the best chance of observing likely developments.

We are also fortunate in that the US government has commissioned a series of major surveys about the availability of the equipment needed for Internet access. Unlike commercial surveys, which have often been subjected to methodological critiques, the three 'Falling Through the Net' studies conducted by the US Department of Commerce Census Bureau for the National Telecommunications and Information Administration (NTIA) used large (48,000 household) samples, which were designed to give a valid representation of the population as a whole. While all surveys suffer from a variety of limitations due to possible error, we can treat these results as reasonably reliable indicators.

The overall findings of the third and most recent report, published in July 1999, based on data from late 1998 and titled *Falling Through the Net: Defining the Digital Divide*, are summarised as showing that: 'Access to computers and the Internet has soared for people in all demographic groups and geographical locations...[but there is also] the persistence of the digital divide between the information rich [...] and the information poor [...] For many groups, the digital divide has *widened* as the information 'haves' outpace the 'have nots' in gaining access to electronic resources.' (NTIA, 1999: xiii). These gaps are based upon divisions familiar to European observers, like income and education, as well as on particularly acute US markers of distinction like ethnicity (or 'race' as the reports put it).

National Income Distribution and Internet Access

Since this is the largest and most authoritative study of what is on most accounts one of the most 'wired' of societies, it is worth looking at its findings in some detail. Overall, 42.1 per cent of US households had a personal computer (up from 36.6 per cent in 1997), while 26.2 per cent used the Internet (up from 18.6 per cent in 1997) (NTIA, 1999: 10). Within those global figures, however, there were wide discrepancies. Only 6.6 per cent of households classified as 'Black non Hispanic' and with an income of less than $15,000 per year had a computer, and only 1.9 per cent of these used the Internet. By contrast, 80 per cent of households classified as 'White non Hispanic' and with an income of more than $75,000 per year had a computer and 60.9 per cent used the Internet (NTIA, 1999: 18 and 27). Similar disparities are observable on a variety of different discriminators, and overall it is reasonable to conclude that the various measures of social advantage and disadvantage map closely on to household computer possession and Internet usage.[5]

Table 3 Percentage of US persons using the Internet by income and location

Income	At home (%)	Outside home (%)	Any location (%)	Overlap(%)
All U.S. .Persons	22.2	17.0	32.7	5.2
<$5,000	9.5	12.1	16.0	5.6
$5,000-9,999	5.1	8.7	12.1	3.6
$10,000-14,999	6.0	9.5	13.9	3.5
$15,000-19,999	7.7	10.5	16.6	2.8
$20,000-24,999	9.9	12.1	19.9	2.2
$25,000-34,999	14.1	14.9	25.3	0.8
$35,000-49,999	22.5	17.7	34.7	4.8
$50,000-74,999	33.1	21.7	45.5	11.4
$75,000+	47.7	28.0	58.9	19.7

Source: NTIA (1999: 43)

5 I have here concentrated on income, but a similar picture of structural differentiation can be drawn from other discriminators like gender, 'race/ethnic origin', family type and so on.

Unlike earlier studies, the 1999 Report also has more detail on Internet usage, and these figures are collected for individuals rather than households. Table 3 gives a breakdown of the location of usage for the US population and for a range of income bands. As can be seen, apart from the very poorest group, whom we might suppose includes students, overall Internet usage is closely related to income level. Perhaps the most interesting figures, however, are the ones in the final column, here labelled 'Overlap'. This is derived by subtracting the number of those who say they use the Internet in any location from the sum of those who say they use it at home and those who say they use it outside the home. This constitutes a measure of the percentage of a particular group that says it uses the Internet both at home and outside the home. This rises very sharply for the income groups at $35,000 per year and above, and it suggests that these people are the ones most likely to have the Internet integrated most fully into the overall pattern of their lives.

Table 4 Out-of-home usage of the Internet

Group	At work (%)	At K12 School (%)	At other school (%)	At public library (%)	Someone else's PC (%)
All US	56.3	21.8	10.9	8.2	13.6
<$5,000	12.3	36.9	32.4	14.2	17.7
$5,000-9,999	15.2	26.8	32.0	19.9	26.6
$10,000-14,999	19.8	31.7	21.7	13.9	28.4
$15,000-19,999	30.0	29.1	18.0	12.3	24.9
$20,000-24,999	37.1	25.6	14.1	14.9	27.1
$25,000-34,999	47.8	24.7	11.1	11.0	20.0
$35,000-49,999	55.7	22.2	8.9	7.5	15.1
$50,000-74,999	64.1	21.2	8.1	7.0	10.2
$75,000+	72.9	16.2	7.6	4.2	6.2

Source: NTIA (1999: 50)

This evidence of a division between those for whom the Internet is integrated into the overall pattern of their lives and those for whom it is an additional, and perhaps optional, extra is supported by the pattern of out-of-home usage illustrated in Table 4. Individuals from the same group of higher-income families who are likely to have Internet access at home are also much more likely to have it at work. For them, the Internet is increasingly part of the everyday life experience in the same way as the car and the telephone already are. The individuals from poorer families are much less likely to have access at either home or work, and to the extent that they use the Internet it is either through some form of public provision or as a result of the charity of their friends. These systemic differences, which have here been traced with regard to income, are also reproduced for other measures of social differentiation. For example, they show up very strongly indeed for educational level: 87.2 per cent of those with a BA or more using the Internet outside the home use it at work, compared with 57.8 per cent of those with High School Diplomas and only 8.7 per cent of those who did not graduate from High School (NTIA, 1999: 52).

Internet Usages

When we move to the kinds of things that the Internet is used for, it is evident that e-mail is the by far the most popular application, both inside and outside the home. Across the whole of the US population, on average approximately 80 per cent of the wired population use email at home, and this varies little with income. In all categories, more than 90 per cent of people use home email to keep in touch with family and friends (NTIA, 1999: 66). Outside of the home, email is less popular, and less used to keep in touch with family and friends, but with 53.6 per cent of respondents using it, it is still the largest overall category, although in some income groups it is not the most common activity. Outside home email is heavily used by all groups to keep in touch with family and friends, but the percentage of usage involving job-related material rises with income and the percentage involving personal relations falls (NTIA, 1999: 71). Table 5 gives some overall figures for Internet usage both inside and outside the home. We might wonder why some of the categories are underreported, particularly since anecdotal evidence from news sites suggests that they have their largest audiences during working hours, and be particularly puzzled by the contents of the category 'info search', but overall a quite clear pattern emerges. I have given figures for the individuals in the highest income group and for those reporting an income which, if they are the sole earner in a family of three, would place them in the category of 'working poor', just below the federal poverty line. Email is integrated into the personal and professional lives of the better off in a way that it is not for the poorer groups, for whom it is much more a means of keeping in touch with family and friends both at home and at work. The richer group also scores much more highly on usage of the Internet for work-related tasks both at home and at work.

Table 5 Selected profiles of Internet usage inside and outside the home

	E-mail	Info search	Check news	Take courses	Job-related tasks	Shop and pay bills	Job Search	Games and Ents
All US at home	77.9	59.8	45.9	36.1	29.1	24.5	14.5	5.8
All US at work	53.6	50.2	–	44.6	38.8	–	8.5	–
Income $20,000-24,999 At home	74.6	59.2	–	41.4	19.1	–	17.9	–
Income $20,000-24,999 At work	42.1	45.1	–	49.2	29.1	–	9.4	–
Income $75,000+ At home	78.7	60.0	–	35.0	34.5	–	11.7	–
Income $75,000+ At work	62.9	30.7	–	49.4	56.3	–	6.6	–

Source: NTIA (1999, 60, 62, 63)

The Nature and Impact of Internet Technology

Our survey of US Internet penetration and usage suggests two general lessons about the nature and impact of this technology:

1 Although the particular kinds and nature of the systemic inequalities of access may be peculiar to the USA, it is notable that the patterns map very closely upon existing and well-known forms of social differentiation. We can therefore suggest that while, for example, the importance of 'race and ethnic origin' as a discriminator may not be so great in other societies as it appears to be in the USA, the locally-significant markers of social inequality will be reflected in every country. Slightly less convincing statistics for the EU, for example, show that while in 1998 Internet connections stood at 8.3 per cent of the total population, for the poorest group they were 3.5 per cent and for the richest 18 per cent (INRA, 1999: 33). We might expect to find that more egalitarian societies, for example the Scandinavian Social Democracies, would have a less extreme distribution of resources, paralleling their less extreme distributions of wealth, income and social advantage.

2 It is clear from the US evidence that for the richest groups in society, amongst whom the Internet is most widely distributed, the Internet has become what we may term an 'integral technology'. That is to say that it has a multitude of functions across their working and leisure

> lives. It is neither essentially a leisure medium, like television, nor essentially a working medium, like the fax machine. Rather, it is embedded in to the routines of both work and leisure, and has perhaps accelerated the blurring of the distinction between the two. For less well-off groups, however, the Internet is primarily a communication device – an extension of the telephone and the postal service – that is predominantly used for leisure purposes. It is not integrated into work routines to anywhere near the same extent as it is for the better-off groups. At its present state of development, the Internet is a technology that shows signs of adaptation to the social patterns of its users, and its usage is beginning to reflect the differences between them.

Overall, the development of the Internet appears to be following quite predictable channels in that unequal societies are giving rise to unequal access to this medium. Social realities are ensuring that, far from realising its potential to allow all the right to public speech, the Internet is developing in such a way as further to privilege those who are already rich and powerful. From the point of view of its diffusion within the most wired of societies, the Internet does not appear to be developing in such a way as to realise its potential as a mechanism to enhance democracy.[6]

The Supply of Public Information

So far, we have dealt with the ways in which the technology of the Internet is distributed, with a view to considering how far it realises its potential of allowing all to participate equally in a contemporary reconstruction of the market place of classical democracy. The right to public speech, however, is more or less empty unless the citizen is able to articulate an informed opinion and in order to do that she needs access to information and interpretation about the most important public issues. Providing this sort of material has always been one of the prime reasons why theories of media freedom are inseparable from theories of democracy. In this section, we will investigate the narrow issue of how newspapers are faring on the Internet.

Here again the potential of the Internet is enormous. Because telecommunications compress time and distance, it is now possible to look at material that has been produced anywhere in the world at more or less the

---

6 The problem of the exclusion of poorer groups from the political process is, of course, particularly acute in the case of the USA, where these sections of society have low political participation rates.

same time as it is published on the Web. Instead of being restricted to the few local papers, perhaps reflecting the limited perspectives of one's own environment, it is now possible to get news and opinion from around the world. Newspapers have certainly adopted this distribution technology in large numbers, as Figure 5 demonstrates.[7] Starting only in the mid-nineties, by the end of the decade thousands of newspapers are freely available online, overwhelmingly through the World Wide Web. These figures underestimate the informational riches available: at the same date in June 1999 there were in addition 3,809 magazines, 2,042 radio stations and 1,311 television sites online (E&P, 1999). The opportunities for the enquiring citizen to gain a rounded view of the world is today unparalleled in human history. Sitting at my desk in London, I can have access to global information resources that were, at best, available to the President of the United States of America a mere decade ago.[8]

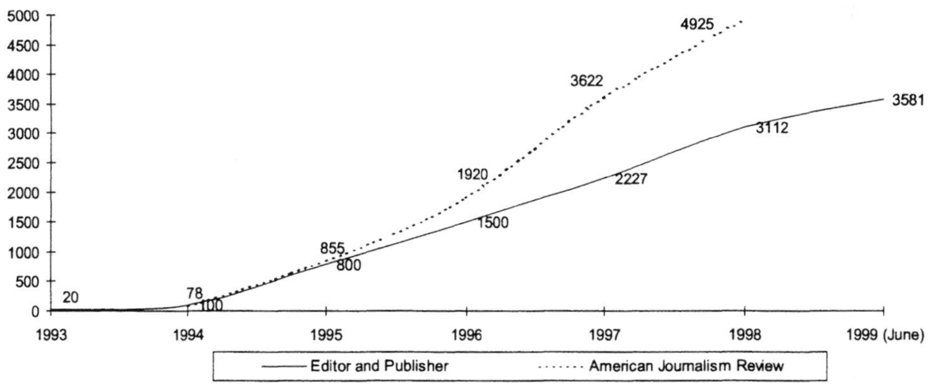

Figure 5 The growth of online newspapers

The reports and interpretations do not, however, reflect in any way the actual distribution of human experience. As Figure 6 shows, there are a huge number of online papers available that originate in the USA, while

7 I have included two data series here. While they differ in their absolute numbers, probably due to differing definitions of a 'newspaper', they both demonstrate a similar pattern of development. We do not, for our purposes, need to choose between the two.

8 There are severe problems with the economics of online news, which I have dealt with elsewhere (Sparks forthcoming b). Whether this free cornucopia will persist is another matter.

Asia and Africa have far fewer titles. Absolute numbers, of course, conceal the realities of relative provision. As we noted above, Asia contains, in India and China, the world's two most populous nations. In Japan it contains the world's second largest economy. It is therefore even more striking that these large and, in one case, wealthy countries produce so many fewer online titles than does the USA. While Africa is, of course, smaller in total population, and does not contain any economic giants, it is still a large and extremely diverse continent, and its under-representation is remarkable. In fact, the imbalance is even more severe than appears from the bald figures. Of the 57 online newspapers available in June 1999, all were written in English or French, or both English and Afrikaans.

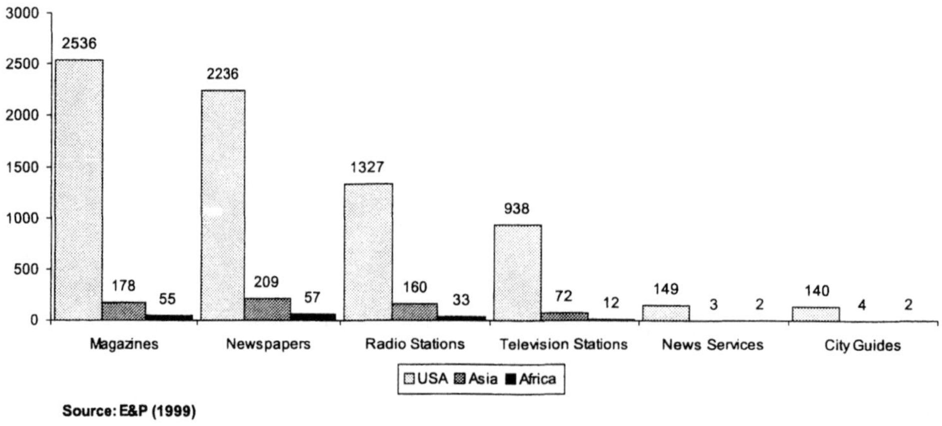

Figure 6 Distribution of online media resources

The claim is often made that the epoch of globalisation is marked by a disjuncture between economic and symbolic resources. It is taken to be one of the marks of the global epoch that the symbolic realm is much less connected to a physical location than is the case for either the economic or the political. To the extent that these newspapers have transcended space and time, of course, it is true that the development of online editions represents a massive step away from the tyranny of place. On the other hand, as Figure 7 demonstrates, there are no grounds for supposing that what we might term the geography of cyberia is any different from the geography of the plain old offline world. In the offline world, rich countries produce large numbers of newspapers and poorer countries have fewer. In the online world, the same is true. If anything, online newspapers are more concentrated in the richer continents than are their offline versions. The force of economic circumstances works even more strongly on the Internet than it does elsewhere.[9] The net result of this is that the same problem of the domination of the news agenda by the concerns of a few rich countries is likely to be reproduced in the online world in an even more severe form than is notoriously the case in the offline world.

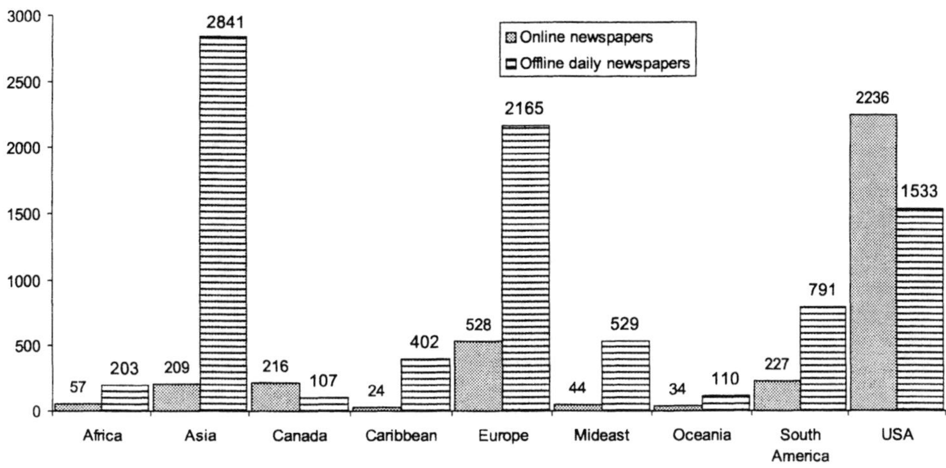

Figure 7 Comparison of online and offline newspapers

It's Early Days Yet

It might well be objected that, since the material under consideration in all of the above sections relates to a very short time period, it is not adequate as a base for firm conclusions about the future. Of course, this is partly true. It is early days. Things will undoubtedly change as the Internet matures and projections from existing data need to be highly tentative. There are, however, three things that can be said in support of the conclusions drawn here. Firstly, this paper is not concerned with

9 There are some obvious problems with this graph, and it should be read as indicative only. The definitions of newspaper used by E&P are not the same as the definition of daily newspapers used by UNESCO – indeed the concept of a daily newspaper loses its meaning online. The geographical areas are probably different. The figures relate to different years: mostly from 1995 in the case of UNESCO and from mid-1999 for the E&P. Even then, the UNESCO figures are not complete, and I have tried to construct a run from the available data. These are definitely not reliable numbers, but the broad trend is probably a reasonably good picture of reality.

gazing in to the far future but with relatively near term, and here the data is surely a better guide. Perhaps things will look different in a couple of decades, and certainly they will look very different in a couple of centuries, but in the next few years it is likely that we will still be living with the consequences of the trends that we have examined here. Secondly, at least the conclusions drawn here are based on some data, rather than the poetic imagination and wishful thinking that seem to mark so much writing in this field. Of course, data does not resolve everything: it is the product of a particular set of theoretical concerns rather than an impartial court of appeal. On the other hand, a conclusion that can show that it has some evidence, however fragmentary, to support it is surely superior to one that is purely based on the desires of its progenitor. Thirdly, we are not completely in the dark as to the course of future developments. There is a body of literature that has examined the ways in which earlier technologies have spread, or failed to spread, through societies. While we should not treat this material as an infallible guide, we can look to these findings to give us some indications about the possible future of the Internet.

The study of the diffusion of innovations records amongst its major finding that there is a normal pattern to the ways in which populations adopt innovations (Rogers, 1992). This pattern is that at first relatively few people adopt something, then once it has proved viable there is a much faster take-up by the majority, and finally a few hold-out laggards are persuaded to join up. If this pattern of behaviour is plotted as the percentage of adopters against elapsed time, the result is a curve that resembles a flattened 's'. This s-curve is said to be a general characteristic of all diffusion processes. The nature of the curve will vary, particularly with the speed of take up, but the basic shape remains more or less a constant. There are, as we shall see, a number of problems with this model, but we can certainly take it as a starting point to consider the diffusion of the Internet.

Uneven Diffusion

The evidence presented in Figure 8 suggests that the diffusion of online newspapers is not taking place evenly across the world. Although this covers a very short time span, it is noticeable that there is no uninterrupted process of growth: indeed the figure for Asia has actually fallen, perhaps as a result of the impact of the economic crisis in the region. Two things can therefore be argued. The first is that the time taken for newspapers outside of the USA to 'catch up' is likely to be protracted. Growth is not concentrated in those areas that are currently under-represented. Secondly, if the first proposition is correct, then it follows that the imbalances in the provision of public information will be with us for a very long time, if not forever.

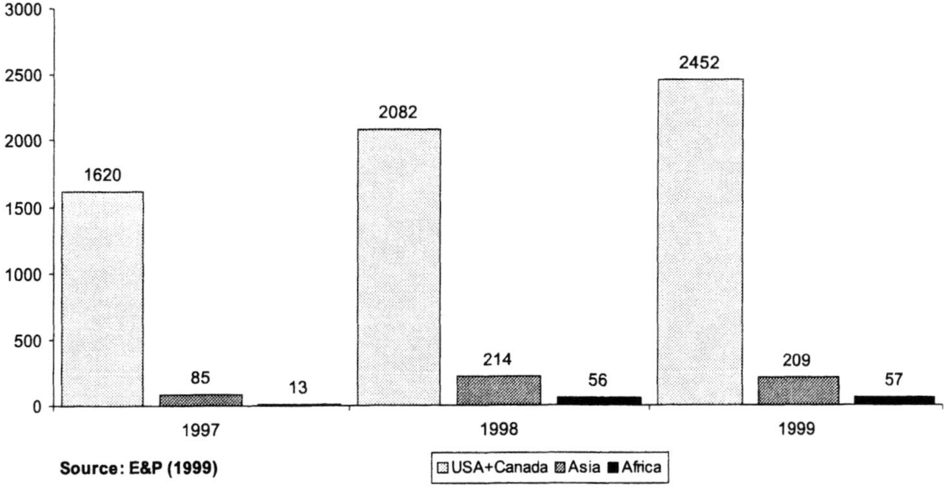

Figure 8 Number of online newspapers 1997-1999

We may use similar reasoning to consider the likely continuation of the disparities of online access that we noted above. We can see no sign of the s-curve with regard to the total number of Internet hosts, so it is reasonable to conclude that we are very far from saturating the potential population for them. On the other hand, if we look at the diffusion of access to the Internet and its enabling technologies within the USA, we can draw some interesting conclusions. Firstly, some of the concerns of the authors of *Falling Through the Net* are slightly misplaced. They record with understandable dismay that that the gaps in take up between the rich and the white and the poor and the black have actually been growing wider over the last few years: they note that the gap is becoming a 'racial ravine' for some groups. From the point of view of diffusion theory, this is normal and not particularly worrying. In any differentiated population, there will be different propensities to adopt innovations. In general, the elite sections will be more ready to adopt than the marginal groups. What is happening in the case of the Internet in the USA is simply the result of this general law: rich, white, elite people are adopting this innovation first. According to theory, sooner or later, other less advantaged groups will also take up the innovation, and eventually they will catch up with the elite. From this point of view, the main issue is whether it will be sooner or later and, if later, how much later? Concerned that it might be quite a long time, the authors of the report suggest a series of public-access measures that can reduce the gap between the different sections of US society.

If we take a slightly more critical view of diffusion theory, however, a different conclusion suggests itself. The prototype of the diffusion of an innovation was hybrid seed corn amongst Iowa farmers, and in time effectively the entire population adopted it. It is, however, by no means certain that any innovation will always diffuse throughout almost the entire population. Some, like television, clearly do. Some technologies diffuse to only one part of the total population: not everybody has a Polaroid camera, for example. Others, like quadraphonic sound systems, Digital Audio Tape, and the first generation of videodiscs, failed to diffuse at all. More significantly, there is the question of what constitutes the appropriate 'total population'. In the case of seed corn, the total population in question was that of cereal farmers. It was not the total population of the state of Iowa: to this day, there are, to my certain knowledge, professors of mass communication at the University of Iowa who do not plant hybrid seed corn. When discussing the diffusion of an innovation it is essential to be clear exactly what the parameters of the population in question actually are. It is therefore quite illegitimate to assume that the Internet is a technology whose natural audience is the whole of the population of the USA, let alone of the world. It might be that it will find a niche that is much smaller than the whole population.

In that light, we can reconsider the evolution of the enabling technologies of the Internet. There are available relatively long-run figures for the availability of computers in US households. These are plotted by income groups in Figure 9. These results illuminate a number of points. First of all, the diffusion of computers in all groups appears to be levelling off, except for the very poorest where it is actually falling. These approximate s-curves suggest that the maximum diffusion for computers in the homes of the US population is approaching, and that it will be different for different social groups. The richest groups will have very high levels of computer penetration, and the poorest groups will have very low levels.

If these conclusions are correct, then there will never come a time that the personal computer, and thus the Internet in its contemporary form, ever reaches all US homes. The inequalities of access that are so evident today will become permanent features of the online world. At the very least, the public provision of online access is likely to be essential for the foreseeable future if any form of inclusivity is adopted as a desirable social goal.

The application of diffusion theory to the available data thus allows us to make somewhat firmer prognoses about the likely development of what otherwise might be dismissed as evidence from an immature phase of the Internet. Within the USA, it looks as though home access to the Internet is maturing, at least in its current form. It also looks as though the online newspaper is reaching the maximum range of its diffusion internationally. The inequalities that we have charted in preceding sections thus appear to be structural rather than conjunctural. At least for the foreseeable future, it is unlikely that the Internet will reach the level of universality that would make it a viable medium for enhancing democratic life in any acceptable sense. This conclusion seems to be true even of the USA, and it is therefore true *a fortiori* for the populations of countries that are at the moment less wired. Such people, of course, constitute the vast majority of the world's population.

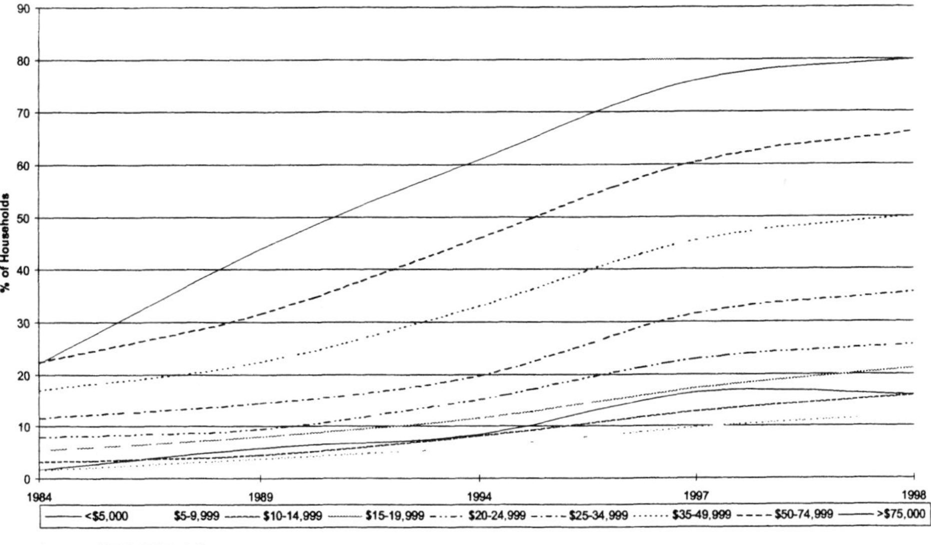

Figure 9 Home computers in the USA at nine income levels

Conclusions

We have reached fairly pessimistic conclusions about the three main questions we set out to address in this paper. It seems highly likely that the Internet will fail to realise its undoubted potential as a medium of democratic life. Both its availability as a mode of participation and expression, and the presence of information and opinion, will continue to be very unequally distributed. To the extent that it is a medium through which people can learn and can debate, it will be for rich, white, people rather than for the mass of the world's population. Secondly, the evidence is that the distribution of the Internet, and the associated opportunities for political and cultural enrichment that go with it, map even more closely on to the existing distributions of wealth and power than do other, older, technologies like the printing press. To the extent that the Internet is a global medium, it necessitates a theory of globalisation that is so crudely reductive as to make Marx himself wince.

There is, however, one possible counter-development that is consistent with the findings we have reviewed above. If we start by asking what exactly is it that is being diffused, then the answer is obviously very much more than simply a set of electronic devices. The Internet is, as we have shown, a social technology that takes at least part of its form from the patterns of everyday usage. Many technologies have been socially 're-invented' in the course of their life, and the Internet is a case in point. It has gone from being a mechanism for massive data transfers to a vehicle for email. In the last couple of years it has again been re-invented as a channel of commerce. The massive recent growth in the number of hosts is, as we have seen, largely a result of this recent re-invention. None of these forms of the technology, however, necessarily imply that the relevant population for the diffusion of the Internet is the same as the total population of any country. But it is at least possible that it may yet be re-invented as something else entirely from what it has been up until now. One of the things that it could be reinvented as would be as an entertainment medium: clearly, substantial efforts are today being made in that direction. If such a reinvention were indeed to occur, then it would be legitimate to compare the diffusion of the Internet to that of television, and predict that universal connectivity, in at least the rich countries, would be a goal of the foreseeable future.

The current 'invention' of the Internet is one that we have seen fits the patterns of life and work of the upper classes well, and it is reasonable to assume that this version has begun to, and will continue to, be diffused amongst them quite fully. A new 'invention' of the Internet as an entertainment medium might fit the social patterns of other groups, perhaps the poorer and less advantaged, rather better. This technology, perhaps based on an adoption of the currently marginal WebTV, might well diffuse throughout the whole of society, at least in countries like the USA. It is, however, likely that this will be a version of the technology in which the democratic potential of the current invention is pushed into the background. If this were to take place, then the Internet would come to resemble the printed press, which we have argued serves quite distinct social functions for different groups of readers. In the case of the Internet, those who used its informational and dialogical potential would find they had enhanced opportunities for public life, and those who used its entertainment functions would find that they had enhanced opportunities for fun and games. The evident divisions of the offline world would be reproduced online.

There is, of course, an alternative. That is to find ways of providing the existing democratic technology, or better an enhanced version of it, to the whole of the population. The authors of the US report cited above, and numerous reform-minded academic authors, devote considerable time to suggesting mechanisms like community access whereby the technology can be made available to groups too poor or too marginal to have any other way of going online. It is the implication of this paper that, however worthy and well intentioned these efforts are, they miss the point. What are embedded in the Internet are social positions and social practices, not wires and microchips. The problem is to diffuse the social relations, not the technology. Only to the extent that it is possible to overcome social inequality will it be possible to generalise the diffusion of the Internet and realise its wonderful democratic potential.

References

E&P

1999 *Editor & Publisher Media Links: Online Media Directory Current Database Statistics*, June 2 <http://www.mediainfo.com/ephome/npaper/nphtm/statistics.htm>.

Hargittai, E.

1999 Weaving the western web: Explaining differences in Internet connectivity among OECD countries. *Telecommunications Policy*, 23 (10/11): 701-718.

INRA

1999 *Measuring Information Society: A Report Written by INRA Europe for the Directorate General XIII*. Eurobarometer 50.1.

ISC

199 *Internet Software Consortium*. <http://www.isc.org>.

Meyer, E.

1998 *AJR Newslink: An Unexpectedly Wider Web for the World's Newspapers*. <http://ajr.newslink.com>.

NTIA

1999 *Falling Through the Net: Defining the Digital Divide, A Report on the Telecommunications and Information Gap in America*. Washington, DC: National Telecommunications and Information Administration of the US Department of Commerce.

Nua

1999 *How Many Online?* September. <http://www.nua.ie/surveys/how_many_online/index.html>.

Rogers, E.

1992 *Diffusion of Innovations*, 4th edition. New York: Free Press.

Sparks, C.

Fc. a Beyond national politics: The emergence of a global public sphere. In L. Bennett and R. Entman (eds.), *Communication and the Future of Democracy*. New York: Cambridge University Press.

Sparks, C.

Fc. b The challenge of the online newspaper. In J. Curran and M. Gurevitch (eds.), *Mass Media and Society*, 3rd edition. London: Arnold.

UNDP

1999 *Human Development Report 1999*. New York: Oxford University Press

UNESCO

1999 *Statistics. Daily newspapers: number and circulation (total and per 1,000 inhabitants)*. <http://unescostat.unesco.org>.

Part v

COMMUNICATIONS POLICIES FOR THE FUTURE

Democracy, Media and Public Policy

Concluding Note

DENIS MCQUAIL
The Amsterdam School of Communications Research *ASCoR*,
University of Amsterdam, The Netherlands, and University of Southampton, United Kingdom

Introduction

This article tries to sketch an overall framework for the topics that have been discussed in the different papers. First of all, I will name the main terms in Figure 1 shown below. 'Democracy' is the key term we started with and have kept returning to. In relation to democracy the central point has been the ambivalent or two-directional relationship between media and democracy. 'The media' is the second key term, located close to 'democracy', because of our specific concerns here and because it is hard to envisage modern democracy without modern mass (and other) media. But media can harm as well as promote democracy. As demonstrated in the upper left part of Figure 1, democracy and media are not occupying a vacuum that is unaffected by other influences such as the state, government, capital and power. In the centre of Figure 1, I have entered the 'conditions' that affect whether or not the media do make a contribution to democracy, according to the discussion. These conditions refer to such matters as the quality and range of media, their independence and accessibility to citizens and relevant interests in society.

The conditions are divided in two sub categories, namely the 'friends' and the 'enemies' of democracy. The use of the terms friends and enemies reflects the ambivalence mentioned above and essentially concerns the features of a media system that are positive or negative towards an open and democratic society. Then there are the implications for 'Public Policy' in the sense of what should or could be done to realise the full democratic potential of the mass media. And finally, as shown in the lower left corner of Figure 1, I name three particular concepts that need to be discussed: *diversity, responsibility and accountability.*

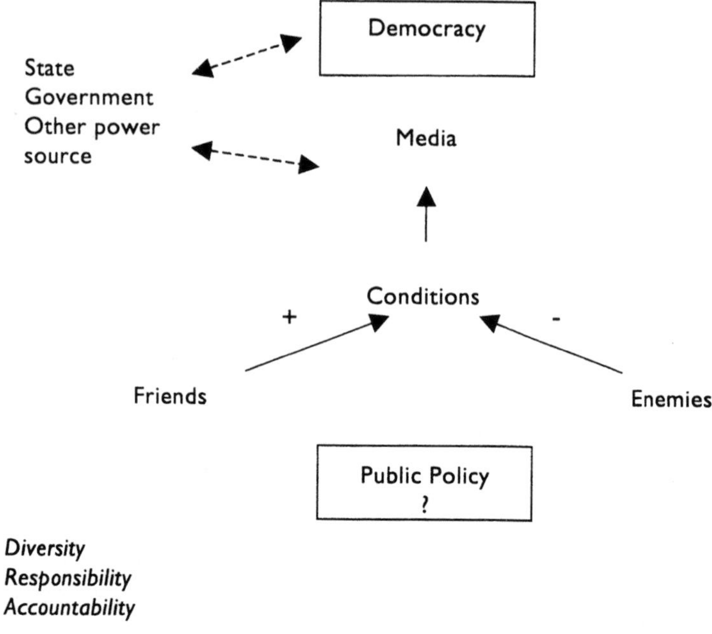

Figure 1 Democracy, media and public policy

Democracy and the Media

Given the limited scope of this article, I will deal rather quickly with *democracy*, because it is too big to deal with in any other way. I think the most important thing here in our context, is to look at certain processes of communication. There is a range of public communication activities that are vital to democracy and also depend on the mass media. These include processes of public information, choice, elections, opinion formation, debate, and expression. It is hard to imagine a democracy in modern society, which is not supported by media. According to the discussion and some of the papers, the contribution of media to these processes are judged according to a number of criteria. The first is 'openness' which refers to more than just an empty space and lack of control or limitations. It should also involve inclusiveness of minorities, special interest groups, and others needing access in the public sphere. So openness is a positive value according to the perspective of the conference. Also the second criterion, that of equality, has not been neglected in our discussion. It is a central criterion in a democratic and open society which does not refer only to material equality but also to universality and broad participation. To some extent it is also covered by the idea of inclusiveness. Thirdly, the process of communication should be assessed by criteria concerning political and human rights, which are deeply imbedded in our social and political orders. Whether the media (mass or not) can contribute to the achievement of democracy involving these processes of communication according to these criteria, has to be seen as a two-way process. There is a tendency to assume that the media are the main motor of democracy but the relationship is not just driven by the media in one (positive) direction. The power of the media to make a beneficial contribution to democracy depends a great deal on political actions, on citizens and on organisations in society. In fact it is more than this; it has to be activated in society, so the first responsibility for seeing that the media enhance democratic processes lies in the hands of citizens and political institutions, in many of the societies we have been talking about. As it happens, not much reference has been made in this conference to the responsibilities of politicians and to their failings (such as the misuse of media for propaganda and manipulation).

Regarding *the media*, no attempt has been made to make an analytical distinction between the different media. Most aspects of the media that have been discussed have related to the national or central TV, press, or to the Internet. We should recognise more that the position of the national newspaper or central television channel is not the same as it was in the heyday of the social welfare media policy of the 1970s and earlier. It is necessary to bear in mind that other media (e.g. local or regional media and all kinds of minority, specialist and even international channels) are increasing in number, variety and importance. These media might be important for democracy and for limiting the growth and dominance of the older forms of central 'political' media. Media tend to change in character over time and there is an apparent tendency away from political functions and more towards business and entertainment importance.

Friends and Enemies of Open Societies

A number of *conditions* necessary or conducive for media to contribute to democracy have been put forward in the discussion, sometimes implicitly and sometimes explicitly. First of all there is the quantitative condition of sufficient media (availability) with universal access (reach). Other conditions mentioned are diversity of structure, diversity of content, access to systems for those who want to publish or start media, access to voices and groups, acceptance of democratic tasks (i.e. social responsibility towards society) by media, willingness to be accountable to society for public service tasks and good practice of media (quality of journalism, high standards of professionalism) to earn the trust of audiences.

Moving down in Figure 1 we come to the *friends*, or positive forces, that help to secure these conditions. A first subcondition is having economic and moral support from audiences. Other friends include: a secure income from advertising or readers; high professional standards within the media themselves; and technological innovation, which produces challenges to the existing status quo and helps to break down fixed structures. Under friendly forces we can also include the qualities of the actual medium with particular reference to interactivity and the consultative power and potential of the Internet. Furthermore, it is still necessary to have an audience of good citizens with their own sense of civic responsibility for being informed and forming opinions. In short we need active, voluntary civil societies where people are willing to and able to debate issues and speak out on important issues. Competition between media in itself seems also to be recognised as beneficial in general. Without competition there would be less pressure for diversity and quality. Another friend is transparency of ownership of the media, of editorial dispositions and ideologies, so that citizens know where the media stand in relation to political and economical power. A last friend is a supportive public policy environment with at least a positive attitude within the political system towards creating the conditions for services to democracy.

Ranged on the other side are the *enemies* or negative forces. Firstly, there is concentration of media ownership. This has traditionally been seen as a potential enemy of democracy because of the strong likelihood that it excludes certain voices and overemphasises the interest of those who own the media. Secondly, fierce or ruinous competition is seen as an enemy in the sense that it destroys diversity. A third enemy is the politicisation of capital. The links between political forces working in a democratic system and the deployment of capital to put instruments at the disposal of openly political actors has a negative effect. A fourth enemy is the existence of strong barriers to access. Not just concentration, but also the way modern media are organised, make that the investments needed to enter into a restricted large scale media market act as barrier. A fifth enemy is the lack of advertising. We could discuss whether over-dependence on advertising is equally negative but not having advertising income, in a market system often means lack of power and presence in the media market and lack of independence. It may also mean lower quality, because of lack of resources to meet the full range of informational and other means. Finally, overcommercialisation of media, as translated in tabloidisation and sensationalism, or the neglect of public tasks is an enemy as well.

Responsibility, Accountability and Diversity

In regard to the concepts of *responsibility* and *accountability* two aspects become important: responsibility *for what* and accountability *to whom.* I will not fill in the first in detail because more suggestions were given in regard to the latter. This concerns the direction of media, responsibility, keeping in mind that other actors (e.g. politicians) should also be responsible. Media should be accountable to society in a general way and to their own (potential) audience. The connection between people that are citizen in a democracy and the media is important. Media may furthermore be responsible to some cause or some wider social, political or moral purpose (whatever it is, this should be transparent and not concealed). Responsibility is also owed by journalists to their own conscience and to ethical codes and values which play part in professionalism and affect the quality of media in certain ways.

Diversity has been discussed in many papers and the main point underlined was that it is too narrow to define diversity only as *variety* or *choice* (quantitative and consumerist criteria). In regard to 'real' diversity the emphasis usually placed on the relation of media to some 'extra-media' criteria in social reality. This includes: the distribution of support for political parties, public opinion, social classes and their needs and interests; cultural tastes and preferences; information needs of individuals and groups; social and cultural minorities. In addition, diversity needs to be defined according to criteria both of reflection and equal access. Also, the emphasis must be on change, progress and innovation.

Public Media Policy for Open Societies

The last element in Figure 1 is *public policy*, which refers not only to the question *what* is to be done, but also to the question *why* things are to be done, is there a reason or aim? And *how* must it be done? Subsequently the question appears, what *can* be done? The primary aim of public policy for media lies in the democratic advancement of the conditions mentioned above. It is not easy to determine what can be done, since the range of circumstances as between Russia, Europe and North America is very large. Nevertheless, it is possible to draw up preliminary general conclusions from specific cases of different national media structures.

So, I will end up by giving a variety of things on which public policy could concentrate. Namely:

- The limitation of private monopoly and encouragement of competition;
- Control and regulation of standards (quality, no harm) on matters that are important to the society;
- Concessions to media that serve democratic purposes;
- Retaining or supporting Public Service Broadcasting to keep open spaces and for other purposes;
- The encouragement of professionalism and public accountability;
- The encouragement of new media uses in regard to political and education aims.

The means for achieving some of these goals in practice are more limited than they used to be, for a number of reasons. Nevertheless, the dependence of democracy on adequate mass media is too important for public policy to be allowed to wither away.

About the Authors

PIET BAKKER is associate professor at the Department of Communication at the University of Amsterdam and a researcher for The Amsterdam School of Communications Research *ASCoR*. He worked as a journalist and worked at the Utrecht School for Journalism before he joined the University of Amsterdam. He published books on media history, the Dutch media and investigative journalism. He specialises in journalism, newspapers, media-concentration, new media and communications policy.

JO BARDOEL is associate professor at the Department of Communication and a researcher with *ASCoR*, both at the University of Amsterdam. Before rejoining academia in 1993 he has been working as a senior policy advisor with NOS, the central organisation in Dutch public broadcasting for many years. In 1997 he defended his PhD-thesis 'Journalism in the information society'. In recent years he also did consultancy work for several Dutch ministries and media institutions. Bardoel teaches on subjects as national and European communications policies, comparative media systems and globalisation (with American counterparts) and journalism and new media; his research interests include changing communication policies as well as the future of public broadcasting and public journalism.

KEES BRANTS is senior associate professor at the Department of Communication at the University of Amsterdam and professor of Political Communication at the Department of Political Science at Leiden University. He is a member of the Amsterdam School of Communications Research *ASCoR* and of the Euro-Media Research Group. He focuses his research on media policy and political communication.

JAN VAN CUILENBURG is professor of communications policy and management at the University of Amsterdam. Van Cuilenburg has been chairing the Netherlands Press Fund, an independent governmental agency for financially supporting newspapers and magazines that are temporarily lacking sufficient means. Van Cuilenburg has been member of the Netherlands Media Council and the Netherlands Advisory Committee on Post and Telecommunications. Currently his research focuses on the relationship between media competition, media innovation and media diversity.

ELS DE BENS is professor at the department of Communication Sciences of the University of Ghent. She is dean of the Faculty of Political and Social Sciences and chair of the Flemish Media Council (Flemish Government). Most of her research activities relate to economics of print media, new communication technologies and media policy.

IORDAN IOSSIFOV is PhD student at The Amsterdam School of Communications Research *ASCoR*. He graduated from the Faculty of Law of the Sofia University, Bulgaria (LM in Bulgarian Law) and from the Amsterdam School of International Relations ASIR (LLM in International Trade Law). He joined *ASCoR* in March 1999 after an internship with the European Commission. Iossifov currently studies the relationships between competition, innovation and diversity in national newspaper markets.

GENEVION KEUNE is facilities manager at Kindernet, a children's television channel. She studied communication policy in Amsterdam, conducted a study for the Dutch Ministry of Economic Affairs on scenario's for public policy to stimulate a diverse supply of television programmes, and was assistant professor at the Department of Communication and assistant researcher at The Amsterdam School of Communications Research *ASCoR*, both at University of Amsterdam. Her research dealt with the interrelations between market structures, competitive behaviour and performance in the broadcasting market.

MARIA LOUKINA is associate professor and deputy dean for media training at the Faculty of Journalism of Moscow State University. She has a PhD in Journalism. She has worked as a professional journalist and currently teaches print journalism. Her new method of intensive professional training has been included in the faculty curriculum. Loukina's current research focuses on new trends in journalism in the context of new communication technologies.

DENIS MCQUAIL is emeritus professor in communication at the University of Amsterdam. He is the author of a widely used text book on Mass Communication Theory. He worked as a consultant for the UK Royal Commission on the Press in the mid 1970s, participated in the work of the Euro Media Research Group since 1982, and has held a number of visiting positions including the USA and Japan. His theoretical and empirical research interests focus on the interactions between public policies for media and media systems, and more in particular the role of the public interest in media performance standards and analysis.

IRINA NETCHAEVA is senior researcher at the Faculty of Journalism of Moscow State University. She has an MA in Newspaper Journalism (1969) and a PhD in American Journalism (1979). Her research on media and communications focuses on African mass media, problems of globalization and the use of new technologies in Africa.

KAARLE NORDENSTRENG is professor of journalism and mass communication at the University of Tampere, Finland. He has worked as a radio reporter and head of audience research at the Finnish Broadcasting Corporation and has been involved in media policy planning in both domestic commissions and international organisations, mainly at UNESCO. He has held visiting positions in USA, Canada and Tanzania. His research interests have covered theories of mass communication, international communication and media ethics. His current research deals with the normative roles of media in society.

ROBERT G. PICARD is professor and director of the Media Group, at the Turku School of Economics and Business Administration, Finland. He was founding editor of The Journal of Media Economics, is currently editor of European Media Management Review. He lectured at universities and to communications groups world-wide, and has been a consultant to ministries and government agencies and numerous media companies and labour organisations in North America and Europe. His research deals with media economics and government communication policies.

RENÉ PLUG is marketing consultant at BrandmarC BV, an Amsterdam based enterprise specialised in strategic media performance assessment through market simulations. After his graduation from the Faculty of Social and Behavioural Sciences (MA Communication Studies, focus on Media Policy) he was assistant professor at the Department of Communication and assistant researcher at *ASCoR*, all at the University of Amsterdam. Most of his research dealt with telecommunications and media policy, and their intermediate convergent trends. Currently he focuses on simulation and media performance.

ANDREI RASKIN is senior lecturer at the Faculty of Journalism, Moscow State University. His PhD is about television coverage of presidential elections in the United States of America. He has been TV news correspondent at the '1st Russian TV Channel' and news director at the 'ITAR-TASS' news agency. His main interests include the history of international journalism, international humanitarian law, TV news production and public relations.

COLIN SPARKS is professor of Media Studies at Westminster University, London. He has a PhD in Cultural Studies, is a founding and continuing editor of 'Media, Culture and Society', has worked as a consultant, and held visiting professorships in Sweden and Finland. Recent research focuses on the globalization of the media, the media in transition from communism to capitalism, and the political economy of the press.

ELENA VARTANOVA is professor at the Faculty of Journalism of Moscow State University, and director of the Russian-Finnish Research Centre in Media and Culture. She has been teaching on global media systems and on media economics since 1981 and acquired her PhD in 1986. She has represented Russia on a Council of Europe specialist group on new communications technologies, human rights and democratic values. She has published books on Nordic media models and on Information Society. Her current research interests concentrate on studies of Nordic media systems, the political economy of the media in Western countries and modern Russia, images of neighbour countries in the Russian press, and the present state of Russian news agencies.

RICHARD VAN DER WURFF is researcher with The Amsterdam School of Communications Research *ASCoR* and associate professor at the Department of Communication of the University of Amsterdam. He studied International Relations, worked as a researcher for the European Commission, and defended his PhD on International Climate Change Politics in 1997. Since then he has been working on (regulation of) information markets and on (electronic) publishing strategies. His current research focuses on the interrelations between market structures, competitive behaviour and performance in professional information and broadcasting markets.

IVAN ZASSOURSKY is researcher at the Faculty of Journalism of Moscow State University. He has a PhD in Russian media studies. He worked as economics editor for the Moscow daily 'Nezavisimaya Gazeta', and as PR strategist and advisor to the Vice-Prime Minister of Russia. He published a book on Russian mass media in the last decade. His area of research is political spectacle and the technologies of social reality construction (and deconstruction) using myth, ritual and drama as well as modern marketing and advertising technologies.

YASSEN N. ZASSOURSKY is professor and dean (since 1964) of the Faculty of Journalism of Moscow State University. He has a PhD in American Literature, lectured on mass media and literature at universities of France, USA, Finland, Egypt, Australia, Ecuador and other countries, and closely co-operated with the McBride International Commission on Communication as a consultant and adviser. His research activities concentrate on comparative studies of Russian and American media systems, images of Russia in American and other Western media, and models and new theories of the Russian media.